From
Sailing Ships
to
Spitfires

The Life and Times of an Immigrant Family,
whose Sons Fought in the Second World War

Canadä

*The Publishers acknowledge the financial assistance of the
Government of Canada through the Book Publishing Industry
Development Program (BPIDP) for our publishing activities.*

Library and Archives Canada Cataloguing in Publication

Walker, Shirley, 1932-
    From sailing ships to spitfires : the life and times of an
immigrant family, whose sons fought in the second World
War / Shirley Walker.

ISBN 0-88887-289-5 (bound). — ISBN 0-88887-287-9 (pbk.)

    1. Rosseland family. 2. Canada—Genealogy. 3. United
States—Genealogy. 4. Norwegians—Canada—Biography.
5. Norwegians—United States—Biography.

I. Title.

CS90.R6432 2005   929'.2'0971   C2005-905915-X

Cover design by Bull's Eye Design, Ottawa
"Y2K Spitfire" image on cover courtesy of Dave Miller,
Sailing Ships image courtesy of Glenn Clever
Printed and bound in Canada on acid free paper.

From Sailing Ships to Spitfires

The Life and Times of an Immigrant Family,
whose Sons Fought in the Second World War

Shirley Walker

Borealis Press
Ottawa
2005

For Bill

Who gave me encouragement
every inch of the way

Preface

IN 1989, I RECEIVED a brief history about my mother's family in the mail. It contained intriguing, albeit sketchy, details, most of which I had never heard before. Included with the history were poems written by my grandmother, and by my Aunt Hildur, my mother's sister. The occasion that prompted the writing of this history was the death of my Aunt Faye's husband. During a period of grieving, Aunt Faye shared some memories with her daughter Sandra, who found it so interesting that she wrote it up as a history and sent copies out to her cousins.

On reading the history, I recalled a collection of family letters that my mother had saved from the late '30s and during the Second World War. I brought these letters out and read them. They took me back to another time, and gave me a glimpse into my mother's family, who had emigrated from Norway, and a story that I had never known. My curiosity was aroused. I wanted to learn more. After I discussed this with a friend, she challenged me to get started!

My first step was to join the Norwegian American Historical Association (NAHA), located at Northfield, Minnesota. New members received a small amount of free research, and this research gave me invaluable data about the family and their origins in Norway, including the names of relatives

still living there. In 1992, my husband and I, along
with my brother and sister-in-law, made a brief trip
over to Norway while touring in Great Britain. I had
dropped a note to one of these relatives before leaving, and to our surprise we had two distant cousins
waiting for us upon arrival at our hotel in
Kristiansand, Oystein and Leiv Knibestol. They
were most hospitable and helpful. Oystein assisted
me in finding and visiting the old family homes,
which I had located through detective work using
maps and data from the NAHA.

The following year, at my request, Oystein
made contact with Margit Uldal, an elderly relative
who, along with her husband, had purchased my
grandfather's family home in the 1950s. From
Margit, Oystein obtained copies of many old letters
and photographs still in the family home. The letters were mainly written by my grandfather and his
brother between the 1890s and 1916 while my
grandfather sailed on a merchant sailing ship, and
later, when the two worked in Kentucky after immi-
grating to the United States. The letters followed
them to their homestead in Alberta and ended in
the latter part of the First World War. More recently,
Margit's son, Arvid Uldal, provided the loan of old
photos from the Rosseland farm from which digital
copies could be made for reproduction.

The letters were most interesting, but that
wasn't enough. They piqued my curiosity, making
me eager to learn more about my grandfather and
his brother, and more about the society that they
lived in at the time they wrote the letters. The years

that followed proved to be a great adventure. While doing research, study and travel, I met many wonderful, helpful people and had better luck at finding information than I had ever dreamed possible. I said many times that I thought someone upstairs was smiling down and directing all these events. My research efforts were nearly always successful, and I never encountered any reason to stop. The story was intriguing.

To the best of my knowledge, the facts in this story are true, but for any errors I must take full responsibility. As an amateur historian, my intention has been to describe the circumstances of the world my family knew. The story pertains to the experiences of one family, but their experiences were similar to those of many families in the generation that settled in this country a century ago. From the small part of Canadian history that one family experienced comes *From Sailing Ships to Spitfires*, a universal story.

In 1999, I overheard one traveller on a bus tour in Norway comment, "I would love to read more about the history we are hearing, but I don't want to read a history book. I want to read a story." *From Sailing Ships to Spitfires* is such a story, about Norway and immigration to the United States and Canada in the early 20th century.

Acknowledgements

I MUST ACKNOWLEDGE the contribution many people made to my research and study. Their generous assistance made the writing of this story possible. Thanks to my grandfather's sister Anna, who lovingly saved the letters she received from her brothers, and thanks to those who cared for them and shared them later. Thanks to my mother, Agnes, for saving her family letters, and to dear Aunt Faye, who shared her memories through many interviews, memories sometimes not easy to talk about.

In Norway, Oystein Knibestol photocopied letters and mailed old photos to me. This story could not have been written without his invaluable assistance. I extend a special thank you to Ingrid Ytterdal of Staubo, Norway, a gracious, intelligent lady who generously made a major contribution in Norwegian research. In a private archive in Norway, Ingrid located letters written by the captain of the sailing ship that my grandfather sailed on, letters written to the ship's Norwegian owners from the era before to immediately after the South African War.

In Kentucky, I was fortunate to make contact with J. Patrick Thomas, who had possession of the early records from the Stearns Company, which had owned a coal-mining and lumber operation in the Appalachian Mountains of southeast Kentucky. We were each researching the early days of the company, and exchanged data pertinent to both of our stories. From the homestead years in Alberta, I learned that my family had become close friends with the Berild family, when both families were homesteading south of Youngstown. In 1998, I phoned Berit (Berild) Hagen and asked if she remembered my family. This bright lady answered, "Oh, yes!" and after almost seventy-five years, was able to name the eight children in my mother's family, in the order of their birth. I had four delightful visits with Berit and Palmer Hagen, when Berit shared with me many stories that I later relayed to Faye, who added more details. Allin Allsop lived in that same area and he also shared with me his childhood memories of the Berild and Roseland families.

I met several old family friends from the period the family spent in Okotoks, Alberta during the Depression years. Ralph Cameron was the little boy next door, an only child who spent a great deal of time with the family. Ralph spent an afternoon with me, sharing old photographs and memories, and showed me the town of Okotoks, pointing out locations significant to their lives at that time. Later, I met with Herb Jacobsen, whose father was the pastor of the church my grandparents attended, and whose mother was best friends with Grandma. Herb read many pages to me from his mother's diary of Roseland family events that she had shared with them. Maurice Ardiel was the son of the physician in Okotoks in the '30s, and was my Uncle Arnold's best friend. This charming gentleman shared many

of his memories of life in Okotoks during the years
that my family resided there. Thanks go to Alice
Halstead, who attended church with my grandmother and put me in touch with these people.

When it came time to write the Second World
War portion concerning my uncle's experience in the
Royal Canadian Air Force, I searched for a researcher.
Several whom I contacted recommended Owen A.
Cooke, who worked for twenty-five years as Chief
Archivist with the Directorate of History and
Heritage. I cannot thank Owen enough for the time
and consideration he contributed to my project. He
read my early drafts and gave me much invaluable
advice. I was also fortunate and privileged to meet
with B. D. 'Dal' Russel, DSO, DFC, and Bar, who
trained Fighter Squadron No. 14 in Kittyhawks, was
with the squadron in Vancouver on West Coast
Defence in 1942, and was squadron leader when
their wing was the first to be established in France in
June 1944, following D-Day. Dal read an early draft
of my story and shared his memories with me. Last,
but not least, I must mention Hugh Morse, DFC,
who lives in the neighbouring town of Maple Ridge.
My Uncle Arnold's wife and Hugh's wife were best
friends. Hugh was with No. 14 Fighter Squadron in
Alaska and remained with the squadron in Britain
and France. He often flew with my uncle on missions
over enemy territory. I had lunch with Hugh many
times, when he shared his memories and memora-
bilia with me.

When I had compiled sufficient research to
commence writing my manuscript, I contacted

Margaret Slavin of "Writeaway!", whom I had met at the Victoria School of Writing. Margaret was an invaluable and supportive partner who offered many helpful suggestions and comments through the writing of the first draft of this story. As an unpublished author I was privileged to have my manuscript accepted by Borealis Press. Frank Tierney and Glenn Clever, and editor Janet Shorten were encouraging and attentive throughout the publication process. They were truly a pleasure to work with.

My appreciation must also extend to two gentlemen who translated letters and other material from Norway, letters that were written in Old Norwegian. Gunnar Warolin did the early translation, and then Per Kavlie Anderson worked with me in the latter years. I should mention here that the family name was anglicized when my grandfather arrived at Immigration in New York. Rosseland became Roseland. In preparation for publication, Mr. Warren Sadler skilfully restored, or enhanced, many old family photographs.

In my quest for research data, many libraries, archives and professional persons made a major contribution. The Inter Library Loan division of the Fraser Valley Regional Library responded to many requests, and staff at numerous archives and libraries provided invaluable assistance. These included Provincial Archives of Alberta, Glenbow Archives, National Archives of Canada, Directorate of History and Heritage, and staff from several archives, libraries and universities in Kentucky and Tennessee. Other assistance came from Australia, New Zealand, South Africa, France and Norway.

Others who provided invaluable assistance: Zabeth Botha, South Africa; Forest Brown, St. Olaf College; Chris Cowx; Greta Cumming; Tom Des Jean, National Park Service, Kentucky and Tennessee; Abner Grover, Special Areas Board of Alberta; Cornelius W. Hauk, Railway and Locomotive Historical Society; Charles Hay, Eastern Kentucky University; Beverly Hermes, St. Paul, Minnesota; Val Hutch, Royal Western Australia Historical Society; Tove Dahl Johansen, Universitetsbiblioteket I Oslo; Paul Lemieux, National Archives of Canada; Patricia Maus, Northeast Minnesota Historical Center; Dave Miller, Artist, Y2K Spitfire: Nina Milner, Librarian, National Library of Canada; Lindsay Moir, Senior Librarian, Glenbow Museum Library; Anne Moretro, Aust-Agder-Arkivet, Arendal Norway; Jeremy Nemanishen; Chester, Nerheim, Muskego, Michigan; Ned Nordine, Ludington, Michigan; Thorvald Ravnevand, Kristiansand, Norway; Charles Rheaume, Directorate of History and Heritage; Dawn Strunk, McCreary County Museum at Stearns; Mark Timbrook, Ward County Historical Society; Ronald M. Wood, White Pine Historic Village; Mona Zahara, Tuberculosis Nurses Consultant, Foothills Hospital, Calgary; and many more.

PROLOGUE
In Normandy with the RCAF—
June 1944

THE SUPERMARINE SPITFIRE IX-Bs landed, one at a time, shrouded in dust. Sod had been lifted from the field, and interlocking steel matting laid over the dusty surface to form the landing strip. Flight Lieutenant A. W. Roseland parked his aircraft and proceeded to the squadron headquarters. It was an eerie feeling, walking on ground that so recently had been enemy territory. Number 442 Fighter Squadron had just been deployed to Ste-Croix-sur-Mer on the Normandy coast on the morning of June 15, 1944, arriving about 0900. The other two squadrons in the wing would follow at half-hour intervals, and the remaining pilots from 442(F) would fly over in Douglas Dakotas around noon. Theirs would be the first complete wing to operate from France in four and a half years. Their aircraft had flown over, strafed and bombed this territory for months. It would take some days before this felt like home.

The pilots were pleased to be located in France. The Spitfire IX-B had a short flying range. While on sorties to France from Ford, Sussex, they had always been at risk of running out of gas and ditching in the channel on their return trip. From Ste-Croix-sur-Mer, they would be over enemy territory almost immediately once in the air.

■ ■ ■

The countryside around was very flat, green and pretty, with the same hay and grass that Arnold was familiar with in Alberta. To the south, he would have noticed the sparkling green orchard and the bomb craters that dotted the nearby hayfields. German equipment lay scattered on the ground— uniforms, rifles, helmets, gasmasks and hand grenades, soon snaffled as souvenirs. This had been the site of a German headquarters. Hugh Morse, one of Roseland's buddies, climbed a tree in the orchard. He found blood splattered through the limbs—probably that of a sniper, they thought, buried in one of the nearby, recently dug graves. There were plenty that looked less than a week old.

The ground crew for 144 Wing had come over by ship two days earlier to set up the facilities from which the squadron would operate. It was no small task getting three squadrons settled on a barren hay-field and orchard. The wing consisted of three squadrons with a total of thirty-nine officers, of which Arnold was one, and 750 persons of other ranks. Each squadron was set up in a separate location.

The Number 442 Fighter Squadron pilots camped in the orchard. After picking up their tents, they chose a site and dug themselves a deep slit trench to sleep in, as protection from the flak and anti-aircraft fire. Then they set up their tents over their slit trenches, and tucked their personal effects away, as they always did. Although they had moved their location many times, they were now on the front lines of battle and they would sleep in the trenches at night, to protect themselves from enemy fire.

They heard the artillery all day long. As soon as night came, enemy bombers and aircraft made their appearance, their target the mass of Allied shipping in the channel, which was only one mile north of their base at Ste-Croix. The noise of thousands of anti-aircraft guns in the channel, and a nearby Bofors cannon shooting at the aircraft over and above their campsite, created a din that was almost unbearable. The shells from the anti-aircraft guns made an unearthly shrill whine, racing through the night air. Naval gunners in the channel opened up with orange tracers that ripped across the night sky. Periodically, the pilots in their tents felt the earth shake with the impact of falling bombs.

■ ■ ■

On D-Day, the Allied forces had established beachheads all along the Normandy coast, with the Americans to the west in the region of Cherbourg, and the British and Canadians to the east in the region of Le Havre. On D-Day, the Canadian army had taken Ste-Croix-sur-Mer, a small village ten miles northwest of Caen, and one mile from the channel, and they had immediately proceeded to establish this airfield. On the same day, the British and Canadian armies advanced towards Caen, but they were held back by a heavy German counterattack. A prime objective of the Allies after D-Day had been to establish an emergency landing strip and refuelling station in France. The next step was to establish a base from which to operate in Normandy, to give their fighters a greater flying range into enemy territory, by not having to cross the channel twice on each flight. The establishment of this base in Normandy was such a momentous occasion in the turning tide of the war that BBC crews arrived to do newsreels and radio interviews for audiences in Britain and North America.

■ ■ ■

The morning after Arnold's arrival, six pilots from 442 Squadron were about to take off in their Spitfires when four Focke-Wolfe 190s strafed their airfield. Later that day, a "Beetle Tank" entered the airfield area—a remote-controlled small tank, about four or five feet long. The tank was filled with explosives and propelled by an electric motor. It was one of several weapons the Germans had developed secretly and used in 1944 to bolster their declining manpower resources. The Canadians were not too impressed. The engineers in the squadron proceeded to fix it up to use as a small vehicle to ride in.

Families from the local farms came over to the base to welcome the Canadian airmen, bringing gifts of fruit, flowers and wine. Arnold and a group of airmen visited with children, who showed them papers and ration books that the Germans had given them. The Canadian airmen gave the small children *bonbons* and gum. One child showed his ration of black bread. It was hard, very dark brown, partly mouldy, and a small portion for a day's ration, even for a child. The children told stories of incidents that took place during the occupation, up to the time that the Allied forces had "kicked *les Boches* out." The Canadians later started purchasing milk, vegetables and wine from the local farmers. While

the war went on around them, the farmers continued to work in the fields.

■ ■ ■

The British and Canadian armies on the ground
were battling to take the city of Caen, only ten miles
to the southeast. Roseland and the other pilots of
442(F) spent many hours on patrol over the battle-
front, keeping the airspace clear of enemy aircraft, to
allow the armies on the ground to do their job. On
other sorties, the Spitfires strafed moving vehicles
on roadways and other targets, and dive-bombed
specific targets such as bridges and railways, in order
to cut off enemy supplies and reinforcements. One
night, when American bombers came over from
Britain to bomb Caen, the airfield was treated to a
spectacle, as nine air crew bailed out of an American
B-17 Fortress before it took its final plunge to the
ground and burst into flames. It crashed only a short
distance from the end of their airstrip.

After a week at Ste-Croix, Arnold wrote to
his sister Agnes in Canada, "... *it's not so bad here,
and we do manage to stay quite comfortable even though
conditions are a bit rugged . . . . It is so much better to be
nearer the battle, and not have all that water to cross—
twice each trip . . . .*" He added, "*It was certainly grand
to receive some mail once again—after what seemed like a
very long wait.*" He stated that he wasn't getting the
opportunity to write the number of letters that he
usually wrote.

Even his wife, Audrey, was not getting her
usual number of letters. He thought she understood, though, that he wouldn't be able to write as

often. She had written that everything was under control at home, and that she and the children were in good health. *"We're both looking forward very much to the time when this is all over and we're back together once again—for good this next time, I hope. I have had enough travelling and adventure in the past four weeks to last one a lifetime, I'm sure. Now I am looking forward to settling down in our own little home somewhere."*

Arnold was twenty-eight years old, almost the same age that his father was forty years earlier, when he wrote of a similar longing to his sister back home.

Flight Lieutenant A. W. Roseland, RCAF 1944

Table of Contents

PART ONE
"Dear Old Norway"
(Norway—19th century until 1903)

1

Chapter 1

"I will find my way home,
as long as I am alive"

"Even if this ship took me to Siberia, I would still find my way home, as long as I am alive." Gustav Rosseland was writing home to his sister Anna in Norway. The sailing ship *Aquila* was in the harbour at Little Bay, Jamaica, in 1903, where the crew had been loading logwood to the load rooms, deep in the hold of the ship. The seamen hated the logwood. The roots were filled with earth and spiders, and other small insects that they would later find in every corner of the ship. They preferred that the wood, with all its little creatures, be stored on the deck, but the captain refused. With over 1,000 tons of wood on deck, and an empty hold below, the ship would be unstable. In three weeks, each of the fifteen crew members would carry about seventy tons of wood to the loading rooms, and then they would sail for St. Petersburg, Russia.

Gustav dreamed of his home in Norway. *"We will likely be here for Easter, as the loading will take about three weeks . . . . It is green everywhere . . . . At this place we don't know if it is spring or autumn, because it is the same temperature all the time. But I would prefer old Norway anyhow, and I will be very happy the day I can see the Norwegian mountains again."* The *Aquila* had left Kristiansand, Norway three years previously, and

3

Gustav now just wanted this trip to end. Several times he had been deeply disappointed when he thought the ship was going home to Norway until the captain arranged with shipping agents to pick up another cargo and travel to another destination.

Anna, whom he planned to marry, had been waiting for him in Norway. She was a poised and petite young lady, with a gentle humour and a caring disposition. He recalled the many times that he had walked the two miles down the old postal road from Rosseland to Skara, where Anna lived. But sometimes Anna walked up to Rosseland. At night they walked home by the light of a paraffin candle, and perhaps in bad winter weather, when darkness came early, they waited for daylight before walking home. They had known each other since childhood and had been sweethearts since his early days of sailing. Gustav eagerly looked forward to every visit home. Gustav wrote to his sister, *"I am tired of sailing and I want to get a job ashore. I guess it wouldn't be that easy in Norway, but one could move to another place."*

■ ■ ■

Gustav had been born on the Rosseland farm in South Norway twenty-eight years earlier as part of a "baby boomer" generation, during a period of the highest birth rate of the 19th century. Late in the century, thousands of young Norwegians searched unsuccessfully for opportunities to enter profitable occupations. But Norway was just beginning to industrialize and job opportunities were very scarce; farm families were struggling because the scarce supply of land could not support their growing numbers.

After confirmation at age fourteen, education ended and children entered the work force. Young boys found work on farms, or in the woods, but often young workers were given only food and clothing for their labour. By going to sea as sailors they could gradually increase their income, and they didn't have to pay any living expenses. They could save most of what they earned. A life at sea also offered opportunities for travel and adventure. Gustav, like many young boys, could see the advantage of going to sea.

■ ■ ■

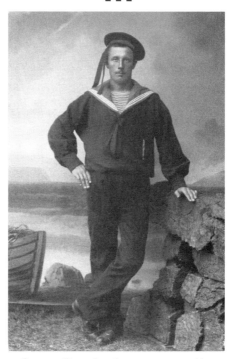

Gustav Rosseland as a young sailor,
circa 1890

Gustav as a mature sailor,
Bunbury, Australia 1902

Gustav was sixteen when he went on his first sailing trip to France, and then to other European ports. From April to November he sailed on the small, 150-ton two-masted brig, the *Mjolner*. The common cargo from Norway was wooden products, and from France they returned with a cargo of corn or wine. To other countries the Norwegians sold fish, and to Britain, pine props to be used as structural supports in coal mines. While in port, the crew unloaded the cargo, cleaned the loading rooms, and reloaded with the new cargo. In his youth, Gustav visited many major European ports. Because winter storms on the northern seas were dangerous for small ships, Gustav was able to spend the winter months at home during his early sailing years.

Gustav began his sailing career as a decksboy. Life for a novice sailor was particularly difficult. Before he served coffee to the officers and the crew at 6 a.m., he had to wash out all the latrines on the ship and scrub the decks. After the main meal at noon, the decksboy always washed the dishes while the others rested. He had the lowest position on the ship and was expected to obey the orders of all the other seamen. Older seamen often reported that they were always tired as decksboys, and sometimes resentful, but they got no sympathy from the rest of the crew, as each crew member had started the same way.

On these small ships, the decksboy lived together with the crew in a small room known at the "ruff," under the front deck of the ship. Two small round windows, known as "cow eyes," provided light. The men slept in narrow berths, with the more senior men in the top berths where they had an overview, and up there it was possible to read from a small paraffin lamp that hung from the ceiling. In stormy weather, they also dried their clothes in this room. They ate their meals sitting on a small wooden chest they brought from home, in which they stored all their belongings. Because the crew worked together all day and lived together in such close quarters, it was very important that they were congenial with each other.

Each week, each crew member was given a pound of sugar and a pound of butter, which he used on hard ship's biscuits or bread. Along with a cup of coffee, this is what he had for his morning and evening meal. At noon, his meal consisted of two or three items, such as salted fish, canned fish balls, herring, preserved meat, soup, gruel or peas. While in port and for a few days after, he might have fresh vegetables. During the 1890s in Norway, potatoes and lemon juice were deemed dietary essentials for improved nutrition and for the prevention of scurvy.

During his second trip to sea in July 1891, Gustav deserted the ship *Albatross* in London. Gustav had some difficulties with crew members, serious enough for him to illegally desert his ship, an offence for which he could lose his licence to sail. The crew always looked for a deserter until the ship left port so, at the age of seventeen, Gustav was a Norwegian-speaking fugitive in the largest city in the world. Gustav eventually found a ship's captain who let him work for his passage home to Norway, and after that he spent almost two years at home with his family.

When Gustav arrived home, his youngest brother, Eilert, was just seven months old. Other siblings at home were his eleven-year-old brother Olav, and his four-year-old sister Anna. They lived with their parents, Andreas and Gunhilde Rosseland, and Gunhilde's father, Eilert Johnson Rosseland, who owned the farm. When Gustav's grandfather died the following year, in the summer of 1892, Andreas purchased the Rosseland farm from the estate.

Gustav remained at home at Rosseland during 1892, and did not return to sailing until the following year. During this interlude eighteen-year-old Gustav and fourteen- year-old Anna became well acquainted at local social events, such as parties at the schoolhouse. Anna's family still lived in their small, older, rented house at Skara. At home with their parents were Anna and her two younger brothers, eleven-year-old Martin and ten-year-old Juergen. The baby of the family was Elizabeth, just five years old.

Gustav worked for his father on the Rosseland farm. According to custom he would receive no pay, except that his father would purchase his clothes and necessities. This was no way for a young man to get ahead in the world. Clearly, Gustav had no great love for life as a sailor, but he returned to the sea as an opportunity to earn and save money. He paid a fine to have his licence reinstated following his desertion, and returned to sailing in March of 1893, on a trip to France. After that he sailed on larger ships and travelled to more distant places.

■ ■ ■

"Gustav, if you would quit the sea, you would make me very happy," his mother wrote to him in June 1894. Gustav had gone to sea contrary to the wishes of his mother, and she was greatly worried about him. *"I think about what happened to Gutter Have, and the same thing could happen to you. I cry when I think about it."*

Life in wooden sailing ships was very dangerous. As steamships came to dominate the market in international trade, Norwegians purchased many older sailing ships that were available around the world for reasonable prices. But these ships were not always in the best condition. A sailing ship was almost like a living creature, in that it required constant care to keep it in top condition. The wood could rot or, in some instances, become infested by parasites. If a ship at sea sprang a leak, sometimes nothing could be done to stop it from sinking. If problems occurred with rigging, masts or sails in stormy weather, the ship could be lost, or a sailor might be swept overboard. Disasters at sea resulted in a large number of Norwegian widows and fatherless children.

In the 1890s, the Norwegian government appointed a commission to study the huge loss of sailing ships, and came up with some astonishing figures. From 1885 to 1894, an average of 300 Norwegian sailing ships were lost at sea each year, with an annual loss of 300 seamen. The record year for losses was in 1894, when 308 ships and almost 600 sailors were lost. That included 42 ships that had "disappeared without a trace." Occasionally, pieces of a wreck were later found washed ashore.

In April 1899, while at sea, Gustav received a letter from his mother. "*I have never been as happy for a letter as this one, because I hear that you have gone through a true conversion . . . .*" Gustav had been raised in the church, but at the age of twenty-four he became deeply religious. In addition to the dangers he faced every day, Gustav experienced great loneliness while at sea. Perhaps the dangers faced by those at sea, and the fear of losing loved ones at sea, contributed to a deeply religious community in South Norway. Gustav maintained an association with a church for the remainder of his life.

By 1899, Gustav was sailing on larger ships to distant ports around the world.

Aquila, formerly the Opawa (Artist Unknown)
courtesy of Alexander Turnbull Library
National Library of New Zealand,
Te Puna Mātauranga o Aotearoa.

■ ■ ■

In Kristiansand, Norway, Gustav met with Sven Stray, of a Norwegian shipping company, in June 1899, and signed on to the crew of the merchant sailing ship *Aquila*. He signed on as a *matros*, or able seaman, at forty-eight kroner per month. On a ship with a crew of fifteen, Gustav had risen to the position next in rank to the officers. The captain gave his order to the officers, who gave their orders to the matros, who in turn gave orders to the crew below him. He could not earn a higher wage unless he returned to school to qualify as an officer. The contract stated that Gustav would remain with the ship until it was back in Europe.

The *Aquila* had been built in Glasgow in 1876, and recently had been purchased by the Norwegians from the New Zealand Shipping Company. It had sailed as a passenger ship, under the name *Opawa*, and traded in all the principal ports of the British Dominion, including twenty trips to New Zealand with immigrants. The *Aquila* was a steel-hulled, three-masted, square-rigged sailing ship—1,076 tons, 215 feet long, thirty-four feet wide, and twenty feet deep. It was known as a fast sailing ship, and a beautiful ship in full sail. Gustav proceeded to London in June, where he joined the *Aquila* after it was refurbished to function as a merchant sailing ship.

After stopping at Métis, New Brunswick for a cargo of wood, the *Aquila* arrived at Buenos Aires, Argentina in December. South of the city, the delta of the Parana River drained into the Atlantic Ocean, a wide delta of many sedimentary islands carved by a multitude of small channels. At the end of the year, when the rainy season begins in the tropical region to the north, many tributaries flow into the basin of the upper Parana. The river begins to rise about year-end and the current becomes stronger, making the trip up-river from the delta very challenging for a sailing ship—one more factor that contributed to the difficulty sailing ships had while in competition with steamships. At the turn of the century, the *Aquila* travelled against the current 300 miles up the river to Rosario, a city located in a fertile agricultural region. Rosario was a place Gustav knew well, having visited there a number of times before.

The population of Rosario had grown rapidly after 1850, and between 1877 and 1900 the population doubled to 112,000. After Argentina achieved independence from its Spanish conquerors in 1816, British companies entered the country, and throughout the latter half of the century, they invested in the sheep and cattle *estancias*, and more importantly, in railroad construction. The railroads facilitated a great deal of trade and attracted large numbers of immigrants from Europe for railroad construction. Wheat and cereal farmers and cattle ranchers settled on the grasslands, or *pampas*, in the region south and west of the river. Wheat, beef and maize became important exports.

At Rosario, the *Aquila* picked up a cargo for South Africa. The weather had been steamy and humid. Captain Olsen wrote that he felt sorry for his crew because they could not work in the heat of the midday sun, even though they had stretched a sail over the work area for shade. Some of the crew had become ill with the heat. They finally got the cargo loaded into the ship, and had an easy trip with the current down the Parana River.

By the time the *Aquila* arrived at Durban, South Africa in April 1900, the British had been at war with the Boers for six months. The Boers were the ruling white class of settlers, of European origin, who had settled the country in the 17th century. They conquered the indigenous black tribes and from them took slaves. The Boers migrated north and east to become cattle ranchers and farmers.

Gold and diamonds were discovered in two independent, northern interior states, Transvaal and the Orange Free State, in the 1860s. When news of the great wealth in the newly discovered mines reached the outside world, fortune-seekers and investors beat a path to South Africa. The two interior states, which owned the wealth in the mines, soon felt the pressure of encroachment from the south. When the president of Transvaal issued an ultimatum to the British to remove their troops from the border of Transvaal, a declaration of war followed on October 11, 1899.

Durban was a beautiful city of 50,000 on the east coast of South Africa, with sparkling, blue water bathing the sandy beaches, and lush green hills to the north. The region enjoyed over 300 balmy days of sunshine a year in a humid, subtropical climate, with warm equatorial waters flowing south along the coast from the Indian Ocean. The city boasted a fine natural harbour in a landlocked bay, with a long narrow entrance between a sandy point and a bluff.

This beautiful harbour proved to be a problem to Captain Olsen and the crew. The city had dredging done in the late 19th century to remove a portion of the sandbar, to allow larger ships to enter the harbour. However, the harbourmaster would not give the *Aquila* permission to go all the way in to the docks, presumably because the waters in the harbour were not deep enough. So Olsen had to pay a fee to have his cargo ferried from the ship to the docks. He suspected that the harbourmaster was in collusion with the small boat owners, requiring his ship to hire their services. The extra cost of hiring the small boats decreased his anticipated profit for the trip.

The delays associated with hiring the small boats and waiting for the ship to be unloaded caused the captain to fear that they would not make it back to Europe before the contract with the crew expired. He would then have to negotiate a new contract with the crew at higher wartime rates, and also run the risk of having them muster off the ship when the contract expired.

Olsen was negotiating with shipping agents in Argentina to get a worthwhile cargo from Rosario, or Buenos Aires, for their return trip to Europe. But he wrote to the *Aquila's* owner, Sven Stray, that the agents he was dealing with could not deliver. Sailing ships relied upon shipping agents to contract their cargo, as the agents had access to telegraph. By this time, some steamships used wireless telegraph. Sailing ships did not have this, another reason why they were having a difficult time getting cargo.

Olsen was waiting for a new sailcloth and he hoped it would arrive soon. But, in any case, they would not be able to leave for a few days because of a dense fog and strong northeasterly winds that were moving north from the Antarctic region. As this was the direction they would be sailing into, he expected that the weather would delay them in port for a few more days.

The *Aquila* did not pick up another cargo. The ship was back at Kristiansand on the 18th of June, 1900. Gustav would now enjoy the rare treat of spending a few weeks home in the summer.

■ ■ ■

Gustav was overjoyed to be with Anna and his family again. After her mother died in 1898, twenty-year-old Anna had gone east to the town of Arendal to work with a family as their "kitchen girl." She returned home to Skara while Gustav was home, so that they might spend some precious time together.

Anna's father, Aanen, now lived at Skara with his three youngest children: Martin and Juergen, ages 19 and 18, and Elizabeth, age 14. Elizabeth had just been confirmed and finished her schooling. Her two brothers were now working in the woods, and Elizabeth remained at home to do the women's work in the house.

At home at Rosseland were Gustav's two brothers: Olav, age 20, and Eilert, age 9. Gustav's sister Anna was now 13 years old, with only one more year of schooling ahead. Gustav's sister and Anna's sister were close in age and best friends.

Anna and Gustav spent as much time together as possible, but the short vacation ended all too soon. Gustav reluctantly left for Kristiansand to join the crew of the *Aquila* in late July. He left shortly after for his last and longest voyage at sea.

■ ■ ■

The *Aquila* travelled the short distance to Sonvik, Sweden in late July to pick up her first load of cargo. Captain Olsen was bringing his wife and two children along on this trip. Only a captain was allowed to bring a wife and children along.

The demand for shipping in the southern oceans had increased greatly in recent months, with the war in South Africa creating an increased need for men and supplies. Captain Olsen had a number of decisions to make. They might proceed to Australia to bring back a load of yarrah wood to either Durban or Buenos Aires. Yarrah wood was in great demand worldwide, for use as railroad ties, or "sleepers." It was also used for bridge timbers and for construction of docking facilities, as it was a durable wood. It could also withstand attacks by salt-water marine borers, and was fire-resistant. But Olsen was also concerned about avoiding the hurricane season in the South Pacific, as sailing ships were at great risk of damage to their sails and masts during a hurricane. He was studying his options. Merchant sailing ships did not sail on schedule. Opportunity and circumstances dictated their operations.

The loading of the ship had gone rather slowly due to the small size of the various containers to be carried aboard. He stated that they could save some time and money by not unloading the ballast. Loading and unloading ballast was heavy work for the crew. Ballast was material of heavy weight, such as rock, sand or steel, stored in the deepest hold of the ship to maintain the stability of the vessel. The weight of the cargo on the ship had to be properly balanced and well secured for sailing in rough seas. An overloaded ship was dangerous, and likewise a ship that was too light. The force of the wind on the sails could roll over a lightly weighted or poorly balanced ship.

The *Aquila* headed south to cross the southern seas to Australia, an area noted for treacherous sailing. In a desperate quest for cargo, Norwegian sailing ships took risks, sailing often in uncharted and dangerous waters. The trip across the southern hemisphere from Buenos Aires to South Africa to Australia was in a region named by sailors the "roaring forties," and "furious fifties." Here the cold Antarctic climate meets the temperate climate from the north, producing unpredictable weather and heavy seas. Westerly winds, frequently of gale force, blow over an open ocean from South America to Australia, unobstructed by land masses. In such winds, damage to sails and masts was common.

The safety of the crew was at great risk in heavy seas. The crew took turns at the rudder and the sails had to be trimmed to keep the ship sailing in the right direction. According to strict convention, the captain and officers walked on the windward side of the ship, where there was least danger of being swept into the seas by rogue waves. The crew walked on the leeward side. The crew worked long hours and took turns at the mast. Sailing into the wind was most laborious, when the crew had to trim the sails almost constantly. The most restful time for the crew was when the ship was sailing with the wind.

■ ■ ■

On Jan. 15, 1901, the crew was at harbour in Australia. The loading had been delayed by a steady summer rain that had been falling for days, and their sails still needed repair. Then, when they were all ready to go, a fierce landward storm followed the rain, and the harbourmaster would not give them permission to leave.

Olsen had had trouble with his crew. He wrote to Sven Stray that they were hardly out of Kristiansand when he saw that one of the men was going to cause trouble. In Australia, several crew members had declared themselves sick. One was back at work, but the other two weren't. Olsen stated that what really ailed them was "ship-jumping fever." He told Stray that in the future he wanted to withhold the greater part of the pay of all unmarried crew members, as this was an effective weapon against ship jumping. Eventually, the *Aquila* was on its way.

■ ■ ■

On April 14, 1901, the *Aquila* was in harbour at Cape Town, South Africa. The harbour was greatly congested with ships bringing troops from the Dominions, and war supplies. Frequently during the war, ships were double and treble-banked, with forty or fifty more ships lying at anchor in Table Bay, waiting their turn at the docks.

By this time the South African War had become a guerrilla war, requiring reinforcements and supplies. At the beginning of the war the British had anticipated a quick end to hostilities. However, the Afrikaners soon organized a fierce resistance in the form of guerrilla warfare. Afrikaners were farmers and descendants of the original European settlers, who adopted some of the language and culture of the indigenous tribes. Although they adopted some of their language and culture, they generally did not intermingle with the indigenous people of Africa. Their language was known as Afrikaans. They were not expected to put up much resistance, but they united to destroy and damage railroads and bridges, and seized British supplies. Eventually, the British retaliated with a "scorched earth policy," burning crops and homesteads, and cutting off food supplies. Later, the British herded Afrikaner women and children into concentration camps, where thousands died.

Cape Town is set in the south end of Table Bay. To the west, the point, or hook, of the bay provides some shelter to the harbour facilities and the city, but Table Bay is widely exposed to the Atlantic Ocean north of there. The city is set on the flat, and on the gently sloping hillsides that rise to the base of Table Mountain. The mountain and two peaks to the east and west partially encircle the city, giving the impression that it is set within an amphitheatre. Table Mountain rises sharply to the rear, is flat-topped and is frequently capped by a flat, white cloud known as a "tablecloth." The wide western exposure of Table Bay leaves it vulnerable to the full fury of winter storms off the Atlantic Ocean. The harbour was safe enough in the summer months, but violent winter storms made it a death trap to many sailing ships. Countless ships were lost until a stone breakwater was completed in 1869, and upgraded again by 1895 after the discovery of gold in Transvaal. The harbour then became very busy; and was even busier during the South African War.

Gustav had great hopes that the ship would now head home to Norway, as the captain's wife was very anxious to return home. Their fourteen-year-old son was due to be confirmed in the fall and it was imperative that they be home for the occasion. Olsen also wanted to leave the harbour because he feared the crew becoming sick from an outbreak of boils in Cape Town. However, opportunities for another trip took precedence, so the captain's wife, with her two children, left the ship on May 31 to make the trip home to Norway. The *Aquila* later left for Biloxi, Mississippi.

■ ■ ■

When the *Aquila* arrived at Biloxi in late October, a letter was waiting for Gustav from his fourteen-year-old sister. It had arrived at Cape Town after they left and had been forwarded to Biloxi via steamship. She commenced writing to Gustav, and this was when she started saving the letters that he wrote to her in reply.

At Biloxi, their ship was lying at anchor far from shore and they could hardly see land. The captain was the only person who would set foot on land in the three weeks that they would be anchored there. Biloxi was a beautiful seacoast town, about fifty miles east of the mouth of the Mississippi River. The long stretches of sandy beaches were protected from the waters of the Gulf of Mexico by a string of islands eight to ten miles out from the mainland, while the rich waters from the Mississippi River provided an abundance of nourishment for the plentiful seafood in the region. At the turn of the century, Biloxi was known as the Seafood Capital of the World, for the large amount of canned seafood and raw oysters exported worldwide.

Three weeks later, on the 19th of November, Gustav wrote to his sister again from Biloxi, where they were still loading cargo. He thanked her for the letters that he had just received. Gustav reminisced that he remembered her as a little girl who used to sit on his lap, and he had a hard time thinking of her as a young woman. He alternated between talking to her as a child and as an adult, but he had little news for her, as all he had done since his last letter was work on the ship. *"Yes, Anna, you must be a nice girl and help your mother as much as you can. I don't think I have to tell you that . . . I will bring you a small gift when I come home."*

■ ■ ■

Five months later, in April 1902, Captain Olsen wrote from Rosario that the *Aquila* was waiting in harbour to take on her load. The long delay in reaching Rosario may have been caused when they passed over the equator, or the "equatorial belt of calm," an area notorious for extreme weather conditions, such as violent storms and periods of no wind, known as the doldrums.

The intense heat in the equatorial belt of calm causes warm, moist air to rise, and along with low air pressure, produces a variety of weather conditions such as cyclones, hurricanes, thunderstorms and squalls. These generally occur August to November. The other extreme atmospheric condition in this region is the doldrums, a state of clear skies, intense heat and no wind. Sailing in these conditions was extremely demanding. Sailing ships might drift for weeks without any wind, and with any light breeze the crew worked all-out trimming the sails to take advantage of the wind while it lasted. While they were stranded in the doldrums, the crews of sailing ships had no escape from the heat. Sailors had to wait helplessly for the next wind in the crew quarters below the deck. With the heat, the tar between the planks on the deck above would bubble, making their quarters below resemble an oven. While on deck, the brilliant reflection of the sun on the still, mirror-like ocean was dazzling to the eyes and bothersome. During his career as a sailor, Gustav crossed the equatorial region many times.

■ ■ ■

At Rosario, Olsen heard news that impacted the whole shipping industry in the southern seas. The news hit shipping circles like a bomb. The reason for all the excitement was rumours of peace in South Africa. Traders and shipping agents were running around trying to secure ships to return troops and supplies from Britain and the Dominions back to their homelands. By the end of the war, 450,000 men from Britain and the Dominions had served the British in South Africa. With talk of peace, those who served the British army were eager to return to their homelands. A huge demand for shipping was forthcoming.

Olsen wrote that four crew members had mustered off the ship that morning, so he was going to hold back the pay for all the others, except for steering mates Gustav Rosseland and Sivertsen. He stated that the rest of the crew really didn't know what they wanted.

Gustav knew what he wanted. He wanted to go home. But again, he was bitterly disappointed. The next news he heard was that the *Aquila* would not be making the expected trip to Europe with wheat, but would be returning to South Africa. It would soon be two years since he left Kristiansand.

■ ■ ■

The *Aquila* arrived at Port Elizabeth, South Africa on May 29, 1902, just two days before the British and the Boers declared an armistice in the three-year war. They had bypassed Cape Town, where the congestion in the harbour was even greater since rumours of an armistice. Their ship anchored in Algoa Bay, at Port Elizabeth, where sandy beaches stretched twenty-five miles along the southeast coast of the cape, the sunniest location of the south cape. In 1820, the city had been the site of the first British settlement in South Africa. Gustav wrote to his sister that they had arrived well and happy. It had been the shortest trip over the ocean in many years, only twenty-seven days. At 4,700 miles, the trip was not exactly short. He had a letter waiting for him dated two months previously.

Gustav was beginning to sound depressed. *"We know nothing about whether we are going to see each other again in this world . . . . A life on earth is just a short breath of air. It is nice to know that there is a better place waiting after this life is over."* He had been sure that he would get home from Rosario, but he had been disappointed so many times that he could only hope now that he would be home by next spring. He knew now that the ship would be making two trips to Australia.

Gustav requested permission to leave the *Aquila* in South Africa for a period of two months, in order to work on British supply ships, an opportunity to earn more money. Because Gustav was reliable, Olsen granted him that permission. He rejoined the crew of the *Aquila* on the second trip to Australia, late in 1902. While in Bunbury, Western Australia, he had his photograph taken, and sent home to the family for Christmas. He couldn't be there, but he sent his photo.

■ ■ ■

Bunbury was a picturesque town of 3,000, about 100 miles south of Perth on the southwest corner of Australia, and situated on the west side of an inlet fed by two rivers. A coral reef protected the entrance to the harbour. The area was well served by railways, with a wooden jetty that extended one-quarter mile into the harbour, providing excellent facilities for loading and unloading. At the turn of the century, Bunbury was an important seaport for the export of yarrah wood, grown in that region. These trips between South Africa and Australia were heavy work for the crew, loading and unloading railroad ties, and sailing through challenging southern waters. From Bunbury, the *Aquila* brought back to Durban two loads of railway ties, probably to replace those destroyed by the Afrikaner guerrillas.

■ ■ ■

On Nov. 14, 1902, they arrived back at Durban after their second trip to Bunbury. Olsen informed Stray that he wanted the ship to go north now, as some of the crew were threatening to leave the ship if they went east again. Three weeks later, the *Aquila* was still waiting in harbour to begin unloading its cargo, because unloading dockworkers were not available. During such long delays in port the captain kept the crew busy on the ship, and the crew was paid the same wage each day of the year while at sea. Ship owners wanted a well-maintained ship, and for the captain it was a matter of pride and safety to have the ship well cared for. The captain always had jobs he wished done, such as painting and repair to sails, rigging and masts, and other routine maintenance that could not be done while at sea. During the time in harbour, the crew could request permission from one of the officers to leave the ship after 6 p.m., or on Sundays.

During lonely evenings Gustav took up the hobby of building miniature ships. He constructed a highly detailed miniature of the *Aquila*, and another ship that he had sailed on, and later took them home to his family at Rosseland, where they remain to this day.

Gustav sent a wistful letter to his sister. *"Last Christmas I thought I would be home with you this year, but that is not possible. Maybe we will not be in the harbour, but at sea."* He didn't know where they were going after they left Durban, but if the ship went to Australia again, he would muster off and then look for a ship to America or Europe. This would mean a financial penalty and also cost him his fare home to Norway. But he resolved that he would be home at Rosseland by the summer. He thanked his sister for her letter. *"Letters from home are the best gift that you can get while travelling the ocean."*

In his next letter, Gustav's spirits were low. *"It is not easy to be on a ship with the same people, who may not have the same interests in life. One can easily feel lonesome. One does not appreciate the home before one goes to sea, and then we miss the family and think about them all the time."*

However, Gustav's wish came true. They headed north from Durban for St. Thomas in the Caribbean.

■ ■ ■

From St. Thomas in the Caribbean they proceeded to Little Bay, Jamaica, where the crew commenced loading logwood. He wrote from Little Bay, *"I am still longing to come home . . . . It will be truly lovely to meet again."* He expected that it would take three more weeks to load the ship and then they would sail for St. Petersburg.

Captain Olsen wrote home to Sven Stray in April 1903 from Whitehouse, Bahamas that he had personally supervised the loading of logwood on the ship. He had several problems with the upcoming trip to Russia, though. He required a telegram of clearance to unload the logwood at St. Petersburg, and he had some problems in respect to insurance for the ship. He thought they might have some trouble unloading in Russia and thought the Scandinavian ship owners had to unite to do something about the totally unreasonable conditions. The Scandinavian ships were mainly sailing ships, so Olsen's concerns about problems were most likely to do with the priority given to steamships in port.

Captain Olsen had also had major problems with the crew that evening. One had brought liquor on board the ship, with the result that some of the crew started fighting, and a few got so out of control that he had to have them tied down. It was well into the night before he had the troublemakers subdued. Gustav did not drink alcohol, so he would not have been involved with the drinking.

Olsen reported that four crew members had mustered off the ship, all with Scandinavian-sounding names, and three had mustered on, with British-sounding names. He stated that the Finn and the German were still on board, so now he had to find a reason to sail via Copenhagen to let these men off. Another one of the Scandinavian crew had deserted the ship, and the steward was bedridden, but the captain thought it was rheumatism and believed that he would be better in a few days.

He hoped that the circumstances on the ship would improve when they got under way again in the fresh sea air. He was sorry that the trip home would be long, as the hull of the ship was badly overgrown with sea growth, causing the ship to travel at a reduced speed. The *Aquila* was due for a keelhauling once they returned to their home port.

■ ■ ■

Once at St. Petersburg, the crew unloaded the logwood. Fabric manufacturers had purchased the logwood for the production of dyes for woollens, cottons and silks, and for dyeing ink. The discovery of dyes in logwood, about 300 years earlier, had changed forever the wardrobes of western Europe. The highly valued wood, harvested from the mosquito-infested swamplands of Central America, was the source of brilliant reds and purple dyes, cheaper than any other known source. After unloading the logwood, the crew scrubbed every loading room on the ship clean again.

Gustav mustered off the ship at St. Petersburg on July 18, 1903. Because he didn't want to wait for the *Aquila* to make the return trip to Norway, he found another ship that was travelling to Norway and paid for his own fare home. It had been just over three years since he had left Kristiansand. He had never expected that Anna would have to wait that long for his return.

Chapter 2
"The Dear Fatherland"

PASTOR BODKER MARRIED Gustav and Anna on September 23, 1903, in the 900-year-old Tveit Church, where Anna's parents had married more than a quarter century earlier. As was the custom in Norway, Gustav and Anna were married in the early afternoon.

The wedding celebration was held later in the afternoon and evening at the Rosseland home, built in 1842 and well suited for a reception. The entertainment area, the living room and dining room, could accommodate a large group in spacious, well-lit rooms, with windows that looked out upon a landscaped garden. Scattered fruit trees provided shade. The home had a basement and several bedrooms upstairs. The Rosseland farm was one of the finest in this area of Norway, one of the few farms with open and flat agricultural land.

The farm comprised twenty-two acres of agricultural land and 900 acres of forested land, nestled in an area of undulating hills and small heavily wooded mountains. Paths and trails wove through the hills, and the old postal road from Kristiansand to Arendal ran past the property. Eikland Lake, on the west, stretched two miles from the town of Vennesla to the west side of the Rosseland property. As small property owners, the Rosselands were members of Norway's property-owning and voting class.

Wedding photo,
Gustav and Anna 1903

Roseland family group 1903: Andreas, Gunhilde, Anna, Olav, with Gustav and Anna sitting in front (missing—Eilert)

Rosseland farm 1923

Friends and relatives brought food to the reception, as was the custom for all important social occasions such as weddings, christenings and funerals. Guests included all the Rosseland aunts, uncles and cousins. Uncle Kristen, with his wife Marie and their children, came from the adjoining farm. Aunt Gusta with her husband Arnt Stensvand came from Arendal, as did Uncle Jacob and his wife Tilda, along with all their children. Arnt Stensvand was a well-known principal of two schools in Arendal, one of which graduated many young women as schoolteachers over a period of twenty-three years. Uncle Jacob was a businessman and hotel proprietor in Arendal. Guests from Anna's family included her father Aanen, who was a woodworker, her two younger brothers Martin and Juergen, and her younger sister Elizabeth. Neigbours from the local area also came to extend their best wishes to the newlyweds, as the Rosseland family had been established in this region for almost sixty years.

■ ■ ■

Gustav's grandfather, Eilert Johnson Rosseland, had arrived at Have in Birkenes in 1838, a farm a few miles to the west of the Rosseland farm. Young Eilert did road work and whatever labour he could find and, in 1840, he went to Rosseland as a brick-layer. These were tough economic times in Norway, but young Eilert knew what he wanted and managed his money carefully. When he received an inheritance, he added that to his savings and purchased the farm at Rosseland in 1846.

Eilert Johnson Rosseland, died 1892

Eilert Johnson Rosseland had been born in 1818, immediately after the Napoleonic War ended. He was twenty-eight years old when he became a landowner, and was ready to settle down. In 1848, two years after he purchased Rosseland, he married Anne Gurine Nilsdatter, who was ten years his junior. She was from the farm Have, where he had originally worked when he arrived

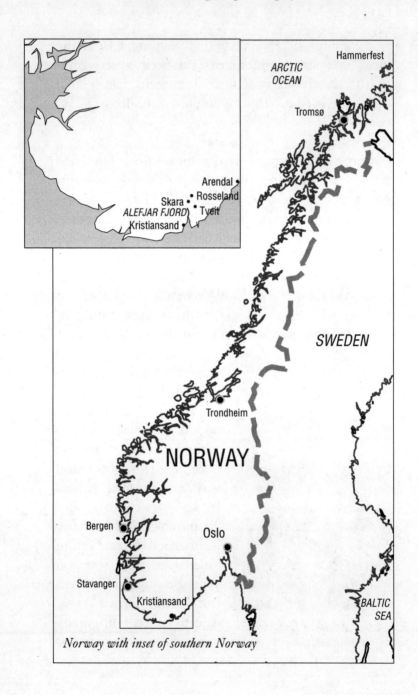

Norway with inset of southern Norway

from Bjelland. Their four children—Gunhilde, Kristen, Gusta and Jacob—were all born in the 1850s. Then, in 1856, Anne Gurine's mother joined the family by purchasing from Eilert a legal contract to live at Rosseland and be cared for there, for the rest of her life. When Eilert obtained the cash from his mother-in-law, he purchased more land adjoining the Rosseland farm. He was fortunate to make his purchase during a period when crops were good and prices for grain were rising. Then in 1866, Eilert's wife, Anne Gurine, died and he was left a widower with four children at home, ages eight to fifteen years, and his mother-in-law, Anna Nilsdatter.

■ ■ ■

The early years of Eilert's life had been during an era of dramatic change in Norway. One of the most significant events in Norwegian history took place two years prior to his birth. Norway had been joined in a friendly union with Denmark for 400 years, until the end of the Napoleonic War. During the war, Denmark had joined Napoleon in a barricade on the seas, in an attempt to crush the British shipping industry and destroy the British economy. This had been a ruinous decision for Norway, as the British allies promised to reward their friend Sweden by ceding Norway to Sweden, as part of the peace treaties. It happened that at this time Norwegians were becoming passionately nationalistic and wanted nothing less than Norwegian sovereignty.

Before the treaty to award Norway to Sweden had been concluded, a gathering of farm-

ers, businessmen and bureaucrats met at Eidsvoll,
Norway to draft a constitution, and on May 17, 1814
declared their country a free and sovereign nation.
However, Great Britain insisted on the transfer, and
late in 1814, Norway became part of a union with
Sweden. The Swedish king now governed Norway
through an executive committee that was an inter-
mediary to an elected governmental body in
Norway. As a "morning gift" to celebrate the union,
the king, Karl Johan, gave the Norwegians a gift of
thousands of Bibles. Later, it was commonly said
that the Bible and the constitution represented the
spirit of the Norwegian peasant homes. The constitution had aroused in Norwegians a new sense of
dignity and nationalism and for the remainder of the
19th century, Norwegians strove for democratic self-
government and sovereignty.

Eilert and Anna Gurine's four children were
born during the years that became known in Norway
as the Golden Age of the '50s. The distribution of
wealth had become more skewed during the depression that followed the Napoleonic War, when
disenchanted farmers and day workers bore the burden of taxation, which supported the government
and aristocracy. In fact, the '50s were the golden age
of the aristocracy, government officials and property
owners who were members of the voting class.

Leaders of the working class began to advo-
cate universal suffrage and abolition of the cottar
system. In lieu of the right to use a small portion of
land, the cottar repaid the landowner by providing
labour. One leader was convicted of treason in 1850

for suggesting the abolition of the cottar system. Cottars, day labourers and owners of small farms began to unite, demanding voting rights, and opposing their heavy taxation and economic repression by the privileged classes. Democratic reform in Norway would take the form of a class struggle.

■ ■ ■

At Rosseland in 1875, Eilert's children were now adults, and his mother-in-law had died. Gunhilde, Kristen and Jacob were still living at home, but Gusta had left home in 1874 when she married Arnt Stensvand. Gustav's mother, Gunhilde, had married Andreas Olsen Moi in 1873, and remained at Rosseland with her husband.

Gunhilde and Andreas had their first son on February 2, 1874 and they named him Andreassen Gustav Rosseland. Children in Norway were named according to the custom of using the chosen name of the father. To the father's chosen name, the sons had the suffix "-sen" added, while the daughters had the suffix "-datter" added. They could also use the name of the farm as a surname.

The Rosseland farm produced barley, oats and potatoes, along with a vegetable garden and fruit trees. Eilert had seven cows, a calf, three sheep and a horse, and he was slowly also harvesting timber from his wooded land.

■ ■ ■

During these years, education was spreading into the rural areas of Norway, and Eilert had a special interest in furthering education in this area. In 1860-61, he was a member of the local government.

In 1875, he sent his youngest son Jacob to a folk high school in nearby Landvik, earning him the wrath of a local priest in Birkenes, who called the school "the devil's work." Folk high schools were a new institution, with the purpose of awakening higher aspirations in the student, through emotional appeal.

Early in 1876, Eilert hosted a meeting at Rosseland to discuss building a new schoolhouse, to be supported by local taxation. Before this time, children had received twelve weeks of education each year from a visiting teacher who taught classes in living rooms and in farmhouse kitchens. At the meeting, the following motion was put forward: "That at Aas there is reason to build a new school-house with the dimensions of at least 8 feet square and 9 feet high, with windows facing south and a smaller roof, which will house a woodshed and a toilet." Fifteen persons attended the meeting and the motion to build the new school was carried, although five people left the meeting in protest. The school was built on the grounds of the Aas farm, one and a half miles north of Rosseland. In 1880, Gustav's brother Olav was born. Also born on the neighbouring farm was Kristen Aas, who was to become Olav's lifelong friend. The Rosseland children and Kristen Aas all attended the Aas School.

■ ■ ■

Waves of high birth rates had followed the large number of births after 1814. Europe was free of the famine, pestilence and disease that usually accompanied war. The herring stock returned to the

North Atlantic, potatoes were introduced to the Norwegian diet, and smallpox was less virulent, all contributing to a healthier population. In the fifty years after the Treaty of Kiel, Norway's population roughly doubled. This put extreme pressure on the small amount of agricultural land, as most of the population was still supported by agriculture. When land was divided among descendants, the parcels became smaller and not sufficient to provide a living for a family.

The effect of the population crisis on farmland was compounded by other changes in the agricultural economy. Following poor crops in the '60s, Norway began importing cheap grains from the United States and Russia. Farmers then switched to dairy farming and sold their products in the market. The economy gradually changed to a monetary-market economy. Farming became more efficient, using newer techniques and implements that required less labour. Trading in the marketplace was enhanced by an era of road building, the beginning of construction of a railway system, and steamship service along coastal routes.

■ ■ ■

The economy in Norway went into general decline in the 1860s except in South Norway, where the Rosseland family lived. The shipbuilding trade flourished in South Norway. The rapid increase in world trade after the industrial revolution had created a huge marketplace to be serviced. The natural resources of the southern Norwegian coast and the available labour supply were factors that shot the tiny nation of Norway to a leading position in the merchant sailing world. The irregular coastline provided sheltered locations for harbours, while the abundance of timber provided raw material for the ships. Kristiansand and Arendal and other smaller towns along the coast were supported by the shipping industries. East of Kristiansand and three miles south of Rosseland was the town of Alefjar, on the northern tip of Alefjar Fjord. In 1881, sixty-six vessels left Alefjar with cargoes of timber. The availability of work in the area attracted workers from other regions of Norway where jobs were hard to find.

■ ■ ■

Aanen Larsen Kylland arrived at Alefjar in 1873. Aanen had purchased his father's farm in Aseral in 1868, but with the poor economy he could not keep up the payments. He travelled south to Mandal, a seacoast town west of Kristiansand where he looked for work as a carpenter and day worker. When he arrived at Alefjar, he found accommodation in a boarding house at Lomsland, about a mile north of the town.

Inger Marie Markusdatter, with her sister Sofie, travelled to Alefjar from Kvinesdal, a town at the tip of a fjord west of Kristiansand, in order to look for work in the area. They, too, found accommodation at Lomsland.

Aanen and Inger Marie were married at the Tveit Church in July 1876. At the time, Aanen was forty years old and Inger Marie was thirty-two. Their first child died, and their second child, Anna, was born in April 1878. In the '80s, they had three more children.

Skara, Anna's family home. Original home has been enlarged. Photo was taken in 1992.

In 1880, Aanen and Inger Marie moved to a rental house on the farm Skara, located about three miles north and west of Lomsland. Skara was an idyllic setting. From the road, the path to Skara rose to a high point, and then went down a slope, which opened into a bowl-like contour. A small lake was surrounded by gently sloping fields, with heavily wooded areas on the higher slopes. The small, older house was a low structure, sited on the far side of the lake and back in the trees. The best agricultural land was on the sloped hillside coming in from the road and down towards the lake; the fields around the lake were satisfactory for grazing cattle.

The land at Skara provided most of what Aanen and Inger Marie needed to sustain them. Aanen worked as a carpenter and woodworker, and also farmed his property. He kept three cows and nine sheep and was able to sell some barley, oats and potatoes to wholesalers in town. These crops grew better than wheat in the short northern season. In town they purchased coffee, sugar and salt. They made their own candles, and purchased some kerosene for lanterns. From the sheep Inger Marie obtained wool to spin and weave, and from that she sewed clothes for the family. To get to market they walked about ten miles over a narrow, wooded path, but sometimes they arranged with a neighbour to take some of their products to the market in town by cart or buggy. Skara never had a horse.

Theirs is the story of a near-subsistence lifestyle still lived by many in the rural areas of Norway at that time, including day workers and the remaining members of the cottar class, who worked for large landowners. In contrast to day workers and farmers, business people, officials and larger landowners now purchased many items in the marketplace. Within this structured class society there were wide variations in materialism and economic levels, and even wide variations within each class and between farms.

■ ■ ■

The world economic crisis of the '80s and the rise of steamships for both the transport of passengers and the international trade of goods tolled the death knell of the sailing ship era. Maintenance and repair was the only sailing business that remained healthy in South Norway. With the loss of so many jobs, there was little money circulating in the economy.

Despite the decline in the economy, Aanen had saved some money working as a carpenter. Finally, in 1893, he was able to purchase Skara by taking out a bank loan and a mortgage to build a new house. He built the house on the slope coming in from the road, looking out on the small lake and pastures. The foundation was stone and mortar, a solid wooden structure with two rooms on the main floor and a loft above. In the kitchen a large stone fireplace provided heat and a facility for cooking. Aanen was a skilled carpenter and built his own furniture. The loft above was where the children slept: it had standing room for an adult in the centre and wooden beds built in against the slope of the roof. The loft was heated in winter from the stone fireplace below.

■ ■ ■

Anna had most of her schooling at the travelling school, when the teacher rotated between the homes of different children, for twelve weeks of schooling during the winter months. The classes were held sitting on benches at the table in the kitchen, with parents sometimes present during the instruction. This had some advantages, as parents could listen in and have their own education advanced, and also reinforce the teacher's instruction for their children.

The short school term always took place in the winter, so at a young age children were able to help on the farm in the summer. Boys eight to ten years old got jobs tending cattle for neighbours. The pay was meagre, perhaps a pair of shoes to wear in the winter. Children commonly went barefoot in the summer, even in the woods, while adults wore wooden shoes.

The usual family breakfast was porridge every day made from barley and oats, along with some milk. The custom was to give the children fresh milk, while the adults drank the milk after it had turned sour. They had taken the cream off earlier and made it into butter, and any excess butter they took to market. The women made *lefse*, a large, thin, dry circular flatbread, made with flour from barley and oats, mixed with potatoes. If kept dry, it remained edible for a long time. The main meal included items such as dried fish or pickled herring, some vegetables and berries from the woods, or apples. Although their diet was limited, some of the foods they ate were quite nutritious. Children whose fathers worked on larger farms, however, could see the richer landowners living in luxury while their serving persons subsisted on meagre rations.

By 1891, residents in that area had built a new schoolhouse at Erklev, about one mile east of Skara, at the junction of the old postal road. New legislation encouraged advancements in education. In 1889, the Norwegian government passed a law determining that girls should be taught arithmetic. Before that time it was thought that girls did not need to know arithmetic, because they would spend a lifetime doing housework and farm work.

Local lore has passed down a story about the teacher who taught at the earlier travelling school, and also during the first year at the new Erklev School. Apparently he did not wish to teach the girls to write because he thought it was unnecessary. The man, who was Anna's teacher, emigrated to North America after teaching one year at the school. Anna completed her schooling in 1892, after turning fourteen and being confirmed by Pastor Bodker.

Pastor Bodker had been assigned to the Tveit parish, where Anna's family lived, two years before the new school opened. One of his responsibilities was the supervision of schools. He visited the school regularly, wearing wolf-skin clothing and big boots, and driving a wagon that had no springs and squeaked loudly. People could hear him coming for miles around.

Bodker became a well-known and well-loved pastor in this region, from 1889 to 1904. The pastor was an important person with many duties. He was always a member of the local School Commission, and usually chairman of the Poor People's Commission, which handled problems of assisting persons who, for reasons of health or lack of money, could not look after themselves. If an indigent person was living in their own home, they might be given grains, potatoes and such items for food. If they had no home, they lived on different farms in the area for specified periods, perhaps a week or two in one home, and then on to the next. Farmers were required to assist indigent persons this way, but the quality of care could vary greatly in different homes. It was a matter of shame and embarrassment for a person to need this type of care. The pastor also visited the sick and the dying, and taught confirmation classes to those who were about to be confirmed at age fourteen. He presided over christenings, confirmations, weddings and funerals, and kept detailed records of all these events, as well as records of his daily activities. The church in Norway was a state church and the pastor was paid by the state.

In spite of the impediments to her education, Anna did learn to read and write well, and perhaps Pastor Bodker had some influence in this respect. After Anna completed her schooling she remained at home to look after her sick mother and the younger children. Pastor Bodker visited the home during her mother's long illness. Years later, Anna was writing poetry in English. The following is one stanza from a poem that she wrote, recalling her childhood at Skara.

> *I think of times as the night draws nigh,*
> *Of an old house on the hill.*
> *Of a yard all wide and blossom starred*
> *Where the children played at will.*
> *And when at last the night came down,*
> *Hushing the merry din,*
> *Mother would look around and ask*
> *"Are all the children in?"*

While her mother was ill Anna shared, and then took over, most of the women's work in the house. Men and women had a distinct division of labour, and the amount of work that was a woman's responsibility is daunting to consider. As well as housework and caring for the children, a woman looked after the animals and milked the cows. She made butter and cheese, and carried the water into the house. She spun the wool, wove the fabrics, knit and sewed clothes for the family, and did her laundry in a creek or lake. She helped with the work in the garden, and worked beside the men in harvest season. If the family had no horse, she helped to carry the hay to the barn in haying season. In addition to this, women usually bore several children and nursed their babies. Anna would have assumed many of these jobs during her mother's illness.

■ ■ ■

Inger Marie was dying a lingering death from tuberculosis. In 1889, in the East Agder region where they lived, over one-third of deaths had been caused by tuberculosis. The real number of TB cases may have been higher, as families submitted the registered cause of death and the disease might never have been officially diagnosed. The number of tuberculosis cases began to increase after 1850; this was puzzling, because it occurred at a time when diets and general health were improving.

In the latter part of the century several scientific discoveries ultimately helped to gain control of the disease, although it took many years before that was accomplished. Robert Koch discovered the TB bacillus in 1882, and the fight against TB began. In 1889, the Norwegian medical establishment decided that education was going to be a big factor in managing the disease, so they prompted the government to print and distribute 10,000 educational posters around the country. In 1895, Wilhelm Roentgen discovered the X-ray, which became an invaluable diagnostic tool, but it was years before many X-ray machines were in use. The main treatment in the late 19th century and up to the middle of the 20th century was bedrest. In particular, it was believed that fresh air was essential for healing, and TB patients were frequently kept outside in their beds every day of the year, regardless of the weather.

Although the disease had been known for centuries it was never well understood. An ongoing controversy questioned whether the disease was inherited or contagious. TB was most commonly found in the lungs. The patient had a frequent cough and spread the germs widely through the air, germs that were very hard to kill and lived a long time. TB most often affected children and women, and one theory proposed that it was because they spent more time indoors in bad air. The patient coughed frequently, and brought up sputum that was eventually tinged with blood. Tuberculosis patients often assumed a delicate and fragile look, a characteristic that caused death by tuberculosis to be romanticized in 19th-century literature, art and operas. A strong and healthy person might recover from a mild case of tuberculosis, but moderate to advanced cases led to death.

Inger Marie died on January 8, 1898 at the age of fifty-two, leaving behind four teenagers.

Anna was almost 20, the boys were 17 and 16, and Elizabeth was almost 13 years old. During the period that Anna cared for her dying mother, Gustav had been away at sea most of the time. He did not return until a year after her death, in January 1899. After her mother's death, Anna found work as a kitchen girl in Arendal, hoping to save some money for the future. Gustav left on his first *Aquila* voyage in June 1899, and was home for a few weeks in June and July of 1900, before leaving on his final three-year trip on the *Aquila*.

■ ■ ■

These were difficult years for Aanen. People who knew him through their family legends describe him as a very strong, industrious and talented man. He was a skilled woodworker, a man of good humour and a talented musician. He played both the accordion and the fiddle. At the age of sixty-two, he was a widower with four teenage children. But that was not his only problem.

Aanen had paid down earlier debts, but he was in financial trouble now. The economy was poor and people had no money to spend, the reason that many left for America during this period. Aanen had borrowed money from the bank, but he was not able to keep up the payments. On June 13, 1902, the courts seized several items from him, including a plough and three cows. In September of that same year, the courts ordered the seizure of more property, including a long list of furniture, another cow, woodworking tools, and what appeared to be most of his personal possessions.

Anna's Father, Aanen—died 1914

Anna's Mother, Inger Marie—died 1898

Anna as a young woman

However, Aanen was not one to give up easily, and he was able to take out another loan from the Hypotek Bank in April 1903. He must have paid down his previous debt in order to qualify for the new loan and was attempting to buy back the personal property he had lost in 1902. It must be concluded that Aanen was a hard-working man still earning an income while well over sixty years of age, in an economy where money and jobs were scarce. Perhaps Martin and Juergen were contributing financially to assist Aanen.

These were the circumstances of Anna's family when Gustav arrived home to marry twenty-five-year-old Anna in the summer of 1903.

■ ■ ■

Anna was waiting for Gustav when he returned home after leaving the *Aquila* in St. Petersburg on July 1903. The long-awaited wedding was a joyous occasion. Gustav and Anna remained at the Rosseland farm after their marriage. Also on the farm were Gustav's parents: Andreas, age 55 and Gunhilde, age 52. Gustav's three younger siblings, Olav, 23, Anna, 16, and Eilert, 12, were still at home, too.

Gustav's parents were thinking of their retirement and looking forward to selling the farm to their children, with a clause that their children would look after them in their old age. Andreas had assumed a mortgage earlier when he purchased the farm, and within weeks of Gustav and Anna's marriage, he took out another fairly large mortgage. Andreas had obtained a commitment from his two older sons that they would send money home to him from America, money that would be credited towards their later purchase of the Rosseland farm.

Gustav and Olav decided to leave for America in the spring of 1904. Olav had worked on the farm since completing his schooling and had recently completed his two-month compulsory military service. Emigration to America presented an opportunity for the brothers to improve their financial status.

They understood that in America a wide variety of jobs in construction, forestry, mining and industry were open to immigrants. Wages in the United States were higher. American sailors were paid three to four times as much as Norwegian sailors. In 1903, if a Norwegian skipper couldn't get a cargo for his sailing ship, he might emigrate, along with his mates, sailors and seamen. Jobs were available on the Great Lakes ferries. Although conditions in Norway were improving with the development of manufacturing industries, pulp and paper, and hydroelectric power, there were more young people looking for work than there were jobs available. And wages in Norway were very low.

After the Napoleonic Wars, the population of Norway doubled twice as fast as the population of Europe, and emigration from Norway was exceeded only by emigration from Ireland. Earlier, it was families who emigrated, but now it was youth, as the farms could not support further divisions and still maintain the families. By 1900, fares to America had come down considerably and steamship lines were in great competition with each other for passengers.

"America Fever" had been rampant in Norway since the first emigrants left about 1850. When the early emigrants went to America, good land was still available in the Midwest and the Gold Rush was on in California, creating dreams of gold and wealth. Three waves of emigrants left Norway before the turn of the century, interrupted by the Civil War and periods of recession in the United States. Overall, the early emigrants did well, and money flowed back to Norway.

Young Norwegians admired America for the democracy and the freedom implied by the American Constitution. They believed that in America, no work was vulgar and that people were respected for the job they did. They would be free of the class distinctions they suffered in Norway, where the working class disdained the privileged, who indulged their sons while at the same time paying their workers a meagre pittance. America truly appeared to be a land of opportunity.

When Gustav left for America in May 1904, Anna was pregnant, expecting her child in June. She remained at Rosseland with Gustav's parents, his sister Anna, and his younger brother Eilert. Gustav and Olav joined the third wave of emigration to America, which had commenced about 1900.

PART TWO
"America Is Not What It Used to Be"
(United States—1904-1911)

Chapter 3
"There are thousands out of work"

"A summer as slack as this is more than anyone remembers," Olav wrote in late August 1904. The turmoil in the labour situation in New York had dashed their hopes of finding employment in the construction trades for the summer. Gustav was working, but Olav was again out of work. Gustav had acquired a wide range of work experience during his sailing years, and he had found a good temporary job. But Olav, with only farm experience, was having difficulty finding employment. They were living in Jersey City, associating with the Norwegian community there.

Gustav and Olav received news of the birth of Gustav's daughter, Magnhild, in early July, shortly after they arrived in New York. Olav wrote, *"I must first send my congratulations to my sister-in-law. I hope it is a sweet little girl that you got, that may never give you any trouble . . . ."*

At the turn of the century, New York was enjoying a boom of construction and growth, a city second in size only to London, England. Waterways divided the city, while bridges and the transit system joined the area together. Brooklyn Bridge opened in 1883, and then in 1903 the Williamsburg Bridge opened, at the time the longest suspension bridge in the world. In 1904, both the Queensborough Bridge and the Manhattan Bridge were under con-

59

struction. The transportation system in New York was on three levels—street level, elevated railway and now the new subway system, which was about to open in October 1904, the longest, brightest and safest subway system in the world.

Skyscrapers were rising in the skyline. The newest skyscrapers were the thirty-storied Park Row Building and the triangular Flatiron Building. The new Macy's 34th Avenue store had opened, and Pennsylvania Station and the Singer Building were under construction. Immigrants supplied an abundance of labour. About half a million passed through Ellis Island that year and about a quarter of them remained in the city. But in 1904, those responsible for this astonishing growth in the city— the builders, employers and unions that represented the workers—were in a state of turmoil and conflict with each other.

Olav wrote, *"It is true that you at home will get no help from us this summer, but where are you going to turn when you are unlucky?"* Gustav and Olav had not been able to send money to their father, as they had promised.

In the construction industry, the Employers Association locked out the unions of the Building Trades Alliance in August for violating an arbitration agreement. The unions said the agreement was forced upon them. They claimed that in every case that was brought before the General Arbitration Board of the Employers Association, the decision was made in favour of the employers. The unions wanted a closed shop for union members, but the employers wanted an open shop, so they could hire non-union workers. The defiant unions were going to take 32,000 men on strike, but the employers retaliated with a general lockout that would ultimately affect the employment of 100,000 workers. The unions sued the employers under the Anti-Trust Law, and then deposed their own president in favour of one who was less antagonistic. The Railway Union, representing the elevated rail employees and members moving over to employment in the subway, were on strike. The union wanted $3.50 per day for a nine-hour day, but the employers held firm at $3 per day for ten hours. In New York, 3,500 meat cutters and butchers went on strike in sympathy for their union in Chicago, but called it off after four weeks when they could see the strike was lost. There was discontent, strikes and riots across the country. *"If we could get hired on a steamboat we would take it until times got better. In the spring I am thinking about going inland to see if things are better there."*

In order to understand the circumstances that Gustav and Olav encountered in New York in the summer of 1904 and in their work experience in the next few years, we must look back on the changes in American society following the Civil War.

■ ■ ■

Industrialization had begun prior to the Civil War, but it was after the Civil War that America made great advances in industry and manufacturing. During the war, the North pushed through legislation for high tariffs to protect home markets for industry, and gave railroads subsidies and land grants to open up the west. Although most good farming land was gone, the Homestead Act of 1862 provided free land for farmers. This increased both the number of customers for railroads and the marketplace for manufactured goods. Those who had made profits from industry during the war were in a position to take advantage of business opportunities during the period of reconstruction. By the end of the century, the United States had risen from fourth place to the position of world leader in industry.

State and federal governments wished to repair the devastation of the war and ease the country through postwar depression and reconstruction. The great increase in capital, an outpouring from governments during the war, was in the hands of business people eager to invest. In less than ten years, railroad mileage in the country more than doubled, creating a great demand for steel as well as for materials necessary to support the growing towns and cities across the country. The industries that saw the greatest growth during this time were involved in railroad construction, steel production and petroleum manufacture. The assembly line method of production arrived, with a wide range of new technologies and advancements, including electric lights, telephones, phonographs, electric street lamps, electric railways, internal combustion engines, automobiles, refrigeration and much more. The buoyant economy was interrupted three times by periods of financial crisis and depression, but these interruptions did not halt the United States's march towards world industrial leader.

Businesses were highly competitive and aggressive. They wiped out competition in order to control market prices and wages and, of course, to increase their profits. Railroads charged high rates, discriminatory and predatory, giving kickbacks to preferred customers by secret agreements. There was no income tax and no government regulation. As an added bonus, businesses could translate their economic power into political power. During hard times, predatory companies bought out their rivals, consolidated their interests, and formed trusts and monopolies. Gradually the great wealth of the country fell under the control of fewer and fewer industry leaders. It was during this period that Charles Darwin released his theory on the survival of the fittest and Thomas Paine taught "That government is best which governs least." This thinking exactly suited the aspirations of business leaders.

The great expansion of industry led to changes in American society. Populations began to cluster around industrial centres. As wheat prices dropped from overproduction, farmers moved to the cities, joining the constant influx of immigrants. Cities grew, but vast numbers of the working poor lived in slums and tenements. The rising business and professional class gained a higher standard of living and the wealthy few lived lavishly.

Business made huge profits based on low wages to workers and an abundant supply of labour. Other workers often resented the steady influx of immigrants and held them responsible for the low wages. Work hours were long, a ten- or twelve-hour day being the norm. Mass production and overproduction brought prices down a little prior to 1900, while wages remained constant. Although wages were low, purchasing power for workers did increase a little during this period.

Changes in working conditions had a great impact on the working class. Former independent craftspeople became wage earners as their skills and products became part of a manufacturing process and assembly line production. Those who once provided services and held positions of respect in the community now became company employees. Workers moved to company towns where they lived in company houses, shopped at company stores, and found all aspects of their lives governed by company policies. Unsafe workplaces were common, with high rates of industrial accidents and deaths, yet there were no social services to provide for those in unfortunate circumstances. Conditions for workers improved little, and workers became increasingly aware of the great chasm between their circumstances and that of the owners and management. This increased awareness resulted in the rise of union activity, precipitating a number of crises between union and management.

■ ■ ■

Across the United States in the 1880s, there were almost 10,000 strikes and lockouts, even though most workers did not belong to unions. A group of unions combined in 1884 to urge employers to adopt the eight-hour day as the standard in industry. When the designated two-year period expired on May 1, 1886, few companies had complied, and workers across the country started going on strike. Leading businessmen combined to quell the strikes, calling in Pinkerton guards and police. At Chicago, an unidentified individual threw a bomb into a crowd, killing a policeman. Although there was no evidence of the bomber's identity, the courts held four labour leaders responsible and they were hanged. Businessmen used strike-breakers, and eventually workers returned to work when they could not hold out any longer. The company black-listed strike leaders and the unions were broken. The eight-hour day did not become an industry standard until 1935.

With the downturn in the economy in 1890, prices and markets for steel declined. At his steel refinery at Homestead, Illinois, Andrew Carnegie kept a firm hand on costs and preserved his profits by reducing wages and letting workers go. Workers objected to the cutbacks by voting overwhelmingly to go on strike. The company called in Pinkerton guards and the state sent in the militia, with ensuing violence. The company refused to talk to union leaders, agreeing only to talk to individual workers. After four months, the resources of the workers were gone and they went back to work. The company blacklisted strike leaders and successfully swept out the union.

A severe recession gripped the United States' economy in 1893, and at Pullman, Illinois, orders for the luxury Pullman Palace Car declined. Pullman ordered layoffs and cut wages of workers by 25 per cent, but not those of management. The company also refused to cut rents in the company town, where rents were already higher than in the surrounding area, and wages were at a subsistence level. Workers formed the American Rail Union, and across the country 2,000 joined the union. When a union committee demanded that Pullman revoke the wage cuts, the company responded by discharging three union committee members. Union members voted to strike and set up picket lines. The union then refused to pull cars belonging to Pullman on any rail line across the country. In response, the management of twenty-four rail companies decided to support Pullman against the union and agreed to send the Pullman cars on mail trains. The union then refused to work on mail trains. The federal government did not want mail service disrupted, so they sent in troops and secured an injunction against a union leader, ordering him not to talk to any union members. The leader later went to jail for defying the injunction. The companies hired strike-breakers and would not rehire workers unless they signed a contract never to join a union while they were a Pullman employee. Union leaders were blacklisted. As intended, the American Rail Union was destroyed.

Demands for reform began to echo through the political system in the 1890s. The Populists demanded reforms such as graduated income tax, government ownership of railroads, loans for farmers and an eight-hour day for labour. In 1896, the Populists joined the Democrats in fear of vote-splitting, and then disappeared from the political scene. One prominent group that agitated for a diverse range of political reform was later labelled "muckrakers" by Teddy Roosevelt. This was an unorganized group of editorialists, writers and speakers who called for a great range of political reforms, including regulation of trusts, honest municipal government, improvements in health and safety, the rights of women and others. This group consisted of middle-class and professional workers. In the early years of the 20th century, journalists and newspapers editorialized their causes. The movement gained strength and became known as progressivism. However, reforms came about slowly.

■ ■ ■

For Gustav and Olav, the prospects for the winter of 1904-05 looked grim. They had worked very little over the summer and had accumulated debts. The harsh winter of the northeast was looming, when conditions would likely get worse. Through word of mouth in the Norwegian community, they heard of jobs available in lumbering in the Appalachian Mountains of Kentucky. This was an occupation they were familiar with from their property in Norway. They could obtain room and board from the company, and the company would repay their rail fare if they stayed six months. Best of all, there were prospects of employment throughout the winter months. They could see nothing better on their

horizon, so they were off to Kentucky in late
September.

■ ■ ■

They transferred trains at Cincinnati for another
eight-hour train ride south towards the Tennessee
border. The train rolled through bluegrass country
to a few miles south of Lexington, where it entered
the rugged terrain of the Cumberland Plateau. This
is a highly irregular area of once majestic mountains,
eroded over time to become a highland carved by
tortuous river channels that snake through narrow
valleys. Trainmen used to call this route the "rat
hole" division because the train darted in and out of
so many dark tunnels. The whole area is carved by
rivers and creeks, some with steep rock embank-
ments, and crossed by numerous bridges. The
hillsides and riverbanks of these valleys were covered with great stands of giant hardwoods, under
which lay a great wealth of bituminous coal. The
Big South Fork River flows north from Tennessee
to the southern part of Kentucky, whence it flows
north into the Cumberland River, west to the Ohio,
and eventually to the Mississippi River. Gustav and
Olav's destination was five miles north of the
Tennessee border on a site near the Big South Fork
River.

■ ■ ■

After the Civil War, southern states were eager to
improve their economies and looked for ways to
convert their natural resources into cash. During a
major recession in 1873, the state of Kentucky
ordered a geological survey to identify and publicize

the great natural wealth of timber and coal in the Appalachian Mountains, one of the most rugged and isolated regions of the United States. During the same period, the city of Cincinnati decided it had to construct a railroad south to enhance its trade with the southern states. The railroad was completed through to Chattanooga, Tennessee by 1880. In order to make the railroad construction profitable, they engineered it to cross through this rugged area of previously untapped rich natural resources of timber and coal. When the Cincinnati Southern Railroad came through, the settlers of the area had daily communication with the outside world for the first time.

Native Americans had hunted and lived on the Cumberland Plateau for thousands of years, but in the previous hundred years, settlers of largely Anglo-Saxon stock had made their homes there, in isolated areas suitable for agriculture. They settled in the coves and hollows of the fertile valleys, along the rivers and creeks that wound through the rugged mountains. They also settled on the meadows of the plateau above the valleys. The grandeur of nature often surrounded their settlements: steep cliffs or escarpments, waterfalls and arches carved by the power of water through the hard rock.

The settlers were blessed with an abundance of water and virgin stands of timber: giant chestnuts, walnut, pine, oak, poplar, hickory, cedar, cherry and maple. In the forests and meadows they found such things as fruits, berries and nuts, as well as numerous livestock, to support them in their subsistence living. To purchase whatever else they required, they brought to market their livestock: hogs, cattle, sheep, turkeys and other products. They herded their animals over dirt trails, some of which later became wagon roads. It sometimes took them weeks to deliver their stock to the cotton planters in the south.

The most established north-south road in this area of the Appalachians was the Somerset-Jacksboro Road. When the Cincinnati Southern came through in 1880, it roughly followed the route of this old road. Settlers, who had previously relied upon couriers for news from the outside, now had regular mail and newspaper delivery and passenger service on the train. When Justus Stearns built his town at the site of the old town of Hemlock on the Cincinnati Southern route, he built an electric plant and the residents experienced electricity for the first time in 1903.

■ ■ ■

Justus Stearns was originally from New York, but he married into a wealthy business family from Ludington, Michigan, and made his home there for the rest of his life. After the 1873 "Panic," he had gone broke, but started over again working as a clerk. (At that time economic depressions were known as "Panics.") By the 1880s, he had established his own store in Ludington and in 1885, a lumberyard. During a lumber boom in Kentucky in the late 1890s, Stearns heard reports of vast tracts of virgin timber in the southern Kentucky and Tennessee region. In 1898, he bought out his in-laws' extensive commercial holdings in Ludington, including a hotel, lumber operations, salt mining operations, electric power plant, railroad and a 50,000-acre property, all of which he incorporated under the Stearns Salt and Lumber Company. He also had extensive holdings in the Midwest, the Pacific Northwest, the Great Lakes, New Orleans and Florida. By this time, Stearns had agents scattered around the country looking for business opportunities, with a special interest in increasing his depleting lumber resources in the Midwest.

In 1900, Stearns sent Al Kinne to Kentucky to secure properties to add to his timber holdings. By all accounts, William Alfred Kinne was an effective and amiable ambassador for Justus Stearns. He travelled extensively through Kentucky and Tennessee, his warm and outgoing nature winning him friendships with the mountain people.

In his travels, Kinne met up with Louis Bryant, a bright young mining engineer who had come into the area a few years earlier to consolidate mineral and land holdings acquired by his father. In 1893, in order to publicize the resources in the Kentucky Mountains, Bryant had taken a one-ton, thirty-six-cubic-foot block of bituminous coal from the Worley mine to the Chicago World's Fair. While Bryant had the expertise and holdings, he did not have the resources for development. The two would become friends, and Bryant later became a valuable associate of the Stearns Company, teaching them a great deal about coal mining. By 1901, Kinne had negotiated a twenty-five-year lease with Bryant that called for the construction of a railroad and the opening up of mines in the area, and gave Stearns the right to harvest the timber in the area. Kinne had secured 50,000 acres in what became known as "The Big Survey."

In the spring of 1902, Stearns had his representative sign the articles of incorporation for the Stearns Coal Company, the Stearns Lumber Company, and the Kentucky and Tennessee Railroad. Legend has it that the papers were signed under an old gum tree that stood next to the site where the first company store was later constructed. The town site was at the location of the old town of Hemlock, at the crossroads of the Somerset-Jacksboro Road and the east-west road from Williamsburg to Monticello. The Big Survey included lands from three Kentucky counties and one from Tennessee. The Stearns Company had become the sole proprietor of the town of Stearns, governing all aspects of daily life for the residents there. In 1903, Justus Stearns sent his only son, Robert L. Stearns, to reside in the small company town in Kentucky to oversee all the operations in the community that bore his name.

When Gustav and Olav arrived at Stearns in late September 1904, the town was just two years old.

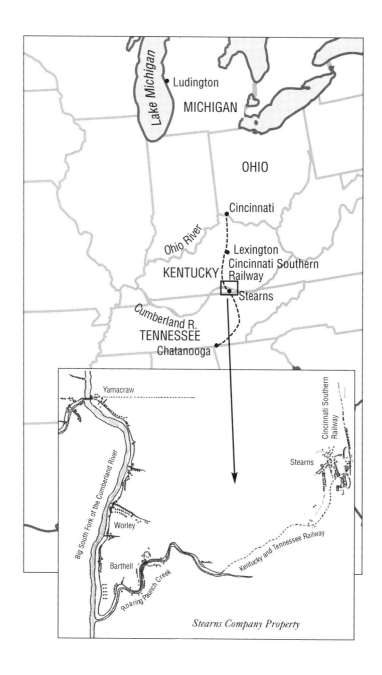

Chapter 4
"If you gain something,
you lose something else"

IN THE EARLY DAYS, the company painted most of the buildings in town white with green trim. The first buildings Gustav and Olav saw when they stepped off the train at Stearns were the train station and the company store, which housed the company offices upstairs. Near the top of a sloped hillside, several hundred feet to the east, stood the new hotel, and residences were under construction on the hills that encircled the town to the north. Across the tracks and beyond, to the south, stood a new electrically driven planing mill, the first all-electric planing mill in the United States. Stearns already had an electric plant in Ludington, so he had no problem setting up another plant in Kentucky.

Stearns office building and railway station. The hotel that burned on Christmas Day 1908 is on the mid-horizon.

75

The company had let out a contract in 1902 to have the first four miles of railroad constructed on the slope down to the Big South Fork River, a drop in elevation of 450 feet. Crews then constructed log booms on the river at the mouth of Roaring Paunch Creek to catch the logs purchased upstream, since the company bought timber from residents in the area, as well as logging their own. Logs were transported on the K&T Railway up to the mill in town, where they were transformed to market grade lumber. The company shipped the first load of coal from Barthell mine in June 1903.

■ ■ ■

The brothers moved into a company boarding house and got to work on October 1, 1904. They started at the planing mill, but the mill was shut down frequently that fall because there were not enough logs to cut. The brothers' income at first was not enough to pay their room and board, so they quit the mill and asked to work in the woods, where they could work at logging every day, except when it was raining.

Their first Christmas was lonely. They went for a walk in the afternoon in "free nature," and ate and drank all day with healthy appetites. They said that nothing of the good food was missing, but they longed for the festive mood of Norway. Christmas Day seemed just like an ordinary Sunday.

Gustav complained that it was hard to write a letter, as the boarding house was so noisy. The room accommodated a number of men, which gave them no privacy. He apologized to his sister for not writing more often, but he wrote to Anna frequently and he knew that she would pass the news along. Gustav wrote frequently to his wife, but only the letters that Gustav and Olav wrote to their sister have survived.

Anna with Magnhild 1905

They found the winter at Stearns surprisingly cold. They had days of sparkling cold weather, days of rain, and one week they had four inches of snow. Olav wrote, *"I have never felt so cold."* Near the river in the Appalachian Mountains the air was biting and damp. By March, the weather seemed like a Norwegian summer.

March 1905 was a month of decision. The company would refund their tickets after they had been there six months, and they wondered where they should go next. But, in April, the company offered them better wages starting May 1st, so they decided to stay at Stearns a while longer, perhaps another year. They believed that their work experience at Stearns might help them get better jobs elsewhere.

They were sorry to hear that times were so bad for the working man in Norway, and they had heard that it was especially bad in Oslo. They were sure they were doing better at Stearns. They expected to save about $12.50 per month, and promised to send some money home so that Father could buy some fertilizer, seed or maybe a plough. They still had a debt to repay in New York stemming from the bad summer of 1904, and they were also putting a little money in the bank in case one of them fell ill.

The brothers were most interested in how their money should be spent at Rosseland. Their father had been thinking of fixing the main house. They thought that should be done as soon as possible, and suggested some new furniture and comforters for the beds, and Gustav's Anna was to get whatever she wanted and needed. Gustav and Olav were obviously pleased with the amount of money they could send home. Gustav's wife had written that her two brothers, Martin and Juergen, wanted to come to America, and Olav assured them that they could get jobs at Stearns.

Their fourteen-year-old brother, Eilert, was finishing school and would be confirmed in the fall. He was going to learn to drive that summer—a horse and carriage. Olav wrote, *"Tell him that I am happy to hear that he is really hitting the books, and that we have not forgotten the promise we made for his confirmation gift."*

In June, Olav commented that last year at this time they were in the middle of the Atlantic. The weather was very bad, and they were seasick. This year they were enjoying the lovely spring weather in the mountains.

■ ■ ■

In 1905 the Stearns Company continued the expansion of its operations. It carried on with the rail construction down the Big South Fork River. The company obtained new leases on properties at Rock Creek, so it ordered the rail construction to proceed north to where Rock Creek flowed into the Big South Fork, and commenced construction of a railroad bridge over the river, a short distance north of Rock Creek.

The bridge over the Big South Fork was a reinforced concrete structure 575 feet long, with five arches, the largest bridge of its type at the time. This twelve-mile section of railroad from Stearns to the Yammacraw Bridge became the heart of the company operations, servicing several coal mines and the massive logging operations that took place in the early years of the company.

Olav had begun working on the bridge in the spring, but he had a problem with the foreman. He was asked to fetch some tools one day, but Olav didn't understand what was wanted, so the foreman fired him, saying, "This guy doesn't understand English!" Olav wrote later, *"The new man got [hit with] a plank on his head three days later, and was killed."* After that, Olav worked at the sawmill again. Each day, sixteen fully loaded rail cars, each sixty feet long, left the mill. The biggest timber cut was the chestnut tree, which grew up to five feet in diameter.

By summer, Olav was working again on the bridge. Gustav and Olav worked transporting concrete out to the bridge via an aerial cableway. One day, during a terrible hot spell of 140 degrees Fahrenheit in the shade, a block broke. The brothers were asked to repair it during the rest period after the noon meal and were run up to the bridge in a chair. They worked a full hour in the hot sun.

After they came down again, they went to a shop and drank mineral water. Then Gustav got sick, and Olav got him into the shade, but by this time he was sick, too.

People who looked at them thought they were resting after lunch. The general manager and the boss looked in. "They are drunk," they said, and went away. Gustav and Olav were quite conscious, but too sick to say a word. Then two locomotives came and the drivers realized that the brothers were suffering from sun stroke, as by this time they were shaking all over. They were taken to a doctor, who looked after them. Gustav was off work a week, and Olav was off for six weeks. Olav later reported that he had lost seventeen pounds in the summer.

In September, Olav was reminiscing about the gardens at home in Norway. They would just be finishing the harvest and digging the potatoes up from the ground. That was the job he hated the most. But, in Kentucky, they had just a small patch of potatoes and some corn. They lived on cornbread, potatoes, pork meat and milk. Every farmer had about ten to twenty pigs running loose in the woods, just eating whatever they could find there. These pigs had no fat on them and had a very poor flavour, unlike the pork meat at home in Norway.

They could hardly eat this meat. The cows were also out all year. Farmers just had to buy hay for a few weeks in the winter.

Gustav and Olav's cousin had bragged to them how much money he made during the harvest season in Norway. But Olav wrote that you couldn't compare the harvest income with what they would make in Kentucky all year round. However, he added that expenses were high and few people were lucky enough to make the big income everyone dreamed of making in America.

■ ■ ■

By October 1905, Gustav and Olav had been at Stearns more than a year. *"Time really flies. We are now at the point when we can start thinking about coming home."* Their plan was to earn enough money to enhance their finances and then return to Norway.

In early October, Gustav visited a Norwegian at Stearns who was sick with rheumatism and had no medical care. Some of the workers had just started a campaign to raise money to send him to a hospital. Many Americans had the disease, so they thought it was the climate that caused it. They hoped they wouldn't catch it.

■ ■ ■

Olav was an avid reader of newspapers. In addition to Norwegian articles, he was starting to read English, sometimes getting different opinions and points of view from different papers. During a period in 1905 when Norway was seeking political independence from Sweden, diverse opinions in newspapers caused Olav some concerns.

The Norwegian government presented a bill to the Swedish king demanding a separate consular service for Norway, which it believed essential to its role in international trade. The Swedish king used his veto on the bill to deny the request for a consular service. However, the Norwegian committee that acted as advisory to the Swedish king refused to countersign the veto, as it was required to do. Instead, committee members submitted their resignations, which the king refused to accept. The Norwegians then realized that as a result of his refusal, the king no longer had a governing body through which he could rule Norway.

On this basis, Norway declared its independence. The Swedish reaction was hostile and threatening. They demanded that there be a neutral zone between the two countries, requiring that the Norwegians demolish frontier fortifications recently built for the defence of their capital city, Oslo. Olav wrote, *"The Swedes can holler and be happy, while the Norwegians will look in shame over what happened . . . I am no politician, but when I think about this I get mad, and I think I should tell you what we think about it over here."* The tense situation continued through November, but the Norwegians did eventually gain their independence from Sweden peacefully, in 1905.

■ ■ ■

The two brothers often worked together in logging operations, and Olav described to those at home the jobs that he and Gustav did while logging. Gustav operated the skidder through much of his working time in Stearns. The skidder was a machine used to move logs from where they were cut to where they could be moved for further transport. In the following passage, which has been translated from Old Norwegian to English, Olav demonstrates a proficiency for description.

"In valleys where it is uneven and full of rocks, it is impossible for horses to get through like they do back home, without long detours. Such is the case here. You always try to move loads from the high points to the low points . . .

"The main railroad goes along the river, but the mountains along the river have many small valleys, and that is where we work. They make a little plateau at the end of a side track, and when that is done a locomotive brings the skidder in on its place and we roll this machine into this plateau. Then we hoist a big pole. It is approximately eighty feet tall and fourteen inches thick at the top. We then take a steel cable, which is approximately five-eighths of an inch thick and approximately 1,600 feet long, and fasten it securely to the top and stretch the cable to the end of the valley, or as far as the line goes. Then we find a solid tree in line with the skidder in the valley, and fasten the other end of the line as high as you can, at least fifteen or twenty feet over the ground, until a steam-driven machine tightens it. On the top of this line is a so-called bicycle. To this bicycle will be fastened four lines, of which three lines also are fastened to three different booms on the skidder. These lines work so it can get the bicycle back and forth on the first mentioned cable. A further line, which is fastened to the bicycle, works so that you can fasten the load to it (at the far end of the cable). This way you can lift the timber over valleys and rocks, just like you could on a level

field. Sometimes you cannot see one end of the line from the other, and you place a man on the height where he can see the man (who fastened the load) and the line from the skidder (skidder operator). This man (from the high point) will give signals to tell that everything is in order. This is my job as long as everything is okay, or when we are moving to another site. In this way we often move 120 pieces of timber a day. I am pretty good at splicing cables now. If it happens that one breaks, Gustav and I must splice them."

■ ■ ■

Gustav and Olav moved to board with an American family in a private home. The husband was one of the foremen in the loading division, and his wife had been a schoolteacher. They had three children, the eldest one married and still living at home with her husband. *"Some Sundays we sing, and that is an uplifting thing . . . ."* They had several invitations for Christmas, among them one from a Norwegian family at Stearns. Olav wrote that it wouldn't be the same as at home in dear old Norway. But, as always, there was nothing they could do about it.

They were living at Worley Camp, which had been opened when the company opened two new mines there in 1905. The camp at Worley was beside the tracks of the Kentucky and Tennessee Railroad, about two miles from the Yammacraw Bridge. The residents, miners and loggers could commute to Stearns via regular passenger service on the train. The settlement included a store, a post office, a school and thirty or forty company houses and boarding homes. The Worley mines had been called the crown jewel of the Stearns operations, because the grade of coal from these mines was superior. It was from a Worley mine that Bryant had taken his one-ton block of coal to the Chicago World's Fair in 1893. The company was also logging these slopes along the Big South Fork River, under which lay the treasured coal.

Stearns had brought down most of his office and management staff from Ludington, Michigan when he established his town. Some were young men who had completed university, and later brought their wives to establish their homes at Stearns. He also brought some foremen and skilled workers for different positions in the company. He hired unskilled workers from the mountains, some of whom returned to their homes on days off, and maintained their families in their original homesteads. Some of these homesteaders had sold the mineral and timber rights but retained the surface rights to their land, where they could produce enough to meet their family needs. Stearns also sought immigrants from New York.

Gustav and Olav spent several days over Christmas with their Norwegian friends at Stearns, and enjoyed this very much. On Christmas Day, they were invited to a coffee party with American families, and one of the families invited them for New Year's. But they were now unable to accept the invitation.

On December 30, they got a message that they were to go to work in the morning. The company wanted the skidder moved—a huge machine—

and just about every work gang was required to make the move. It would be located about ten minutes from where they lived. They expected to work on New Year's Day as well.

On December 31, they worked all day to assemble the skidder, which had gone off the railroad tracks four times. Then a railroad car went off the tracks, and then a locomotive. Crews were still working late in the night to get them back on the tracks.

Olav added a note to his letter, saying that it was ten o'clock and he had to go to bed, as they got up every morning at five o'clock to start work.

■ ■ ■

In 1905, Gustav and Olav wrote mainly about their work and their lives at Stearns. In 1906, they were more concerned with family and social life.

In January, they received letters telling them about Christmas in Norway. Olav longed for home when he heard about all the meetings and parties. He said that the last party he went to was at the schoolhouse at Erklev, and he thought that he would feel strange at a party now. *"Yes, my dear, if you have chosen to travel in the world, you must be ready to live with all kinds of longing. If you gain something, you lose something else."* He was looking forward to seeing his friends in Norway again, so that he could shake hands with everyone. *"That would be a double happiness."*

Eilert wanted to purchase a pocket watch and a rifle with the money that Gustav and Olav had sent for his confirmation. But Olav thought that he should buy only one good and lasting item. He asked for a photo of Eilert in his confirmation suit.

Eilert had said that he was interested in coming to America. Olav advised against it. It would be too hard on him to come over before the heat of the summer began. Besides, Gustav and Olav did not have money for his ticket right now, because they had just bought Anna's brother Martin a ticket. All travel arrangements were already made for Martin. They thought that if Martin liked it in Stearns, that he would send for his brother Juergen in the fall. By that time he expected that Eilert would have forgotten about coming over.

Their sister Anna was now nineteen years old, a tall, elegant-looking young woman who had been helping on the farm since finishing school at fourteen. She had applied to Nedenes Girls' School a year ago for one of the limited number of positions, but she was not accepted. The school taught girls high standards of housekeeping skills, as well as some academic subjects. She re-applied in 1906, and was accepted. She left excitedly in February for the eight-month course at the Nedenes School in Arendal.

Gustav's sister and Anna's younger sister Elizabeth were each the youngest of their family; they were close to the same age and good friends. Elizabeth had also moved to Arendal and they were pleased to be together. Gustav wrote in February, *"You and Elizabeth are a little bit more than friends now, as you are both aunts. I suppose you are both looking a little older and more serious since you became aunts . . ."*

He asked about his little daughter, if she was still as sweet and nice. He wished he could see her. He heard that she could walk now, and that she was running around the whole house.

Gustav wrote another caring letter to his sister in March. He was pleased that she was selecting her friends carefully. *"You have to be careful with yourself, because when you are young and you come from the country to the city, you have to keep your eyes open. People from the city look down on country people. They think we are dumber than they are."* He advised her to be careful of city boys because they used a lot of tricks. He didn't want to suggest that his sister was dumb and blue-eyed, but he told her she couldn't be too careful.

His sister missed Magnhild after she left for Arendal. Gustav said he missed her too, even if he had never seen her. *"I miss Daddy's little girl and her mamma so much, that I must be patient and hope that one of these days I will be home with them forever."* He was very pleased to hear how much everyone was bragging about his daughter. The brothers sent a generous gift to their sister, equal to one month of savings. They suggested that she didn't have to tell their father, if she didn't want to. Then their father would still give her the usual amount that he had promised.

Anna's brother Martin arrived in Stearns in late March. He had some trouble adjusting to the climate and food, but was feeling better by the end of May. Olav told a story about him. Martin had said that the only thing English and American people did at Easter was eat plenty of eggs! On Easter morning, just as they sat down at the table, Martin broke the silence. "*What is this? I have never seen anything like it*!" He extended his hand to a tray full of painted eggs. "*We don't have any hens in Norway that lay eggs like that*!" Everyone had a good laugh.

Gustav seemed more undecided about when they would return to Norway. He wrote that they were longing to go home, but then suggested that it might be years before they returned. However, he asked the family to postpone maintenance work on the outbuildings on the Rosseland farm until he got home.

Olav was equally undecided. He wrote in late May that he wasn't sure if he would return home to Rosseland that summer. As a young single man, he frequently mentioned how he missed the social life in Norway. He recalled that the next Sunday would be Whitsunday, and how nice it would be to be at home. "*Just imagine us coming to visit you at Nedenes. Then maybe I could see some of those nice chickens that you say you have plenty of. If I was allowed, then I would take one or more of you under my protecting wings, like a hen does to her chicks . . .*" He had sent a photo to his sister and had a reply back that one of her friends thought he looked very attractive in the photo, and sent greetings to him. Olav wrote, "*Say hello, and tell her that I look better than I do in the picture.*"

Olav added that yesterday a little baby four months old died in their house. The married daughter of the Michigan family had her first child in

January, and this baby had now died. Both parents were taking the corpse to Michigan and Gustav was keeping them company to Stearns. Gustav had been off work for two weeks with a recurring problem with his foot.

■ ■ ■

Gustav wrote his sister an affectionate letter in September 1906. He apologized for not writing more often, but said that he was thinking of her often and was happy every time he heard from her. *"You are the only little sister that we have. Is it any wonder that we love you so much?"* He wondered how long it would be until they met again.

The date of their return to Norway was uncertain. They were doing well financially at present, so they thought they might stay longer. *"We are never in money trouble here, which was sometimes the case when we were home . . . ."*

Gustav and Olav had sent Juergen a ticket a while earlier and expected to see him at the end of October. They thought it would be nice to have another Norwegian there with them, because there weren't too many in Stearns. They didn't know if they would stay at Stearns for the winter. They were thinking of going to Florida, but would not make a decision until Juergen arrived. If they left, they thought that the family they stayed with would come along also. *"They are so nice and friendly, and we would like to stay with them, and we think they like our company, also."*

Because they were doing well financially, they were in no hurry to return to Norway. No letters exist today that they wrote during the winter of 1906-07, but sometime over that winter they made the decision to extend their stay in America. Gustav made arrangements for Anna and three-year-old Magnhild to join him at Stearns in Kentucky in the spring of 1907.

Chapter 5
"Right now it is hard times all over"

ON FRIDAY EVENING, May 17, 1907, a weary Anna alighted from the train at the Stearns station, accompanied by tired and excited three-year-old Magnhild and sixteen-year-old Eilert. Gustav wrote that Magnhild and Eilert were very alive and in good spirits. Anna was a poised young woman with a sparkling smile, but on this occasion her face was drawn with fatigue. They had just made the trip across the ocean and taken the train from New York, with a transfer at Cincinnati.

There to meet them at the station were Gustav and Olav, and Anna's two brothers, Martin and Juergen. For Gustav especially, the occasion was momentous. He saw his daughter for the first time, and he knew that after years of waiting to be together, he and his wife would never have to part again. Gustav wrote, *"I am so happy to have my dear ones back with me."*

Later Anna wrote to Gustav's sister, *"I guess you understand how happy I am. I have accomplished what I have longed for—for so many years. Don't think I have forgotten you people back home. Oh no, I am thinking of you all the time and I wish I could hug you . . . I couldn't say much when I left. I cried inside and couldn't say a word."* Anna wondered if she would ever see the family again. Gustav wrote that he hoped God would look after them so that they could meet again at their childhood home.

Gustav, Anna and Magnhild in 1907

Anna and Magnhild moved into the Tibbetts home at Worley Camp with Gustav. She wrote to Norway that these people were very kind to her. Grandmother at Rosseland had worried whether Magnhild would get enough milk, but the Tibbetts family had bought a cow, just for Magnhild.

On her first Sunday at Worley, Gustav, Anna and Magnhild attended Sunday School and were invited back to the doctor's home, a short distance away, for dinner. The doctor had children the same age as Magnhild. *"They are so nice, but it is too bad that I cannot talk to them."* Anna did not speak any English. The next Sunday, Gustav and Anna went to Sunday School and for a walk, while Magnhild stayed at home with her uncles.

Anna wrote home to Norway, explaining that she had written a letter to her father to tell him about the voyage over, so she would not repeat that as they could read his letter. At the age of seventy-one, and in failing health, Aanen was living at Rosseland with Gustav's parents. Martin and Juergen had made an agreement with Andreas to send money home regularly to pay for Aanen's keep. Three of his children were in Kentucky and his youngest daughter was not married, so Aanen had no one else to care for him in his old age.

"Magnhild is a real gold nugget. She has given us so much pleasure here in our new life," wrote Gustav. Magnhild was everyone's darling. Anna wrote that she cuddled her father every evening when he came home from work. She played with the two Tibbetts children, Clare and Jenny. Magnhild spoke to them

in Norwegian and they answered her in English, and they all understood each other.

Young Eilert was thoroughly enjoying his adventure in America. *"You should see how much there was to see in New York. We saw hundreds of steamships. I think we can say that we saw thousands of streetcars and railway cars."* Eilert liked almost everything he had seen so far. He started work on the first Monday after he arrived and he was being paid $1.65 per day, almost as much as the others received.

Gustav was working with Eilert, and found him a good worker and pleasant. Eilert was eager to please; energetic yet relaxed, with a ready smile. In Gustav's family there were short genes and tall genes. Gustav was of average height, while Olav was shorter than average. The youngest two siblings were tall. Eilert was over six feet tall and his sister Anna was also tall. Gustav continued, *"I think it was best for him to come over to us, because he is at an age that could lead him into trouble. There is not so much danger of that here, because there are not so many youths here as at home. Youths here do not get so much out of line as they do at home."*

■ ■ ■

The family needed more privacy and space, so Gustav applied for a company house at the new camp at Yammacraw, two miles further down the river, at the end of the K&T Railroad line. Yammacraw had opened in 1907, with the same services there as at Worley—a store, post office and school.

This was a strange new environment for Anna. She had lived the past four years in the spa-

Yammacraw on the Big South Fork River

cious Rosseland home in Norway, on a fine farm in an open valley, surrounded by stands of tall evergreens on the low rolling mountains. At Yammacraw, the camp houses stood on the recently logged, steep slopes, on both the lower and upper sides of the railroad tracks, overlooking the Big South Fork of the Cumberland River. Each thin-walled, wooden dwelling had two rooms and a kitchen, with a kitchen stove, a small coal-heated stove, and one small electric light bulb in each house. In the camp, several families shared the water from a drilled well, and the use of an outdoor privy. Housekeeping and family laundry were labour-intensive chores for a housewife with no running water. Anna tended one of the small gardens on the sloped hillside of the rough, recently logged terrain. One book on the region mentioned a local joke about " . . . falling off a garden." In August, Gustav wrote, *"I guess Eilert told you how we live here, and that frightened you."*

The residents of the camp were company employees. Middle management included foremen, shop mechanics, storekeepers, schoolteachers and doctors. Most labourers for the logging and mining operations were members of the agricultural community in the mountains.

Gustav decided that he should build his own house as he found renting from the company very expensive. Company housing generally created a profit for the company, but Stearns made it possible for workers to build their own homes. It made for a more stable work force. Then he again demonstrated his indecision about whether to stay in America. First he said that he was settling soon and then could send some money, but he quickly followed that statement with *"I have decided not to stay over here."* He asked his sister to tell Father to do the best he could, and the brothers would send money as soon as they could, to help him over the winter.

The family at Rosseland had expected Olav home that summer. He frequently wrote that he was lonely and dreamed of returning, and they had misunderstood and expected him home. But Olav wrote that he was still considering his options. California was too expensive, but Canada sounded attractive. He had seen Canadian government advertising offering 160 acres of farmland for $10. He wrote, *"Canada should be perfect for oats and wheat . . . . On government land you can raise cattle and harvest all the hay you want. Many people make good money doing this."*

But he decided to try farming that summer in North Dakota. He had heard that farm wages there were about three times what they could save at Stearns, and the job included room and board. Olav headed north to chase a higher income.

■ ■ ■

In mid-July Olav travelled by train to Chicago and then to Minneapolis, where he obtained a contract for farm work. He had travelled north with a friend from Norway, Martin Severinson, who had come over to Stearns in the spring, just a few weeks before Anna arrived. Since coming to America, twenty-six-year-old Olav had learned to speak English well, and was anxious to see more of the country. Gustav wrote, *"Ole can take care of himself. He knows the language and the American system well."*

Olav found the prairie land awesome, amazed that he could see so far in all directions. *"When I am working I dream that it is my land; then I would be rich enough to go home."* The farms around there were all new, so there was not much cultivated land. One afternoon when they were working, a thunderstorm began, and then the rain started. Olav had never seen rain like this. Before they got to the house, they were both soaking wet. He wrote a letter quickly so the farmer could take it in to town. The farm was near Sarles, North Dakota, six miles from the Canadian border.

"The farmers here all think they are champions when it comes to ploughing, but if some of them went to Norway they would have more to learn than we have here." Olav said that the only thing he had learned

was to drive several horses at the same time, more difficult than one or two. The owner had eighteen horses and seventy cows, and three more farms with the same number of animals on each. Olav liked the job, but found the hours of work very long. He thought he would try something new next year.

Olav was undecided about where to go when his contract on the farm finished in the fall. He wanted to go home to Norway, but the wages there were starvation wages. He hadn't had much luck in America, like others had, but he hoped his luck would improve.

Photography was Olav's passion, which he had discovered years before. He carried around with him on his travels a large, box-like camera with a tri-pod, of early 20th-century vintage. He had found a good man in Stearns who wanted to go into a part-nership with him, but the man drank a little too much, so Olav declined the opportunity. Had that man been in North Dakota, he would have started a partnership with him there, because the sale of alco-holic beverages was forbidden in North Dakota. The Roselands did not drink alcohol.

Olav received shocking news from Kentucky in September. *"Poor old Aanen, he must have been heart-broken to hear of Martin's death. It was so unex-pected, that I had a hard time to believe it."* Olav could hardly believe the news. Anna's brother, twenty-seven-year-old Martin Kylland, had died suddenly at Stearns. He had fallen and re-injured a broken leg. He died very quickly when an infection rav-aged his body. The weather was so intensely hot

Anna's brother Martin, who died August 1907, at Stearns

that he had to be buried on the same day that he died. Anna and Juergen were deeply grieved to lose their brother in such a sudden, unexpected and tragic manner.

Olav and Martin Severinson continued to work hard through to the middle of October. When they finished the harvest they had threshing to do. After that they ploughed the acreage again. By early October they had ploughed 100 acres and still had 400 acres left to do.

Olav and Martin returned to Stearns in late October. In the face of a sudden economic crisis that had swept across America in the past two weeks, Olav and Martin went to Yammacraw to bunk in with Gustav and Anna. By late October it was clear that the Stearns operations would be affected by the financial crisis.

■ ■ ■

The "Panic of 1907" began in mid-October, and with it good times in America came to an abrupt end. The economy had slowed down in 1906, followed by a decline in the stock markets in 1907. Money and credit had been tight on the international market, which caused a rise in interest rates and a slowdown in the expansion of business. Complicating the crisis in America was the lack of a central bank to accommodate fluctuations in the money market. The economic health of the country was in the hands of businessmen and investors whose aim was to protect their own interests by removing as much of their funds from the banks as possible.

On October 16, a failed takeover bid by a New York company precipitated a series of events which spread like wildfire in the financial world. Investors rushed to get their money out of banks before they became insolvent. Many businesses and banks did become insolvent, or fail during the crisis. A number of businesses across America folded, with the loss of all jobs, and in others workers were laid off, or had their wages cut.

The financial world blamed President Teddy Roosevelt for the regulatory measures he had introduced and his prosecutions under the anti-trust laws. But he claimed that the financial world engineered the panic to force the government to relax in their enforcement of anti-trust laws. However, Roosevelt's enforcement had not cut corporate profits, and it seems the reasons for the panic were many and complex. One of the principal reasons was the lack of regulation in the financial world, a factor that later initiated financial legislation. Economic instability followed this crisis, which persisted until the First World War.

What all this meant in Stearns, Kentucky was that there was a slowdown in orders for lumber in the fall of 1907, and the subsequent near-collapse of the lumber business. As winter was coming on, the demand for coal remained good for the time being. But the next couple of years would bring more unexpected changes in Stearns.

■ ■ ■

In their small Yammacraw home, Olav, Martin, Eilert and Juergen joined Gustav and Anna. With their incomes threatened or non-existent, the young men could not afford to pay board at a company boarding house. Gustav never seemed to have any spare time, because when he wasn't working he was shopping for Anna. She spoke very little English, but was learning. Gustav did the shopping for the seven people who now lived in their small home.

Gustav had hoped that Ole and Martin would find a place up north where they could all settle. Once settled in Stearns, they had found it difficult to find work and move to another place. Travel was expensive and they ran the risk of depleting their funds before finding a satisfactory job. The recession had now made it even more difficult, as jobs became scarcer.

Gustav wrote in early December, *"I guess you are short of money. It is the same here. We haven't had any wages lately, and we will not get any until Christmas either, other than a bank cheque."* They couldn't cash the bank cheque immediately, so it wasn't much use to them at that time. They could buy necessary items at the company store on credit, as long as they had income owed to them.

The recession put financial pressure on Justus Stearns. He had expanded his industrial operations rapidly in the past ten years, and made investments through the use of loans, for which he was indebted. Companies relied on their income from housing and company stores during slow economic times, so the amount of credit they could extend their employees was limited. The wage earners in the family had to find an income.

Gustav concluded his letter, *"It is nearing Christmas time; I will therefore wish you a Merry Christmas and happy and blessed New Year. . . . Think about it, it is the fourth Christmas since we left. I didn't think it would be that long until I could come home . . . ."*

■ ■ ■

A few days after Christmas 1907, Olav, Eilert, Juergen and Martin became coal miners. Gustav remained at his old job, trying his hand at a variety of different tasks. The demand for timber had fallen off and logging operations were in minimal operation. Olav and Juergen worked inside the mines, while Eilert and Martin began their coal mining experience, sorting and transporting coal outside the mine. Olav wrote, *"You should see how black we look when we come back from work. We look like chimney sweeps."* Olav hoped to begin work as a photographer during the day, while working in the coal mines at night. He explained that he was unable to send money home right now, because he had just sent away for $25 worth of photography equipment.

Working in a coal mine was a dirty and dangerous job. Once the crew dug an entry tunnel into the coal seam on the hillside, the workers laid tracks for moving the coal. Then the miners worked in pairs, creating rooms, or shafts, off the entry tunnel. Working close to the floor, one miner cut a wedge deep into the coal seam. Then they drilled holes into the coal above, and tamped it with explosive powder, which they then fired. This brought down the face of the wall. After the dust and the coal settled, they loaded a coal car, and mules pulled the car out to the main tracks.

Once the coal car was outside the mine, other workers sorted out the rocks and impurities. Then a weighman, appointed by the company, checked and weighed the coal to determine the grade of coal and the weight. A machine then pulled the coal car over to the tipple, where it was stored for loading into railway cars. Miners were paid by the weight of coal they delivered outside the mine, rather than an hourly wage.

Many miners lost their lives in mining operations. Newspapers gave dramatic and sensational reports of mine explosions caused by the ignition of toxic and explosive gases. However, far more miners lost their lives in solitary incidents when the roof of the mine fell in on them. These incidents went unnoticed by the public. Miners were held responsible for their own safety, while coroners' inquests ruled most deaths accidental, regardless of the safety practices of the company. Five miners died on December 29, 1905 when an explosion at Mine Number 1 at Stearns threw three of the miners from the entrance of the mine into Roaring Paunch Creek. The large numbers of miners who died were a significant factor in the continuing poverty of the mountains, as most who died left behind a wife and family with no means of support.

The Norwegians found that Americans did not have the same prejudice against those who worked at dirty jobs as was the case in Norway. It didn't matter how dark and dirty they looked, the Americans greeted and talked with them on their way home from work. *"In this way the Americans are different than they are back in Norway."* For those who came out of the mines black and dirty, the company provided bathhouses, for which the workers paid extra. The bathhouses were not available to other members of the community.

The presidential election would be held in the coming November, and the brothers were very interested. Roosevelt had stated that he would not run again, but they were hoping he could be convinced. Teddy Roosevelt was hugely popular with the working class, as they believed he understood their problems and was working for them. *"This time Gustav and I will be able to vote. We haven't been here long enough to vote, but they aren't too fussy about that here . . ."*

In March, Olav reported that they were only getting two or three days of work each week, and some weeks they got no work at all. Company management had lowered the wages for workers in February. Olav had worked very little in recent weeks, barely earning enough to pay his board. *"Right now it is hard times all over."* They had heard that it was better times out west, but the cost of travelling was too high. They could go broke looking for work. *"We hope that things get better, but they won't get very much better, because it is always bad in the United States during election year."* Olav had made this same statement about poor times in an election year when he was in New York in 1904.

■ ■ ■

Andreas had written to tell his sons about a possible land deal with Hunsfoss, a pulp and paper factory just two or three miles from their farm at Rosseland. The thrust of negotiations was that Andreas would trade some of his treed land for fertile land owned by Hunsfoss. Gustav and Olav sent a letter to their father to say that if they got all of the fertile land in the land deal, then maybe they would all come back to Norway. But once again, Olav ended his letter with an ambiguous statement. *"Well, if times get better here, it should only take a year before we can send some money home to help defray expenses."*

It should be noted here that immigration officials anglicized the Rosseland name to Roseland when Gustav and Olav entered New York. This was commonly done to the surnames of many immigrants. So, after their immigration the family used the altered name of Roseland as their surname.

■ ■ ■

In early June, Gustav and Olav received an urgent request from their father for money. They immediately sent $40, which was all they could afford at that time. Olav explained to his father that Juergen had sent two months of his income to his younger sister Elizabeth, who needed assistance, and Juergen was just about out of money. Olav's response suggests that Andreas had again asked

Juergen to send some money for the care of Aanen. Since Martin's death, Juergen was under great pressure to send the money they had promised to send to Andreas. The downturn in the economy and lack of work had increased his financial problems.

Andreas had asked again if the brothers were coming home to Norway. They responded that if the Hunsfoss deal went through, maybe they would come home—some of them, or all of them. But they thought it might be more sensible to stay in America for another year or so, and pay for a man to help Andreas. *"I would very much like to come home, but I don't want to come home as poor as when I left."*

■ ■ ■

By early August, Olav had found a suitable partner for a photography business. The man was an American, Charles Hixon. He had worked as an office man, but in the last twelve years he had learned a great deal about photography. They would work in a tent and travel to various places. They had two tents, one for a kitchen and dining room, and one for a studio. They had purchased equipment for $250 and received their first order for $137. Olav didn't want to spend the rest of his life working as a labourer, and he loved photography. He wanted a business of his own.

■ ■.■

Eilert wrote one of his occasional letters to his sister in October 1908. *"It is starting to be cold here. The leaves are turning yellow and now falling from the trees."* He wrote that he was working in the mine again, the only place where you could make money. He wasn't as fat as he had been last winter, but he expected to be fat again when the cold weather set in. Olav, Eilert and Juergen were living in a company boarding home again while they were working in the coal mines. He had heard that the Norwegian economy was improving, so he thought perhaps he could be doing as well in Norway as he was here. *"In this place nobody knows anything about what goes on in this country, or in the rest of the world for that matter . . . . The river runs in the same direction as before, and that is about the only thing we see here."* Always whimsical, this teenage immigrant was not finding life in the Appalachians very exciting.

Gustav began his letter in early November with good news. They have all been in good health and feeling fine. The bad news was that incomes had been poor. Gustav had worked only half-time in the past few months, and that would set him back financially. He answered his sister's question about the kind of work he was doing. He had taken on a variety of odd jobs, and doing what he had been doing for a long time, operating the skidder. He was used to this machine and could do a little bit of everything with it. He had also tried operating locomotives, and he worked on the river doing repairs. The booms always have to be ready for logs. Gustav had become well known in the lumber operations. Although lean and of average height, he was known to his co-workers as "Big Gus."

Eilert and Juergen had been working together in the mines for a while, and Gustav reported that Eilert was in good health and strong as a horse. Olav was still at Stearns working with photography, but it was starting to get chilly at night and too cold to live in a tent. "*There is no money around and people do not have enough money to feed themselves.*" Up until now Olav had done well, but with the cold weather he wanted to move back in with Gustav and Anna for the winter. They were also expecting Martin Severinson to move in with them the following week.

■ ■ ■

Gustav reported that Olav had taken their photograph and they would be sending a copy to Norway soon. The group was posed at the kitchen table, the usual setting for a family photo, with the men in their Sunday best suits. Gustav sat on the left, with Anna on his left, eight months pregnant. Eilert was poised to play his violin, and dapper Olav was holding Magnhild. Juergen sat on the right holding his accordion. Juergen had inherited his father's musical talent—Aanen played both the violin and accordion. Gustav thanked his sister for sending the photo of Rosseland that he had asked for.

"*Magnhild is so active that she doesn't know which foot to stand on. She runs around playing by herself from morning until bedtime. She is everybody's sweetheart.*" Anna was busy doing chores every day—very time-consuming under the circumstances at Stearns. She always intended to write a letter to Norway, but the time flew very quickly for her. Anna was pregnant, expecting her second child in late November.

Their good friends, the Tibbetts family, had returned to Michigan. The doctor who was there

Family Portrait at Yammacraw, November 1908. Left to right: Gustav, Anna, Eilert with violin, Olav holding Magnhild, and Juergen.

Rosseland home in Norway 1908

had gone to California and they liked it in
California. They had a new doctor now, "a very nice
and good man." Gustav and Anna had visited them
a few times, and they had visited Gustav and Anna's
home. The doctor and his wife had four children,
two boys and two girls, one of them just a year older
than Magnhild. So Magnhild had good friends to
play with.

Gustav asked how the land trade was going.
He wanted to hear the latest news right away,
because he had a lot to do to get ready to leave. *"We
have a lot of furniture and twenty-four turkeys and hens.
I also had four pigs, but I sold them a while ago. So, you
can see that we can't get away from here in a day's time."*

Gustav asked the family to send some
Norwegian newspapers to them. *"It makes no difference how old they are, it will be new to us."* He wrote
that the way things had gone lately, they had been

*Gustav, Anna and Magnhild on the left, and doctor's family
on the porch of the doctor's home, 1908*

Magnhild with their turkeys and chickens, 1908

unable to send money home, but they promised to send some as soon as things got better.

"I think that often after the election things will either get better, or they get worse. The day after tomorrow we have the election, and then we will know what the next four years will bring us. We hope the right man gets in. It is William Taft that we want."

Chapter 6
"We can't make up our minds what to do"

ON NOVEMBER 7, 1908, the Republicans won the U.S. elections William Taft became the next president of the United States. Olav explained that this was roughly the same as a Left victory in Norwegian elections. But, he explained, in America, elections have a bigger influence on the times and the people than in other countries. Olav had been reading newspapers and was well informed on the election and election issues. He was not short on opinions.

"I guess you are unfamiliar with the name Standard Oil Company. It is one of the richest companies in the United States. I just read that this company yearly pays $3,000 to $5,000 to editors of all kinds, of small papers across the land. Just tonight I read in a paper how big business owners 'buy' editors of many papers, so that these can slant news stories to favour the rich man and to trick the working man. When some government job is to be filled, these lousy editors write up candidates that are friendly to these big companies. There are three or four men in the States right now who spend millions yearly for this kind of stuff. And you can bet they get their money's worth."

Standard Oil was the first major trust formed in America and became the subject of much criticism by muckrakers. A trust was a group of companies that acted in concert to control resources, freight rates, wages to workers and prices. Their primary aim was to reduce costs and increase profits, while at the same time having no moral responsibility towards society. Because of the great wealth they controlled, they were also able to purchase political power, especially in an era of very little effective legislation. *"There is lots of dirty stuff going on during elections. Money talks."*

Progressivism in American society sought political change to correct the perceived injustices and evils brought about by the power of those who had accumulated great wealth. A growing number of voices claimed that the trusts and combines had reduced wages and raised prices. They believed that these same wealthy individuals, who were associated with the trusts and combines, dominated the major political parties, and that the government had come to represent business interests, and not the people. Olav wrote, *"It helps to get workers to work for maybe one or two dollars less every day. Then companies set up prices for their goods."* He believed that Roosevelt was a man who tried to stop this. He hoped that if Mr. Taft used the same policies as Roosevelt, maybe they could enjoy the same good times that they had earlier.

Olav added that he and Gustav and Juergen had talked about going to New York that spring and then maybe going home in the fall. *"If times don't get better, it is our hope to go home as soon as possible . . . the way it is here now, we can do just as well or better back home."*

■ ■ ■

No sooner was the 1908 election over than the Stearns Company and its whole enterprise at Stearns was thrown into a crisis. The United Mineworkers of America had come to Stearns in the fall of 1908 in an attempt to organize the company coal operations. However, there were indications of some union activity prior to that time. The company had evicted several union-leaning men from company housing in the previous year.

In November of that year, the company and the union were in dispute over the right to hire and fire men, and the miners were seeking the right to elect the "weighman." After the coal was mined, the weighman weighed it, and judged the impurities in it, meaning that his decisions determined how much the miner would get paid for his work. The company had introduced a new "docking rule" in respect to the weighman, and the miners thought this unfair. When the company refused to meet with a union committee on the 17th of November, a strike began and the company began to seek replacement workers. One week later, on the 24th of November, the company evicted seven more union-leaning men from company housing.

In the years since coal mining had been established as an industry in the United States around the mid-19th century, the lines of conflict between miners and operators had been clearly drawn. The major issue for the miners was wages and working conditions. The only power the miners had was withholding their labour by a strike against the operators. The operators had several sources of power against the miners. They could evict miners from company housing without notice, a measure that was greatly feared by miners. The operators used the courts, both state and federal, to seek injunctions and orders to restrain union activity. Operators could also lock out their workers and hire replacement workers, and blacklist troublesome miners so that other operators would not hire them. Coal operators competed with each other, and keeping the cost of labour down was an essential element in their competition. While the operators competed in the marketplace, they were united in their opposition to unions.

Anthracite coal had reigned supreme in the industrial area of the north until the latter part of the 19th century. After the Civil War, and after railroad construction in the Appalachians, softer bituminous coal in the south became the marketplace leader. There were several reasons for this. The veins of anthracite coal in the north ran much deeper in the earth, making mining more costly and more dangerous. The bituminous coal in the Appalachians was much more accessible, as miners could enter and bring the coal out on a horizontal plane, through shafts opened on the sides of the mountains. Because it was so easy to open a mine in the south, the market became flooded with coal mined by small operators. The operators had to remain competitive by keeping the cost of coal down. That meant keeping the unions out of their operations.

■ ■ ■

In the middle of all this unsettled activity at Stearns, Anna gave birth to their second daughter, Gudrun, on November 27, 1908. Eilert later wrote home to Norway about the birth of the " . . . *first Norwegian-Kentuckian born at Stearns.*" At the time of Gudrun's birth, Gustav was unable to work as he had dislocated his shoulder. Olav wrote, ". . . *he can't do anything for a long time, where he must use that arm. But, when I talked to the foreman, he said he would try to find some easy work for him.*" An injured man, unable to work, did not get paid.

Olav had been offered a job in the mine, but he didn't want to cross the picket line. As usual, Olav held strong opinions on the matter. He believed that the workers were not paid enough, so he told the company that he wouldn't work in the mine. He was afraid, however, that the strikers would lose, because it was a foolish time of year to strike when it was bad times all over. He had offered to work in the woods, but since that is not where the company wanted him, he thought it was highly doubtful that he would get any work. *"But they know that they cannot keep me unless they give me a good-paying job before spring. It looks like stubbornness will be fought with stubbornness."*

Olav believed that the timing for a strike was wrong, during a severe economic depression. And it was a bad time to seek increased wages when the Stearns Company was short on sales and strapped for cash.

Throughout November, a number of employees continued to cross the picket lines to work in the mines. This was greatly reassuring to the company. Olav wrote in December, *"There are so many ignorant farmers who have been used to making $1 to $1.50 per day, and when they are offered $1.75 to $2 per day in the mine, they think this is big money."* A number of miners still maintained their farms in the mountains, and some became *de facto* seasonal workers, as they returned to their farms when needed there. Some supplemented their incomes by operating "Blind tigers," an illegal whiskey or moonshine business, a long-time practice in the mountains. These families had lived a subsistence lifestyle prior to becoming miners, so their mining income merely supplemented an economic standard that they were accustomed to.

Christmas was coming, so Olav took the opportunity to give his family in Norway a bad time about the small amount of mail they had received in 1907. *"I hope you sent as much mail as you did two years ago, because then there was so much they had to send it on an extra train."* He sent greetings to his family and friends in Norway, and wrote that Eilert, Anna and Gustav had all sent their mail yesterday.

■ ■ ■

As the days rolled towards Christmas, tensions surrounding the strike mounted, and the lines between the company and the union were more harshly drawn. On the 10th of December, the company sought a federal injunction against the union for a trespass order, restraining certain evicted union members from trespassing on company property. On the 11th of December, a United States marshal served a restraining order on several union members. Later, warrants went out for the arrest of men who had violated the order. On the 17th of December, a U.S. marshal came to Stearns with warrants for the arrest of several more men. On the 23rd of December, one of the men confronted a company official, allegedly threatening his life, and a warrant went out for his arrest.

On Christmas Eve, several U.S. marshals arrived in Stearns by train, with warrants for the arrest of the troublemakers. When three more marshals arrived on Christmas morning, a group of about thirty marshals encircled the hotel where the fugitives were holed up. The stand-off began about 10 a.m. At noon, the marshal in charge shouted a warning, and then proceeded towards the hotel. As he neared the hotel, someone shot down at him from above, and he died within minutes.

All afternoon, tempers ran high between the marshals and the renegade union leaders. In the late afternoon, after allowing the guests to leave, the marshals torched the hotel. As the fire blazed, the fugitives ran for their lives. One was shot dead as he ran from the hotel door. The others ran for the bushes and the hills, and escaped. Reporters converged on the town and the incident hit the front page of *The New York Times*. Rob Stearns, son of Justus Stearns, came to town and defused the situation for the company. After the shootings, he declared that this was now a matter between the federal U.S. marshals and the outlawed union men.

■ ■ ■

"1908 was a bad year for America, a worse year than many can remember," eighteen-year-old Eilert wrote home to his sister in January 1909. But, he added optimistically, he hadn't lost faith yet. He still hoped for good times in the next couple of years, and then he could return to see his dear family and Norway again, in 1911.

Then Eilert, always playful, put words to a chanting song. For their amusement socially, children in Norway followed a custom of putting their own words to a chanting song. *"We have heard about gold in this country. One picks it up with the fingers and places it in the hand, and piles it until it is full . . ."* He added that he always understood that the Norwegian-American stands high among the girls in Norway. *"I will see if that is so when I am home once again."*

Eilert wrote that he and Gustav and Olav were "shook up" to hear that their cousin Anders had returned home to Norway. Anders hadn't liked America, but Eilert said that no one liked America when they first came. *"It was a good thing he went to South Dakota, because if he had come to Kentucky he would never have seen Norway or his home again."*

■ ■ ■

The strike continued into 1909. It was still on in April and Olav didn't think the strikers would win. *"Most of the workers are so dumb they don't know what is good for them."* While Olav supported some of the reasons for the strike, he had no support for the strike at that time. He did, however, have opinions on how the power within the system favoured the operators. *"Yes, it is legal for the rich to unite in trusts and monopolies, but when a few poor workers try to unite to get more wages, the law is not on their side. Beautiful times, don't you think? I, for my part, cannot say that I know too much about the way things are run. But from what I can see, I think everything is in favour of the power and government, in the hands of men of tyranny."* In all the letters the brothers wrote home, they never made any specific complaints about the Stearns Company. The company prided itself on being benevolent towards its workers; however, that benevolence did not extend to union sympathizers.

The strike at Stearns was still on technically, but the workers who were union leaders had disappeared after Christmas. Not much was happening in respect to any negotiations.

Times were poor all over the U.S., Olav wrote, but from what he understood, it was better in the north and in the west. They were all in good health and in good spirits, even if the job situation was not too good. What money they made went to feed them. There was no money left over. Wages had gone down quite a bit but the price of food and clothing hadn't.

Olav had worked with Gustav and Eilert in logging operations for the last month. Juergen and Martin Severinson were in North Dakota where Juergen worked for a Norwegian farmer. Olav thought he might go back there for the harvest. He still thought about returning to Norway, but just couldn't decide what was best. From the beginning, he had been determined not to go home broke.

"It is awful how people get engaged back home. Pretty soon there will be no bachelors or unmarried young people left. If Eilert and I come home, there will be no one for us to choose." Olav was lonely. There were no single women available in Stearns and no social life for unmarried men. At the age of twenty-nine, Olav's opportunities for female companionship or for finding a mate were either limited or non-existent. He then asked his sister about friends and relatives in Norway and sent messages to them.

■ ■ ■

"You remember that we have written about a flood that destroyed the company's loading booms in the river?" The Big South Fork had flooded that spring, as it sometimes did after a heavy rain or snow. Flooding had been more severe since the extensive logging that had taken place on the mountains. The river had been rising quickly for hours when the company booms broke, releasing nearly a million feet of logs into the river.

Thousands of logs piled up against the new bridge in a solid mass, and the new bridge withstood the assault. Many logs floated downstream. Some workers were sent down river to catch the logs that were flowing away, and workers risked their lives trying to save as many logs as possible. A remarkably small number of logs were lost.

Gustav, Olav and Eilert had been hired on the crew to rebuild the new booms. It was good-paying work, and in May they each had 29 days of work. *"We just take all the work we can get, because if things are going to continue the way it looks, decent wages will be beyond the reach of the working man within a year or two.* " Those who were working in the coal mines were not getting much work. Some of them got only two or three days of work a week, and at reduced pay, their income was not even sufficient to pay their room and board. *"So you can figure out for yourself what kind of work it is, and what they have left to feed their family on.*"

■ ■ ■

The family in Norway asked how the strike was going, and what had happened to one of the leaders, Berry Simpson. He had been appointed manager of Number 4 mine at Worley Camp when the mine opened in 1904, at about the same time that Gustav and Olav moved in with the Tibbetts family at Worley. In this small community, Gustav and Olav became well acquainted with Simpson and his family.

Simpson was in good favour with the company, as was his wife, who was from Alabama. The company had appointed her manager of their new hotel when it opened. But Berry Simpson had become one of the organizers for the union and the company evicted him from company housing early in 1908. He had been forbidden to trespass on company property, for presumed union activities, and the couple was separated by the trespass order through the fall and Christmas, 1908. Rumour had it that Simpson had run for his life from the burning hotel on Christmas Day, and taken a train south.

Olav wrote that Simpson and his sons had surrendered voluntarily early that spring. Along with three other men, they were still in jail. A hearing had been scheduled for April, but no witnesses came forward, so the hearing was postponed until July. Olav stated that he wasn't aware that Simpson had anything more to do with it than to assist in organizing the strike. However, he understood that the authorities wanted the men sentenced to hard labour, and wanted Simpson tried for arson which had caused the death of one man in the burning hotel. The allegation was made despite a total lack of proof that he was at the scene or had anything to do with it. *"Three good lawyers are defending them. I hope that everything will be taken care of, and that justice will prevail in this case."*

■ ■ ■

Eilert and Olav were home alone that day. Two young speakers from Texas had been holding revival meetings at the schoolhouse every evening that week, and Gustav and Anna had gone each evening. They had gone that morning for another meeting and were stopping at the doctor's house for dinner. Olav and Eilert had just been looking at the calendar and figured out that it was Whitsunday, an important day in Norway. *"Over here they don't really celebrate it at all."*

Olav returned to the subject of logging on the Rosseland farm and asked about Father's money problems. Olav wondered how long their forest would last if Father cut twelve or thirteen acres per year to provide himself with an income. He said he had a good idea now about how they could rig up a steel cable and transport the logs by utilizing the water power on the farm. *"Has Father a boy to help him or is he managing by himself?"*

Olav then went into a lengthy and detailed narrative about the possible land deal at Rosseland. The brothers had discussed the subject extensively and had many suggestions and questions for their father. They proposed a detailed plan of action that entailed outright ownership of some parts, the use of some parts at certain times, water rights, fishing rights, road use, new roads, etc. After making many suggestions, Olav then insisted that Father should make all decisions. Olav wrote, *"If I live and have good health, it is very likely that I will be in Norway this time next year. Maybe we can all be home at the same time . . . but we can't really make up our minds what to do . . . I will leave when I can't take America any longer."*

■ ■ ■

In June, Mrs. Simpson was back at Stearns; Olav had seen her on the K&T passenger train that ran between Stearns and Yammacraw. She was with one of her daughters, but they didn't get a chance to talk to her. Simpson's two sons, and another man who had been in prison, were now out of jail and on bail. They had been talking to this third man who had become so fat in the six months that he was in prison that they hardly recognized him. Berry Simpson was to appear at a court hearing in July, but the outcome of this hearing is unknown.

In 1909, the Stearns property straddled three Kentucky counties and stretched south to include a portion of Tennessee. McCreary County was formed in 1912, bringing all the Stearns Kentucky property within one Kentucky county. Official records up to that time are difficult to locate, as they were dispersed through several counties in Kentucky and Tennessee prior to 1912. Newspapers from the area carry no report. The brothers never mentioned the strike again in their letters. There is no record of further activities of the United Mineworkers of America in Stearns until the winter of 1922-23.

■ ■ ■

Everyone had been healthy, but the weather was hot, up to 95 degrees Fahrenheit at midday. The extreme heat no longer bothered Olav. He had the "appetite of a horse." A week later, heavy rains began and the air cooled. It looked like the river would flood again, and they would have to go out to work on the booms. During flooding on the river, the waters were turbulent and dangerous. Floods could come at any season with heavy rains, because water drained quickly off the large, flat areas of the Cumberland Plateau, especially in areas where large stands of trees had been removed.

■ ■ ■

Olav wrote his sister again in August, continuing his discussion on the proposed land deal that his father was making with Hunsfoss. He had various suggestions about how Father might negotiate the deal to their advantage. Then he added, *"Naturally, it is up to Father to do what he thinks is best, whether he wants to make the purchase or not."*

Shortly after writing this letter, Olav and Eilert left Stearns for North Dakota, where they found farm work for the threshing season.

■ ■ ■

The family had witnessed great changes in the Appalachians in the early years of the 20th century. Large areas of the mountains had been denuded of their great stands of virgin hardwoods. The hillsides had been eroded and scarred by logging and mining. Agriculture declined. Railroads, roads, schools and medical care had come to some regions of the mountains, and with them came company towns, with absentee owners. Now, the company towns were declining, as jobs and incomes eroded in the economic downturn. With the slowdown in industrial and construction activity throughout the country, the Stearns Company shut down the sawmill and closed its lumber operations in 1909.

Gustav and Anna remained in Stearns until the spring of 1910, when they moved to Ludington, Michigan, the hometown of Justus Stearns.

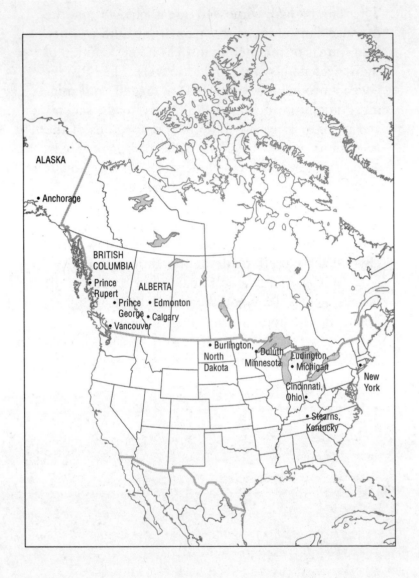

ALASKA

• Anchorage

BRITISH
COLUMBIA
• Prince   ALBERTA
Rupert
• Prince   • Edmonton
George • Calgary
• Vancouver

• Burlington,
North
Dakota
• Duluth   Ludington,
Minnesota • Michigan

Cincinnati,
Ohio •

New
York •

• Stearns,
Kentucky

Chapter 7
"Sometimes things do not go the way we want"

Bunk house at logging camp, Ely, Minnesota, 1910

OLAV AND EILERT TRAVELLED to North Dakota for the threshing season, and in late October they found work through an employment agency at Ely, Minnesota, 115 miles northeast of Duluth. The job was with a construction crew laying a "corduroy road." Some workers cut down the trees, while another crew lopped the twigs off and laid the logs crosswise over the soft, uneven surface to make a passable road for wagons. Olav worked on the second crew. *"One day after lunch, I was with a group of five men, resting after a meal. While talking together, we*

found that we were from different nations, all six of us."
But they didn't like working there, so they returned
to Duluth in early December.

Travelling together, Olav and Eilert were a
distinctive pair. At thirty years of age, Olav had a
small lean build, and held himself straight and tall
to take advantage of every inch of his five-and-a-
half-foot frame. While Olav was more serious and
restrained in his demeanour, the handsome, eighteen-year-old Eilert was more playful and
spontaneous. He held his over-six-foot frame

Olav and Eilert, Duluth, Minnesota, 1910

straight and tall, giving away his not-so-secret problem of finding pants long enough for his long legs. Both brothers liked to present themselves well in public. Young Eilert was quickly becoming knowledgeable about American society under the watchful eye of his older brother.

They arrived at Duluth in early December of 1909, and found jobs at a new opera house under construction. The Duluth newspaper claimed that the new theatre would be one of the handsomest in the Orpheum circuit and would provide "nothing but the best in vaudeville shows."

Duluth was a city of 78,000, situated at the westerly end of Lake Superior, with its sister city, Superior, Wisconsin, a short distance to the south on the other side of the St. Louis River. The motto for the city was "At the Heart of the Great Lakes— Where Rails and Water Meet." Both cities were important ports that funnelled most of the east-west trade across the northern United States. From the end of a long, narrow sandbar that reached up from Superior, the Duluth Aerial Ferry Bridge connected the two cities. A ferry ran back and forth over the narrow channel on a truss that was fixed on a high tower at either end. A building boom was on at the time in Duluth, with the "construction of residences and buildings of a solid nature."

This was the coldest place in Minnesota, and construction work was often curtailed during harsh winter weather, but Olav and Eilert hoped to keep this job over the winter so they could save some money by summer. Jobs were easy to get in the summer and the pay was good, but jobs were hard to find in the winter and the pay was poor.

Travelling around looking for work had been expensive. The money that funded their journeys would have paid their fare home to Norway twice. *"But we can't help that. If we want to find a good job, we have to pay to get to different places."* They had wanted to go home for Christmas. *"But sometimes things do not go the way we want them to go."*

■ ■ ■

Juergen and Martin Severinson had written that they were leaving for Norway in the fall, but then Olav and Eilert had heard nothing further from them. Olav thought they may already be in Norway. If they weren't there, Olav feared that they might have had some misfortune, and perhaps did not want to let their families know.

Juergen had promised Andreas that he would send money for the care of Aanen as soon as the farmer paid him for his work. Olav wrote that if his father had not received money for Aanen, some decision would have to be made about how to handle the problem in the future. But Olav did not want to be involved in that decision. His father would have to decide whether he could let Aanen stay for free. The problem was particularly difficult because Aanen was also Gustav's father-in-law.

Olav learned more details about the land deal at Rosseland from Gustav. They were waiting for the municipality to approve the deal. Olav wondered if the delay was because of the mortgage on the property. He thought it was a very good deal and that it would be a shame if it wasn't approved. In their letters, the topic never arose again. After negotiating extensively with Hunsfoss to get agreement on the details, it appears that the land deal was never approved or concluded.

Since they didn't know for sure where they would be over the winter, Olav asked that they send his mail to Gustav. They would go back to Stearns if they could find no other job. They were sure they could get a job there, but the wages were low in the winter.

In the month of April, Olav and Eilert worked on a ship that freighted cargo on the Great Lakes, travelling as far as Buffalo, New York. Over 400 vessels carrying cargo and passengers were registered to sail from Duluth, from April to December. There was no commercial sailing in the harsh winter months.

Six months passed after Olav wrote his last letter in December before writing home again in June 1910. They didn't have any good news. "*All winter I have been thinking about sending some money home, but my luck is against me, so I have not been able to save anything. If you are in need of some money, I should be able to send some in a few months . . .*" They were back in Duluth working for a building contractor. Their jobs had not been steady and their living costs were high. Most of what they earned went to pay for clothes and room and board, with not much left over.

■ ■ ■

"*Everything is green around here, and the weather has been clear and sunny. Maybe a little bit dry for the farmer,*

I think." The summer began very warm. By the end of June, numerous heat records had been broken, and some records still stood unbroken ninety years later. *"There are many lovely parks here, but the air is not as fresh as we would like it."* Air pollution in Duluth was due to the extensive use of coal in industry. Olav frequently commented on his memories of springtime and flowers in Norway. *"I can remember the smell of the flowers in the evening, when we were out for a walk in the beginning of April. I always enjoyed Norway in the summertime."*

■ ■ ■

Although Gustav and Anna moved from Stearns to Ludington in early spring 1910, Gustav did not write to the family in Norway until early July. The family had sent several anxious letters because they hadn't heard from either Gustav or Olav. *"We have talked for months about writing you, but we can never get started. I have started letters before to you, but I can never finish them . . . . This time I am going to finish it."* On this letter-writing day, Gustav was in an upbeat mood and determined to finish the letter he started.

He wished that the family could see how well they were living. They had rented an upstairs suite in a near-new, large comfortable home, built by a young married couple. The rooms were beautifully furnished, with hot and cold running water in the kitchen and bathroom, and electric lights in all the rooms and the hallway. *"We don't need any lamps, just push the button on the wall and the lights come on."* They entered the suite by a side door, with a stairway upstairs that opened into the kitchen. There were three rooms off the kitchen, a full bathroom, a bedroom, and a large dining room. The dining room had a door to a second bedroom and opened into the living room, with a third bedroom off the living room. The owner of the house operated a coal business, so the home was always comfortably warm. *"But it costs money to live in a house, especially in the city.*

"I think about everything I had in Kentucky, which I practically had to give away because it would cost too much to have it moved here. But I am happy we left Kentucky, and I guess you are also. Now we are among civilized people."

Ludington was a scenic waterfront town on the east side of Lake Michigan, about half-way between the north and south tips of the lake. Commercial activity in the area had originally been based on the logging and lumber industries, but later diversified into salt mining when the timber

Ludington: Gustav and Anna lived upstairs

supply started to diminish. In the flat land of this region, during the warm summers, the fruit industry flourished with crops of peaches, cherries, apples and berries. In 1910, a new cannery for fruits was about to open. Ludington had become a business centre for that central region of Michigan and was becoming known as a resort town. The Pere Marquette car ferries transported rail cars and passengers across the lake to and from Ludington and Manitowoc, Wisconsin, and Ludington was connected by rail to destinations south.

The economy of Ludington was diversified and there were many jobs available, but the wages were poor. Gustav had just lost his job, the day before writing the letter, as a salt-wheeler at the salt factory. Salt mining had been thriving with the rise of the chemical industry, but the economy was in a recession, and the salt plant had been standing still for more than a month because of poor sales. It looked as if the plant would be closed for quite a while. *"There is a lot of other work here, but the pay is no good, so there is no way you can feed a family that way."*

They also had another mouth to feed. Their third daughter, Faye, had been born in May. *"We didn't know if we dared to tell you about the little girl, because you would say that we are going overboard now. But you should see how nice our small girls are. Everyone loves them and adores them."*

Gustav went on to tell about a party at their church called Children's Day, a celebration that was held every year. The church that they attended was the Norwegian Methodist Church, so all the Norwegian children and the Norwegians were there. The church was full. He explained that every child had a verse to say both in English and in Norwegian, and one child at a time came forward to give their performance. Gustav was immensely proud of his daughter Magnhild. He wrote:

"She wore a pink dress and she looked so lovely in pink—China doll shoes and a pink bow in her hair. I wish you could have seen her that evening. When she came forward people whispered to each other and asked whose child she was. She did her act like a professional, much better than the other children that were in her confirmation age. But most of all she was admired by all when she sang, so at the same time I felt proud and embarrassed over what people whispered to each other. Even the children themselves said that Magnhild was the best. The minister said to me later that Magnhild had a special voice. It was the nicest voice he had ever heard, and she was so natural and at the same time shy.

"Magnhild is not afraid of anything, whether it is hundreds of people, or she is alone at home—she is the same. I write this so you will know more about Magnhild. I know you all love her, and she is still as sweet as she was when she came over here. She is just a little bit older."

■ ■ ■

Gustav passed a message on from Anna. She promised to write the family a letter, but Gustav didn't think she would have time, because she had her hands full with her three little chickens: Magnhild, Gudrun and Faye, ages six years, nineteen months and two months.

Gustav wanted to go home now, as soon as he could. He wrote that America was not what it used to be. The wages were going down, and prices were going up. *"If you worked in Norway like you work here, I think I could make a good living. So, if I come home, don't expect me to come home with lots of money."*

■ ■ ■

In September, they had Gudrun and Faye christened at the Norwegian Methodist Church by Pastor Ole Roland. Their landlords, Steffen and Mabel Nerheim, were the godparents. They had become friendly with several Norwegian families during their stay at Ludington, including the Lunde and Soli families. Their friends from Kentucky, the Tibbetts family, had returned to the Ludington area a year previously, to their home in nearby Scottsville. However, they had now left to seek homesteading land in Alberta, Canada, before Gustav and Anna arrived at Ludington.

Gustav and Anna had a difficult time that next winter in Ludington. Gustav was unemployed most of the winter, and they all suffered from coughs and colds. Juergen came to their rescue by giving Gustav an $80 loan to help them through their financial crisis. That amount of money represented savings from many months of work. With the poor wages offered in Ludington, Gustav had little prospect of ever repaying this loan.

■ ■ ■

Olav and Eilert were working in Duluth in July 1910, but the job they were working on was finishing soon. They would be looking for work again, unless their employer got another contract. Many workers were searching for jobs. Thousands had obtained employment on farms the previous year, but the intense heat that summer had wiped out most of the grain crops. There was no farm work, but Olav had no interest in ever doing farm work again.

"I am not going there whether it is good or bad years. I have had enough of the Dakota farming work. Where we were last, we worked 12 and 15 hours every day, and at the end we lost $15 and $20. That man we worked for was a so-called Christian. We thought he was a good man, until we had pay-day. That day he swore and banged the table, so that the cups danced, and he got up from the chair to do the same to me as he had done to the cups. If he hadn't sat down again, I guess some of us would have got a good beating."

■ ■ ■

Olav wrote that he and Eilert wanted to help Gustav go home with his family, because the way things were going, Gustav would never be able to save enough money to take his family home. They hoped to return to Norway the next summer.

■ ■ ■

In November, Olav thanked his sister for her letter, and also for the letter he had received two months earlier and never replied to. The brothers had been working steadily, and were heading north of Duluth on a job that would last three weeks.

Their income had been constant for several months, but the cost of essential items had risen. *"Everything is different than it was four years ago. Shoes, clothing and food are two to three times more now. Rent is also higher, but the wages are rather less than they were four years ago."* Olav had borrowed money from Gustav to start his photography business in Stearns and he had repaid most of that. But he hadn't been able to save anything from the months that he had worked regularly.

■ ■ ■

Olav and Eilert travelled to Burlington looking for work in the middle of March 1911. They went three weeks without work, but then found temporary employment. *"We are thinking about working in a brick factory this summer, and in the winter we will try to get a job in the coal mines, if we decide to stay that long . . . ."*

The industry in this area was seasonal, mainly agriculture, ranching and mining. The first coal mining in the area began in 1884, and then the Soo Railway came into the area in 1892. Coal mining expanded until 24 coal mines dotted the landscape, each operated by an independent owner. Like the mines at Stearns, Kentucky, the mines in this area were drift mines, but the coal here was the softer lignite coal. The Stearns Company mine was the largest at Burlington, and the Davis mine was the second largest. It was Mr. L. M. Davis who had found a fine quality of clay when he built his tipple. Later, he decided to use the clay by starting a brick factory to keep the miners in the area during the off-season, when the coal mines were not in operation. Work in the mines was plentiful in the fall, but in the harsh winter months it was too cold to keep the mines open. Olav and Eilert found little work available in March and April, prior to the opening of the brickworks.

Burlington, North Dakota
Photo courtesy of Ward County Historical Society, Minot,
North Dakota

Olav wrote, *"I have gone to a big school in America, which is called 'The School of Life,' and here I learned to be a socialist."* Olav asked his sister if she could find out the cost of having a socialist newspaper from Kristiansand sent to him.

■ ■ ■

In 1889, with the first boom of homesteaders and ranchers to the area, North Dakota was admitted to the union of the United States. A second wave of settlers arrived after 1905, many of whom were Norwegian immigrants. During this period a socialist movement grew among workers, for labourers and farmers believed that their state government was giving preferential treatment to out-of-state corporations, which were taking profits out of the state. Labourers and farmers began demanding fairer taxes, better government regulations for workers and better government services. Political debates on socialism swept across the state. By 1910, Minot had become a hotbed of the American Socialist Movement. Socialist thinking had been prevalent in rural Norway, so Norwegian immigrants found it easy to relate to the movement in North Dakota.

The town of Burlington was located about fifty miles due south of the Saskatchewan-Manitoba border, a moderately dry area of extreme temperatures—hot in the summer and cold in the winter. Grassy and low, flat-topped mountains, or buttes, were carved by coulees, steep-sided valleys. The tree-lined Souris River flowed through one of these wide irregular valleys. Burlington was a town of wooden buildings strung out along the railway tracks, with a dirt road joining it to the town of Minot, six miles to the east. Minot was the more rowdy town, and the place where miners went for entertainment. Olav and Eilert worked at the Davis mine, a flagstop between the two towns. Most companies operated stores for their employees and some had boarding homes, generally of low quality and hard to find, especially when the mines were closed. Olav wrote that Gustav was thinking about moving there in the summer, so that maybe they could all live together again. *"If times will be good like it was before, it is our hope that we should be able to get ahead again."*

Juergen was also in Burlington. He had bought ten acres of fruit land in Texas, and was making payments on it. He had dreams of planting oranges and fig trees, with prospects of an annual income from a fruit crop. Olav wanted to get land also, but he didn't know yet where he would go. The large number of immigrants entering the country increased the demand for agricultural products and drove up prices for farm products, making farming more attractive.

"I hope that Father can keep going a few more years." Andreas was now sixty-three years old, while their mother was sixty, and they wanted their sons to take over the farm. Olav thought that their forest must have grown quite a bit, so their father should be able to make enough money to pay expenses by harvesting some trees each year. *"I understand that you would all like to have us at home . . . but if it would be the same poor conditions that Father and Mother have had, it wouldn't be any fun for any of us."*

Their sister Anna was now twenty-four years old, and had remained at home to help their parents. Olav appreciated that this had been a personal sacrifice for her. He thought that she should be compensated for her work each year with a set sum of money. *"Father knows best how this should be handled, and decided. And any way he has decided . . . I have no objection to any arrangements that you make."*

■ ■ ■

Gustav and Anna moved to Canada in the late spring of 1911, and Olav wrote in November 1911 that he had just had a registered letter from Gustav. They had moved to the new "boom town" of Castor, Alberta, and were not getting their mail, and their letters to Norway were not arriving there. *"There must be something wrong with the mail service . . ."*

Gustav had obtained a job as soon as he arrived at Castor, with Crown Lumber Company, a lumber supply business. He thought it was a good job at $2.50 per day. Olav wrote that things hadn't gone

146 From Sailing Ships to Spitfires

well for Gustav and Anna in Ludington, but the reason for that was sickness. *"Eilert and I helped them as much as we could, but at the same time we were moving around so much and did not make much money. They needed more help. Lately things have changed for the better."*

He and Eilert were working in the coal mines, working hard and earning good money. The railroad industry purchased some coal year round, but mainly their work was seasonal. The brick plant offered some work during the off-season. Then, residential and business owners purchased their winter supply of coal in the fall. The mines closed again when the cold winter weather set in, in December. Juergen was still working there with them. Olav thought that the money Juergen owed Andreas might be paid back now.

They had met two men from Norway, who came from a farm near Alefjar. This group of Norwegians enjoyed each other's company. Olav asked about their cousin Anders, who had returned to the U.S.A. again. They wanted his address. If he wanted land, they thought that he should go to where Gustav was living. *"It is supposed to be good land, and the railway goes through . . ."* He added that since people in America had a hard time pronouncing "Eilert," he had changed his name to Albert.

■ ■ ■

With the mine closure in December, Olav and Albert decided to join Gustav and Anna in Alberta. In the week between Christmas and New Year's, 1911, they made the move from Davis, North Dakota to Castor, Alberta.

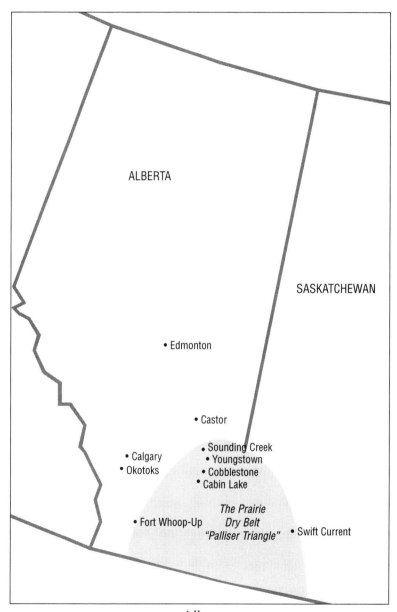

ALBERTA

SASKATCHEWAN

• Edmonton

• Castor

• Sounding Creek
• Youngstown
• Calgary
• Cobblestone
• Okotoks
• Cabin Lake

The Prairie
Dry Belt
• Fort Whoop-Up   *"Palliser Triangle"*   • Swift Current

Alberta

PART THREE
"Canada Should Be Perfect for Oats and Wheat"
(Canada 1912-27)

Chapter 8
"There is not a stump on this land, or stones to break"

"The Last Best West" —
Canadian Government advertising poster

IN THE SUMMER OF 1911, Gustav and Anna stepped off the train with their three little girls, Magnhild, Gudrun and Faye, at Castor, Alberta, about 100 miles northeast of Calgary. The new Canadian Pacific Railway extension from Lacombe, east to Castor, went no further. From the train station they saw before them a brand-new modern main street. The town had risen swiftly since its birth two years previously, as business in Castor had been brisk.

Gustav and Anna's friends from Stearns, the Tibbetts and Johnson families, had taken land southeast of Castor in 1910. Other friends from the United States acquired land in that same area. These friends had given Gustav and Anna information about the opportunities here, and encouraged them to come to the western prairies in 1911. Free land had run out in the United States and the economy of Canada was booming. Immigrants were coming into the country in record numbers.

■ ■ ■

Castor, Alberta, 1911

Canada's economy had been on the upswing since 1900. The federal Liberal government had attracted investors' money by guaranteeing their investments for railroad construction. This brought money from foreign investors into the country at low interest rates. Railroads were under construction across the country, and cities and towns grew all along the rail lines. In the west, these settlements were the centres of business for homesteaders putting down roots in the area. In 1909, the government for the new province of Alberta was up for re-election. They recognized the success of the federal government and offered the same security of investors' money for railroad construction. This brought in workers and contributed to the growth of cities and towns. As an added bonus for the economy, the western provinces had been blessed with adequate rainfall since 1900 and world wheat prices were rising. The thriving economy attracted large numbers of homesteaders and day workers to the area.

The region east of Calgary to the Saskatchewan border, and as far north as Castor down to the Red Deer River, was opening up for homesteading. In 1909, Castor was established, followed by Youngstown three years later. During those years, settlers came north from the CPR mainline south of the Red Deer River, fording the river with their horses and wagons at Steveville. From there they travelled north to Youngstown.

The town of Castor originated when investors planned an extension of a rail line east from Lacombe and Stettler, which connected with the north-south Calgary-Edmonton line. In July 1909, a land auction was held, at which time a piece of bald prairie was sold off in city lots. This piece of previously unoccupied land became the townsite for the new town of Castor. Immediately after, a great rush of developers beat a path over the open prairie with their horses and wagons, bringing loads of building materials. Construction began that summer. By December, Castor was up and running, with a wide range of business services. Citizens were out to welcome the first train as it chugged into Castor on December 17, 1909. Just seven months after the land auction, *Castor Illustrated Annual* noted. " . . . Our popular hotel proprietor has left nothing undone for the comfort of his guests. His hotel is among the finest in Alberta, being a three-storey building equipped with all modern conveniences and furnished in first-class style. It is hard to realize that such accommodation can be had in a town which seven months ago was open prairie."

Castor grew rapidly as a business centre, as it served that whole region east to the Saskatchewan border and down to the Red Deer River. As settlers laboured to create their homesteads, many purchased their building and other supplies there, and these materials were taken out of town almost as fast as they came in. Castor also sat on the edge of a large coal basin and sandstone quarry, and it was bricks made from sandstone in this quarry that contributed to the construction of many buildings in the new town. By 1911, Castor boasted a public school with five teachers, five lumber supply businesses, three hotels, ministers for five different churches, nine livery barns, a weekly newspaper, an electric light plant and a grain elevator, as well as other business and professional services, and an opera house. The Sisters of the Holy Rosary constructed a modern new hospital that opened at Castor in 1911, further contributing to the importance of the town. Two years after construction commenced, Castor had an official population of 1,400, and the population of the larger area it served had grown considerably.

■ ■ ■

Gustav and Anna met Olav and Albert at the train station at Castor in February 1912. They hadn't seen each other for two and a half years. *"When we arrived at the station in Castor, I saw Gustav on the outside. I went out to say hello to him, but he didn't recognize me."* Eilert now weighed 190 pounds. He wrote that Gustav just stood there and laughed at him.

The three brothers each filed an application for land under the Homestead Act, which offered 160 acres to settlers for a $10 fee, with the land being transferred to the homesteader after he had filled the requirements of the act. The real estate market was active at that time, and prices were high. The brothers had great optimism that they would become landowners, and that the land value would increase. Albert expected that the value might increase by $1,000 per year, and thought that they should stay on the land for a few years before selling. *"People who came here two years ago own from $4,000 to $8,000. I believe we could do half of that.*

"This piece of land is totally flat, not a stump on it, or stones to break. All one has to do is to use the plough and then throw in a potato, or a handful of oats, or wheat in the furrow, plus some fertilizer like we used to do in the old country." Olav and Albert had chosen land located near the very shallow Antelope Lake, attracted by the promise of moisture. The land was stark with no shade, as only willows grew in the area of the near-dry lake. Other than the willows, the growth on the land was stubby, dry grass and that hated weed, the Russian thistle. Gustav had located two miles south, near Sounding Creek. A railroad was to be built next to their land, and that would make it more attractive for resale. The new town of Youngstown was only five or six miles away, so they wouldn't have to go too far to sell their products and to shop.

A Norwegian friend had returned to Norway, and Albert heard that he had lots of money. *"Well, back home they say that a man has lots of money if he has more than, say, 1,000 kroner. Americans are always thought to have lots of money, even when they do not have a dollar to their name."* Albert didn't intend to go back with such a small stake.

They had heard that their cousin Anders had taken land in Canada, but they hadn't heard from him. Gunhilde, another cousin, was contemplating coming to America, but Albert advised that the pay for women was even worse than the pay for men. *"In places like Minnesota, Wisconsin, North Dakota or the southern states, the women only get $2 to $3 per week for their work."*

Albert told a little story about an incident that occurred when they went hunting.

The brothers had headed out near Castor the day before, and shot a wolf. Gustav carried it home and placed it at the front door where they lived. After he put it down, the wolf got up and walked away, back to the woods. Anna stood there and laughed. *"It was alive on the way home and all the time it played like it was dead!"*

He concluded his letter. *"Say hello to everyone at Rosseland and don't forget all the nice and pretty girls at home . . . ."*

■ ■ ■

While still living in Castor, in April 1912, Gustav and Anna celebrated the arrival of their fourth daughter, Agnes. Magnhild was now six years old and had started school in Castor, Gudrun was three and Faye was almost two. They would have a full house when they moved to their new homestead that summer.

■ ■ ■

Olav, Albert and Juergen had been working in Edmonton since the middle of June. *"This city is a nice place. 25,000 is the population. There is a lot of building going on and people say that it will be the largest city in the west in a few years. There are a lot of green trees, and a big river runs right through the city, which makes it beautiful."* Like the rest of Alberta, Edmonton was experiencing a real estate boom. The city covered twenty-five square miles, and the population was growing by the day. New subdivisions were being planned and were burgeoning throughout the city, a land speculator's dream. The noise and activity of construction was everywhere, with so many workers and new-comers in the city, that the city council threw open schools as sleeping quarters. Over 2,000 people camped in tents along the river, and scattered elsewhere throughout the city. The weather had been good up to July, in 1912, and was a cause for optimism. It had rained every three or four days followed by sunshine and warm weather. Everything in the fields was lovely and green.

The brothers were moving to their land in August and were required to live on their land for six months of the year. But to start out, they all intended to live on Gustav's property, which was two and a half miles south of Olav and Albert's properties. Juergen had still not decided what to do, as he hadn't been able to make enough money to meet expenses. He was thinking of going back to North Dakota.

They had heard from their cousin Anders, who was living on his homestead. Olav added that it was a tragedy to hear that the *Titanic* had sunk. He hoped that Gunhilde was not on that ship. Gunhilde never did come to America, perhaps discouraged by the news of low wages for women.

■ ■ ■

"We are no longer living in Castor," Olav wrote from Youngstown in October 1912. *"We are now living in Gustav's homestead. We have been here for two months."*

The brothers had chosen land north of the new CNR line to Youngstown. James Young had

Gudrun, Faye and Magnhild, 1912

come over from the Lacombe area in 1909, with a team of horses and all his building and household supplies on wagons. He set up a homestead and a store, and early in 1912, he sold his property to developers, who subdivided the land and sold lots to create Youngstown, named after him. By the summer of 1912, several businesses were already established, including a bank and hardware store, which operated from a tent on the main street until their building was completed later in the fall.

The already experienced Tibbetts and Johnson families assisted Gustav in building his first sod house in August 1912. The Roselands camped with their friends on the adjoining property, while the sod house was under construction. *"There are very few Scandinavians around here. All our neighbours are Americans. But many of them we knew before."*

Many homesteaders built their first home from sod. Late summer and fall was the time to build a sod house, when the roots of the sod were tough and dry. The sod was free, and the houses were cool in summer and warm in winter. The homesteaders would first place four pegs in the ground to determine the size and parameters of the structure, and then dig into the floor area until hitting hardpan, or solid dirt, several inches or a foot deep. With a plough or sharp cutting tool, they cut several inches into the dry, grassy turf, creating building bricks about three feet long and a foot wide. So as not to weaken or damage the tough root system, they carefully carried the "Alberta brick" on a board to the construction site. They laid it root-side-up in a careful pattern to construct the walls, leaving a space for the door and windows. The roof was the most difficult part of the structure to build. They used different construction methods on the roof, depending on what was available and practical at the time. The two greatest problems with sod houses were their tendency to leak in heavy rains, and the little creatures that might appear out of the walls. However, if the turf was cut cleanly, the inside walls could be plastered. Faye remembered well the plastered inside walls of their sod house, and family photos show a nicely finished interior of the Roseland sod home.

Olav continued, *"It is our idea to sell the land when the time comes and then move back to Norway."* To Norwegians born in Norway during the years of the highest birth rate of the 1800s, with scarce agricultural land, the offer of free land by the Canadian government seemed a golden opportunity. Land ownership was a privilege in Norway, an impossible achievement for large portions of the population. The Roselands were determined to become successful farmers, to gain title to their land, and then sell it. They had become land speculators, like many others.

■ ■ ■

Until 1670, this land had been inhabited chiefly by nomadic tribes and bison. About 15,000 years ago, the most recent Ice Age ended, and the western prairies became a great lake. This eventually drained, leaving a great sandy wasteland carved by coulees, through which the water had flowed away. The rivers and creeks that drain the region today were probably established about 6,000 years ago, when the climate became hot and dry. Vegetation returned to the area; then came the bison and other animals, followed by nomadic peoples. The British government, which had claimed the land earlier, granted a charter for the land to the Hudson's Bay Company in 1670. The company established a fur trading industry west of Ontario and across the prairies.

Great Britain had concerns about the administration of this vast and remote land. In the 1850s, the British government sent John Palliser to survey the land to determine the resources and possible uses for the lands. Palliser determined that the area, which later became southeast Alberta and southwest Saskatchewan, was not suitable for agricultural use. This region of the western prairies became known as the Palliser Triangle. In order to be relieved of the administration of the land, Great Britain urged the Hudson's Bay Company to sell the western lands to the Canadian government. At that time Canada consisted of only four provinces.

The problem escalated after the American Civil War, when demobilized soldiers headed west and north in search of land, threatening encroachment into Canada. The British feared that the United States had designs on their territories in western Canada. British shipbuilders had built a ship for the Confederates during the Civil War, which did a great deal of damage to Yankee shipping, so the American government demanded that the British grant them the British North America lands as war reparations. Great Britain refused. The Canadian solution to the threatened encroachment was to purchase the western lands from the Hudson's Bay Company and form a new government, in 1867, in the form of a confederation. When British Columbia joined in 1871, Canada was united from the Atlantic to the Pacific.

In January 1870, Prime Minister John A. Macdonald wrote, "*It is quite evident to me that the United States Government are resolved to do all they can, short of war, to get possession of our western territory, and we must take immediate and vigorous steps to counteract them.*" Macdonald determined that a transcontinental railway should unite the country, and that the western lands should be settled. He brought in the Dominion Lands Act in 1872 to open up the prairie west for homesteading, and embarked on an era of railroad building, financial scandals and remarkable accomplishments that ended with the completion of the railroad from coast to coast in 1885.

A new threat to the west emerged in the 1860s and '70s, when American traders ventured north into Canada via the Missouri River and Fort Benton in Montana, to southern Alberta. They offered "hooch," or adulterated whiskey, to the natives, in exchange for buffalo hides. For a number of years there was a well-beaten 210-mile mule-train trail, known as the "Whoop-Up Trail," between Fort Benton and an American trading post near Lethbridge known as Fort Whoop-Up. Considerable lawlessness prevailed, but Macdonald put an end to this by sending a newly formed North-West Mounted Police force to Alberta in 1875. The end of this era also saw sickness, disease and starvation decimating the native tribes, caused partly by the loss of their main food source, the buffalo. In 1878, there were great fires on the prairie grasslands and the declining numbers of buffalo went south for the winter, never to return. A way of life and an abundance of wildlife had been destroyed by the white man within a generation.

In the late 1890s, Prime Minister Wilfrid Laurier appointed Clifford Sifton Minister of the Interior, with the responsibility of establishing settlement in the west. Prior to that time the government had granted grazing leases to ranchers, but settlers had been slow in coming, frightened by reports of drought, early frosts, floods and grasshoppers. Sifton embarked on a massive program of publicity and enticements to bring "desirable" settlers to the west. In the first decade of the 1900s, the Canadian government widely distributed an array of posters seeking homesteaders in the United States and Great Britain: "40,000 American Citizens Needed," "The Last Best West, Homes for Millions," and "Canada—The Prize Wheat Belt of the World." Olav had been attracted by the Canadian advertising in Kentucky when he wrote, *"Canada should be perfect for oats and wheat."* In 1905, when homesteaders began migrating to these western lands, the federal government formed the new provinces of Alberta and Saskatchewan, from land previously known as the Northwest Territories.

After 1900, the economy in Alberta began to change. Railroads were under construction. Ranching declined sharply with the severe winter of 1906-07, when large numbers of cattle froze to death. In increasingly large throngs, settlers came in to claim homestead lands, and towns grew quickly along the rail lines to service the settlers. Edmonton, the newly appointed capital of the province, grew quickly, while Calgary commenced an annual stampede and served the business needs of the southern part of the province. With readily available money for investments, the real estate market and the economy of the province soared.

The prairie west was rife with activity and optimism in 1912. The future for the province of Alberta looked bright indeed.

Chapter 9
"If nothing unforeseen happens"

"It is inexpensive to get land, but it is hard anyway to get things going when you have nothing to start with." In addition to building and equipping a home, the new homesteaders required a plough, horses, a cow, fencing, a barn, perhaps chickens and a henhouse, and they also had to plant a garden to supply their food. These were just the basic items; Gustav also had to provide for his family. They hoped to buy some horses in the spring, and then buy the farm machinery they needed.

The weather in 1912 proved favourable for wheat crops, so in the fall Gustav was able to work assisting neighbours with threshing. He hoped to work with them through most of the winter. The next spring these people would repay him for his labour with the loan of their farming equipment.

Threshing season was a busy and exciting time in the annual cycle of wheat farming. After the wheat had been cut in late summer, the farmer had his crop tied in stooks to dry, waiting for the time when the grain could be "threshed," or shaken from the stalks it had grown on. A steam-powered threshing machine was common in those early years. The fuel might be hay or wood, and the steam drove a belt that powered the thresher. Eighteen or twenty men were required to throw the bundles into the thresher and keep the machines operating. The men worked hard for long hours, and might be paid for their work by earning the loan of much-needed equipment or horses. It was a time of sharing, working together and making friends.

Women also participated in the threshing ritual. The woman on whose farm the threshing was being done was responsible for feeding the crew three hearty meals each day. Other wives came to assist her, while they all still had their routine chores to do and children to care for.

■ ■ ■

In the early fall, Juergen applied for a homestead and then the three bachelors returned to Castor to work in the coal mines there. But their income was poor. *"All the Englishmen and Scots that came over here are so green and dumb that people can get them to work from when the sun comes up in the east, until it goes down in the west, all year round. There is a law which says you can only work eight hours a day in the mines, but these numbskulls work ten or twelve and fifteen hours a day for less money than they are entitled to get for eight hours."*

Laurier's Liberal government had advertised heavily in Britain to seek English immigrants, with a bias for developing an English-speaking society, so many came from Great Britain who were not accustomed to the work and circumstances that they would face on the western prairies. English and Scots would work for low wages, driving down the pay for others. The economy of the country slowed down in late 1912, with a worldwide recession. Money for construction projects became scarce; so many railway and building projects came to an end. Olav wrote,

"Albert, Juergen and I have not made very much money. That is the case for workers all over Canada . . . ."

A friend from Norway was thinking about coming to Canada, and wanted to find an easy job. Olav wrote, *"Easy jobs are what everyone is looking for, but I don't think one in a hundred finds it."* Skilled workers such as blacksmiths, carpenters and bricklayers earned the best pay. If a worker was skilled in any of these trades, he could earn from $4 to $6 per day, but *" . . . any man who doesn't understand these occupations must work a lot harder here than back in Norway."*

■ ■ ■

Their father wrote that Juergen owed him for the care of Aanen for two years. Juergen had sent money to Andreas after farming in North Dakota in 1910, but he was in arrears again. Olav wrote that Juergen had so many expenses that there was no way he could pay for Aanen at this time, and suggested that the money for Aanen's care should come from the money that Gustav had sent home to his father over the years, because Gustav still owed Juergen $80. Gustav had been sending money home to Andreas for years, money that was being credited towards his purchase of the farm at Rosseland. And Aanen was Gustav's father-in-law.

■ ■ ■

The three coal miners spent Christmas at a boarding house near Castor, as Gustav's house was not big enough to accommodate them all. They felt none of the Christmas spirit that they were accustomed to in Norway. *"Everybody is so busy in this country that people don't get a chance to think about the festivities until it is over."* But the boarding house served a very special meal for Christmas—turkey, cake, pie, oranges, candies, and fruit and nuts. *"Turkey is the favourite American food like the lutefisk is for the Norwegians."* Lutefisk was a traditional Norwegian specialty made of dried cod, soaked in lye to preserve it, and then later soaked and boiled. Norwegians served lutefisk with a nutmeg-flavoured white sauce as a special dinner at Christmas.

■ ■ ■

Olav and Juergen returned to Edmonton after Christmas, while Albert remained at Castor working in the coal mines. January was a poor month, but they earned more in February and March. Olav was discouraged. They had been working hard for years and seemed to be getting nowhere. *"We, who were born in poor conditions, have to work hard, but that should not be necessary if we use our brains. Under this government we work hard to make others rich, but if we could unite and say, 'stop this tyranny,' we could make this a good place on earth to live in peace and be able to tolerate each other. Then we wouldn't have to work as much as we do now and maybe make three times as much as we do now* . . . ." Throughout 1913, investment money disappeared from the economy, and construction came to a halt. There were no jobs and men poured into the cities looking for work.

January was very cold; the temperature went down to minus 55 degrees Fahrenheit. But, in March, the snow had almost disappeared and it was starting to look like spring.

■ ■ ■

In April, they were all working on their homesteads. The Homestead Act required that they have ten acres ploughed and seeded that spring, and ten more acres had to be ploughed in the fall. Olav estimated that it would cost them $150 each to pay for the use of ploughs and horses owned by others, but they didn't know how much it would cost them to live for the next six months, when they were required to live on their homesteads.

■ ■ ■

Gustav ploughed two wheat fields. One was ninety acres and the other was ten acres. In addition, he planted a big garden of vegetables and potatoes for the family, and Anna canned vegetables for winter use. They stored other vegetables in a hole in the ground prepared for cool dry storage, called a dugout. Later, Gustav wrote, *"The crop was not good this year, so we didn't make much money, but I will try for better luck next summer. The weather was dry in the spring, so it took a long time for the seed to grow."*

■ ■ ■

Olav and Albert returned to the coal mines in the fall, but went to a new mine at Sheerness, just 15 miles south of the CNR line. *"Gustav followed us here and got a large load of coal."* Settlers depended on coal for their fuel as there was very little else available to burn. In the fall, farmers travelled with a horse and wagon to get their coal, and sometimes would be away for several nights as they waited in line for coal. They slept under their wagons on the nights that they were away. If Gustav was going to be late getting home, Anna put a lantern in the window, but the horses could always find their way home.

■ ■ ■

Andreas asked again if one of his sons would like to take over the farm. Olav wrote his sister that they would all like the farm. But they wondered if they could manage it, because they had been away so long that they didn't know the prices or the way of living in the old country any more. *"To buy the farm creates debt, and to have to go through the same slave labour in life as mother and father have done would be sheer stupidity."*

Even if he sold his homestead, Olav would not have enough money to pay for the farm, as he expected to pay what the farm was worth in the marketplace. He thought it might be better to use what money he made on the homestead to start another business in Norway, without carrying any debt. *"It could be possible that Father would sell it cheaper to one of us than to someone he doesn't know. But that would mean that he would take from the three of his children and give it to the fourth. Even if that is what is done to most of the farms at home, it would be considered a shady deal."* Olav always wanted a deal that was fair to everyone.

■ ■ ■

Andreas had again asked for money for the care of Aanen, so Gustav wrote a separate, special letter to his father. Gustav explained that he had not been able to repay the $80 that Juergen had loaned him in Ludington two years previously. *"It was understood that Juergen would wait for that money until I*

could manage to pay him with money from here . . . .
*Juergen does intend to pay for his father, but he has his
hands full with his financial obligations over here. As you
know, he has land in Texas, and when the worst is over he
will be a rich man . . . if nothing unforeseen happens."*

Gustav made some interesting revelations
about his financial status with his father. Starting
from the time that he first went sailing, Gustav had
continued to send the largest portion of his income
home to his father. Before he left Stearns in 1910,
he had 1,800 kroner on credit with his father,
excluding the money he had sent to pay for Anna's
ticket and travelling expenses to bring her over to
Kentucky. Based on his income over the years, this
was a large sum of money.

Gustav had not been able to send money to
his father recently. *"I know, dear Father, that all this is
not much help for you at this time with your expenses. I could
probably scrape together this money if things got really tight.
But I would prefer not to spread myself too thin, as it is
hard enough to make it through the way it is. My expenses
are not small and there is no credit to be had on food* . . . .
But you must not let Aanen go elsewhere for help." The
only place that seventy-six-year-old Aanen could go
now would be to a nursing home, or "poorhouse," that
had been established in recent years in that area.
There was great shame for a family that sent its father
to the poorhouse, and Aanen was Gustav's father-in-
law and his wife's father. Gustav pleaded, *"Juergen is
willing to pay just as soon as he can. I am not afraid to
vouch for Juergen, if you can help him in any way."*

■ ■ ■

Juergen wrote in response, "*I received your letter yesterday and I have to tell you that I have no money. To top
it off I have no work. I have worked seven days the last
six weeks, so what I had saved this fall is gone now. It
doesn't matter where I go, everywhere is unemployment. I
have written to Edmonton, where we were last winter, but
they told me there are hundreds of people looking for a job.
Gustav sent me your letter and I also had a letter from
Olav. Olav told me that they had worked up until
Christmas but didn't make more than to just feed themselves. He asked me if I knew of a job.*

"*You know that this summer I had to live at the
homestead, so then I made no money, and I had only
expenses. It looks like I may have to let my land go and
that would mean a big loss to me. Sixteen months from
now I can get a loan from the bank. I could get $1,500 then,
but not a cent now . . . . I understand, Andreas, that you
have problems, but I cannot do a thing about it. If I make
some money this winter, maybe I can send you something
this spring, but I cannot tolerate to see old father to go to the
poorhouse . . . . It might look like I don't want to pay you,
but that is not so. You will get every cent I owe you . . . . You
are right about (my brother) Martin, and that he always
paid on time. I know that, as I paid half of it myself, but
then we both had steady work. Now I am alone, and can
only work six months of the year, because I have to work
on the homestead. That is the difference . . . . You do what
you can. It must go as it will. I can do no more.*"

■ ■ ■

Gustav had not written home to Norway for many
months, and he had no excuse for not writing. As
busy as he had been, he could have written. He

wrote that they were all ashamed for not writing more often. They had no good news, except that Gustav would be able to apply for the deed to his property in just over a year, when he had fulfilled his three-year obligation. He didn't think it would be hard to sell the land because it was so close to Youngstown. They already had one railway and two more lines were planned, one north to Coronation, and one south to Steveville. After that he expected that the prices for land would be good.

The family, including Olav and Albert, spent Christmas together at Gustav and Anna's home, the first Christmas together since 1908, at Yammacraw. *"We will at the same time wish you a Merry Christmas and a Blessed New Year . . . . Yes, dear parents and sister, I wish we could sit down and have a talk with you for a while. It is rather dry writing letters . . . ."*

■ ■ ■

Through the winter months that year, Albert and Olav remained on the homestead without work. *"When everything is lonely and sad, and the evenings get longer and darker, I thought I would pass some time by writing you a few lines . . . "* Olav wrote that marriage was something that they seldom heard about, even if most single men wanted to get married. *"Unluckily there is only one single girl to fifty men here, so you don't have to worry about me getting married."* They never heard about much sickness and seldom heard about deaths.

■ ■ ■

They were not able to find work after Christmas. Olav wrote that they had to be very spartan to get through the winter without an income. They still hoped to buy some horses, a wagon and plough, and some other machinery. Olav and Albert lived part of the time with Gustav and Anna after Christmas and before spring work commenced. The winter was very cold after New Year's, down to minus 40 and 50 degrees Fahrenheit. *"We have had eighteen inches of snow for a long time, and people have had a chance to use their sleighs."*

Juergen was working in a lumber camp out in the mountains several hundred miles away. He had been travelling from place to place trying to get a job. Olav wrote, *"It is getting harder with every year that passes for the working man, and if nothing is done to stop it, many workers will starve to death in the next year."*

■ ■ ■

More sad news came about Aanen. *"It is hard when he won't accept the doctor's treatment. I guess it looks like the end for him. If he dies, the best thing is to burn all his personal effects like clothes, bedding, etc."* It appears quite clear from Olav's comments that he believed Aanen had tuberculosis, which was understandable because of his close contact with his wife, Inger Marie, who had died of the disease. People now understood how infectious tuberculosis was, so this may have been a worry to Andreas, Gunhilde and Anna, who were caring for Aanen in their home. *"I know it is sad to talk about these things, but we have to think of the health of other people. With this kind of disease you have to take precautions."*

■ ■ ■

The brothers worried about the family at Rosseland. They had cards at Christmas, and wrote several times enquiring about the family. Finally, in April 1914, they were relieved to receive several letters. Gustav and Albert each bought two horses. By April, Gustav had finished sowing his property. *"Last night it started to rain and it is raining today, so horses and people have a day off today."*

Olav reported news about friends from Kentucky. The Tibbetts family lived a mile from Gustav, and had 320 acres. One son-in-law lived on the adjoining property and the other had a property close by. Their son had a homestead, gave it up, and then started to apply for another one. Mrs. Tibbetts played the piano and the organ, and she taught Magnhild and Gudrun to play the organ, since the Roselands had acquired this instrument.

Olav and a friend obtained a contract to build Diamond School about one and a half miles from Gustav's homestead, six miles northwest of Youngstown. This is the school that the Roseland girls started attending in September 1914. At this time Magnhild was eleven years old, and Gudrun was seven. Before they left the homestead, Faye also started school. She remembers the walk to and from school, crossing Sounding Creek. The children used to play there on the way home, catching frogs and minnows and putting them in their lunch pails. In bad weather, or cold weather in the winter, Gustav used to drive them back and forth in their democrat buggy. If there was snow on the ground he took them on a sled, with the horse pulling the sled.

■ ■ ■

"I guess it won't be long now before the Norwegian-Americans will travel to Norway for the 100-year celebration. I guess there will be many Norwegians visiting the old country this year . . . ." Norway had great celebrations planned for the summer of 1914. It was one hundred years since the Norwegian Constitution was drafted and signed at Eidsvoll, on May 17, 1814, laying the groundwork for Norway's eventual independence from Sweden in 1905. Norwegians celebrated in 1914, and have continued to celebrate each year since. It was then, and still is today, the most important holiday of the year in Norway. *" . . . Believe me, I long for Norway every day . . . . Many stores over here also make something extra to celebrate the 17th of May."*

As usual, Olav was thoughtful and philosophical. *"Most of the Norwegians out here are thinking about old mother Norway. They have started a fund that will go to needy people in Norway, but so far they have only $40,000. So, why can't the rich Norwegians here give more? Why did the Norwegian immigrants leave Norway? I will tell you. Most of them left because the so-called rich people in Norway would only offer them poor wages and bad living conditions. I love Norway, but I am not sure how much I love the Norwegians in Norway."*

While the Norwegians in northern Europe celebrated the 100-year life of their constitution, trouble was brewing to the south. On June 28, 1914, Archduke Franz Ferdinand was assassinated in Sarajevo, initiating a whole series of events that led to a world war. Western farmers had been suffering through crop failures and political discontent in

1914, and the troubles in Europe seemed a world removed from the western prairies. But, like the rest of the world, those in the west soon felt the impact of the events in Europe.

Chapter 10
"It is a disturbing world we are living in"

THE OUTBREAK OF THE First World War took many by surprise. Up to the last minute nobody believed that war would come, but when Great Britain protested the German occupation of neutral Belgium, and Germany failed to respond, the British declared war on August 4, 1914, and notified the Dominions immediately that they were at war. Germany and Austria-Hungary lined up against France, Russia, and Great Britain and the Dominions. The French fell back in August 1914, as the Germans marched through neutral Belgium and into the heart of France. They finally held the Germans back, on the 10th of September, a few miles northeast of Paris, at a cost of 250,000 French casualties. Meanwhile, Canadians responded to their entry into the war with enthusiastic support. The unemployed and those of British origin rushed to recruitment centres. Canadian newspapers were filled with shocking stories of the German advances.

■ ■ ■

"Quite often we hear about how many German ships the English have sunk, or how many Germans they have captured. But then, all of a sudden, these German ships come back again, so we don't believe all we see in the Canadian newspapers." As usual, Olav had been devouring

179

newspaper stories, looking for the stories behind
the news. Canadian newspapers had come out with
some fantastic stories of war events, some of which
turned out to be false. The British government had
started withholding some news, and releasing
reports favourable to the war effort, some of which
were fabricated.

Olav continued, *"In Winnipeg, U.S. papers
were banned on account of the news from Europe, which
Canadian newspapers are not allowed to write about . . . ."*
The United States was not in the war, and American
newspapers sometimes printed news that contra-
dicted British reports. When war broke out, President
Woodrow Wilson had admonished Americans that
*"every man who loves America will act and speak in the
true spirit of neutrality."* Belligerents from both sides
sought favourable press in America by spreading
propaganda that promoted their own war interests.
Immediately following the declaration of war, the
Canadian government had passed the War
Measures Act, giving the government extraordinary
powers of censorship, control of all means of communication, the right to arrest, detain or deport
aliens, and other powers.

*"Hate for the Germans and Austrians is so bad at
work places that they often fire them and let the English
have their jobs . . . . The English are sure they are going to
win over the hated Germans."* Some persons of
German origin felt loyal to Germany, while others
were loyal to the British cause, but prejudice did not
distinguish between them, or between persons from
Germany and other German-speaking countries.

Olav continued, *"It is hard times, and as usual, the working class is the one that has to suffer. There is a lot of unemployment."* Olav had just finished working on the schoolhouse, but was now out of work again. Jobless railroad and construction workers were everywhere looking for work, in the cities, in the towns and on farms.

■ ■ ■

After the collapse of the 1912-13 economic boom, world wheat prices declined. Then, in 1914, drought caused an almost total failure of the wheat crop. *"The weather has been bad, so the harvest has also been bad."* Gustav and Albert both worked on the threshing machine for about two weeks, but expected to be finished early in the season. They had about eighty acres of hay stacked, but in another week would be able to cut another eighty acres.

Norwegian-Americans attended gatherings all over Norway in 1914, joining in the centennial celebrations. Olav wrote, *"It is nice to see that the Norwegians and the Swedes can tolerate each other again . . . . Have you seen any Norwegian-Americans around your area this summer?"*

■ ■ ■

"It is a disturbing world that we are living in. Canada can also feel the impact of this awful world war." The German Army had advanced north towards the small Belgium town of Ypres, a shockingly rapid advance in the direction of Great Britain. Many young men from the west were eager to join the forces, and others intended to join later.

Even though Norway remained neutral, the brothers feared that the Scandinavian Peninsula could be involved before the war was over. They hoped not. *"But it is scary. No, war is something awful and I pity the country where the war is on."* Gustav had seen in newspapers that prices had temporarily jumped in Norway, when people started to hoard groceries. Later on, prices returned to normal.

"The summer has been so short that it is hard to do half of what one sets out to do, but one should take time to write home." Gustav was replying to his sister's last letter that he had received four months previously. He said that he always forgot how long it had been since he wrote, and then he would promise himself to do better next time. But, with the crop disaster in 1914, he had little good news to report to the family.

"Our crop wasn't too good this summer. It was too dry from the spring, and later on in the summer it got so hot and dry that we were afraid everything would burn." The Canadian government brought in legislation to provide loans to those in the drought areas, so that they could purchase food for their families. *"I think this is very nicely done by a government, because there would be much hardship this winter without this help. The price of food is rising, and I am sure it will be a hard winter for many."*

Gustav had one happy announcement to make. *"I am almost ashamed to tell news that is so old that it is no longer news, but I guess you have heard that we got another girl."* Their fifth daughter was now five months old. *"Her name is Hildur. You might think the name is not pretty, but she is, however, a beautiful girl.*" The family were all healthy and in good spirits. Magnhild and Gudrun were attending school and it was only a ten-minute walk, not as far as Gustav walked when he went to the Aas School.

■ ■ ■

In the fall of 1914 the war was deadlocked on both fronts. The Germans had intended to take France, destroy her army, and then turn their attention to the Russian front. But the Russian front was in a stalemate, and the German army had been stopped in its attempt to take the Belgium town of Ypres. With winter weather coming on, the Germans entrenched themselves on the western front in a long series of deep trenches, in hard-baked clay fortified with barbed-wire entanglements and machine guns. Bunkered down and facing the Germans, with a "No Man's Land" in between, the British and French entrenched themselves in a battle line that stretched 500 miles from Belgium to the Swiss border. The German army remained on the defensive, wiping out enemy attacks with their rapid-firing machine guns. The trenches were especially uncomfortable in rainy and snowy weather, but they became home to the soldiers on the front lines. They slept in the trenches, and were plagued with cold feet, influenza and body lice.

■ ■ ■

In early December, Gustav wrote that they would not send Christmas cards that year because they weren't sure if they would cross the ocean safely. "*We must also be careful about what we write these days, on both sides of the ocean, if we want the letters to be delivered.*"

Canadian newspapers had written about critical times in Scandinavia. Gustav and the others thought they were lucky not to be in Norway, because they could have been called into the Norwegian army. Gustav wrote that countries in the British Commonwealth had put up notices requiring immigrants from those countries to report, and they had no excuse for not showing up. Gustav had seen the notices himself. *"We hope that Norway will not be involved in this war, which will be the worst in history, and we hope that it will soon be over."* Many had believed that it would be a short war, over by Christmas, but new weapons of warfare soon altered those illusions—high explosives, rapid-firing machine guns, poison gas and submarines.

Anna's sister Elizabeth had written to say that Aanen was very sick and the situation for him was critical. Sometime during 1914 Aanen had been moved from the Rosseland farm to a poorhouse. He had become a ward of the state in one of the nursing homes that had been established by the Norwegian government in recent years. This residence was only about five miles from his old home, and about the same distance from Rosseland. Word came shortly after that Aanen had died on December 14, 1914. He was buried at the Tveit Church where he had married, and where Gustav and Anna were married. Faye later recalled the day the sad news came of her grandfather's death, and the tears that her mother shed for Aanen when he died. Faye was not quite five years old at the time.

Olav and Albert spent Christmas Day with Gustav and Anna and the family. Then, on Boxing Day, Olav and Albert entertained the family on their homesteads. For Christmas, the family in Norway sent Norwegian newspapers and photos of the family.

■ ■ ■

For Olav and Albert, winter on the homestead was lonely. Juergen and three other young men visited with them several times over the winter, when they passed the time listening to music and playing cards. *"Juergen and Albert played the accordion and another young man played the violin. If we only had some girls, we could have danced also."* In the summer they had about seventeen hours of daylight, but in the winter only about eight hours. They had only candles to burn, or kerosene lamps, so there was not much amusement for these young men in the dark hours of winter.

They wrote that the snow covered the ground for three months that winter, but it was only a foot of snow, or maybe a little more. They hoped the snow would be gone by the end of February, so they could get started on their spring work.

Olav loved reading newspapers from Norway. They especially liked the column called "City and Country News." It was just like being back in Norway when reading about the places and people they knew, and seeing the pictures of people they used to know so well. *"But you wake up from your dreams and feel funny. It is just like one gets sick for a while, but you soon know what it is. It is that longing for the old country and the dear old places."* Both Olav and Gustav asked many questions about old friends in Norway, and people they saw in the photographs, and sent their greetings.

Olav asked where Anders was living. He had heard that he was living in British Columbia or Alaska. If he was working in a place where the wages were good, Olav wanted to go there the next summer. The only jobs available to them in the winter were in the coal mines, but there were so many workers that they only earned enough to pay their room and board. *"It is still very bad times, and it doesn't look like it is going to get better very soon. Not as long as the war is still on. It looks like the working class is better off in Norway than on this side of the Atlantic."*

Gustav, Olav and Albert were counting the time now until they could apply for the deed to their land. They had made application for the land three years previously, so they could soon make application for the deed. But, Olav and Albert had not yet applied for their citizenship papers, so the earliest they could apply would be in the summer of 1915. Juergen would be able to apply for his land later in the summer, as well. They could then sell their land.

They hoped that the harvest would be good that year, because the price of wheat was high. There had been two bad years of crops, so buyers had no interest in purchasing land in the area. If they had a couple of good harvest years, they hoped that land prices would go up and the buyers would return.

■ ■ ■

With the war came the prospect of a demand for wheat and, as a result, better prices, but in 1915, not all farmers had been able to save sufficient seed from the previous year. In April 1915, in collaboration with the federal government, the government of Alberta passed the Seed Grain Act, allowing farmers to purchase seed under a loan program, with the loan charged against the sale of their property. The expected wartime rise in prices and improved markets for wheat inspired farmers to purchase seed grain in this manner, while at the same time increasing the total acreage of wheat planted in 1915. After the disastrous year for wheat in 1914, circumstances combined in 1915 for perfect growing conditions. There is no record of how successful the Roseland crops were that year, but they perhaps did as well as other farmers in the west.

■ ■ ■

To break the stalemate in the war in April 1915, the Germans resorted to chlorine gas. Against the French Army at Ypres the Germans released 160 tons of the yellow-green gas, crumpling the French defences when the soldiers' lungs were seared. The Germans then made significant advances into Allied territory. The second German gas attack was against the First Canadian Division, recently arrived in France. In forty-eight hours over 6,000 Canadian men were killed and injured, more than one-third of their division, but they held their ground and proved a formidable force against the enemy. Battles continued on the western front, but during 1915 the Germans concentrated their forces on the eastern front in an attempt to wipe out the Russian army.

■ ■ ■

While the wheat farmers in the west were blessed with a magnificent crop in 1915, the Roselands were blessed with another addition to the family. Arnold Walter Roseland was born on Aug. 31, 1915. Faye recalled the event in later years. The custom in the homestead areas was for a "midwife" to come and live in with the expectant mother about two weeks before the anticipated birth. The midwife was a woman who had children herself and had earned her expertise through the school of experience. If a doctor was available in the area, the midwife would call him once labour began, to be in attendance for the birth. The small dwellings on the homesteads were prepared to become a labour and delivery room, so it was necessary for the older children to be boarded out with friends in the area until the mother and baby were both doing well after the delivery.

Faye and Agnes were sent to stay at the teacherage, with the teacher from Diamond School. This was a lonely time for five-year-old Faye, as she waited and watched at the window for Gustav to come for his daily visit. Three-year-old Agnes was quite gleeful, thought this was a great adventure, and showed no signs of homesickness. Their personalities were clearly identifiable at this age. Gustav brought them very special treats on his visits, little liquorice pipes and candies, which they rarely saw otherwise.

■ ■ ■

During the summer of 1915, Canadian Prime Minister Robert Borden spent two months in London. He returned to Canada concerned about the course of the war. Battles continued on the western front with horrible casualty lists, more deadly for the Allied forces than the Germans, who were better organized and better equipped. The war was now a worldwide war as Japan and Italy had entered on the side of the Allies. On the last day of 1915, Prime Minister Borden announced that the government would support a Canadian army of 500,000, a formidable number for a young nation with a small population. Yet this promise of the government met with a general clamour of approval from the Canadian public.

■ ■ ■

In spite of the war in Europe, life on the homestead was not much changed. The family was all together for Christmas. *"We had as nice a Christmas as we could have, but we don't have as many parties and fun as we had in Norway."* They hoped that the coming year would bring to an end the horrible war taking place in Europe. *"I think there are many who hoped that the fighting would stop at New Year's, but no, it looks like they are fighting more than ever . . . . Whatever happens, I hope that the Scandinavian people will remain neutral."*

Olav wrote that a while ago it looked like a few Norwegian ship owners, who let their ships carry war materials, almost pulled Norway into the war. He hoped that the Norwegian socialists were strong enough to keep Norway out of the war, even if some ship owners wanted to make a little money. *"These capitalists have a good guarantee for the risks they take on the ships. But, if it brought the country to war, the ordinary citizen has no guarantee of anything better than misery and hard and horrible times ahead."*

Andreas asked his sons again for a firm answer regarding their purchase of the Rosseland farm. Olav wrote that it looked like none of them could buy the farm. *"But we wouldn't like it sold to strangers either . . . Gustav has such a large family that it would cost too much for him to come home."* This was the first time they admitted that Gustav would not return to Norway. *"We have talked about getting acquainted with things back home, and we have to make a decision about what we are going to do. Albert is just as excited to come home as I am."*

Olav wrote to his sister Anna that her brothers wanted her to be compensated for the help she was giving their parents, now and in the future. *"We wish that you would get just as much as if you worked for someone else."* They didn't know how much she should be paid, because they no longer understood the Norwegian economy. Her father had given her some compensation earlier, but not cash. They wanted her to be compensated again, and on a regular basis in the future.

Olav asked his father to verify the amount that he and Gustav had sent home over the years, and let them know how much of that money was left. Olav said that he had records of the money he had sent home. The amount was 1,200 kroner, a significant amount of money.

■ ■ ■

Olav and Albert suffered a setback when they applied for their deed. They had lived with Gustav for a while, so that time was disqualified, and they were required to plough more land. Olav paid out $200 for ploughing in the spring. He hoped that he could recover this money if he had a good crop in the fall.

In the spring of 1916, westerners began to feel a labour shortage and Olav was no longer short of work. Unemployed skilled workers had gone elsewhere looking for work, and those willing to serve in the forces had been recruited. Voluntary enlistments to the Canadian Armed Forces began to drop off, while Allied forces were suffering heavy casualties and fatalities. The Canadian government was looking for more recruits to the army.

■ ■ ■

In February 1916, the German army launched an attack on the ancient fortress-ringed city of Verdun. The Germans knew that the French would not give up the city easily, and intended to literally bleed the French army until it begged for peace. The fierce battle would continue until the year-end, on a tiny piece of land about six miles square.

In another battle in late spring, the Germans attacked the British and Canadians at Mt. Sorrel, blasting whole sections of trenches to oblivion and sending trees and bodies flying through the air. On the 2nd of June, the Canadians led the attack to take back the ground lost and suffered almost 8,500 casualties.

The French sent a frantic appeal to the British in the early spring of 1916, requesting that they commence an early attack on the Germans on the Somme River, as a diversion that would decrease the intensity of the German attack on Verdun. The British attacked in the Battle of the Somme on July 1, 1916, and on that day alone the British lost 60,000 men, killed, wounded or missing. It was the worst casualty toll for a single day in British history. The British casualties at the Battle of the Somme later rose to over 600,000, including 24,000 Canadians. The Germans repulsed the attack on the Somme, but their losses were also high. The heavy losses being suffered in the war started politicians talking about conscription.

■ ■ ■

"They try to get every man to join the army from over here, and many have joined. Several from Youngstown have joined, and some are already dead, and others have been casualties . . . . One fellow from this area joined in the beginning of the war, and after he had been in France for a while he was sent to hospital in England for half a year. For this they made him a captain and sent him back here to help recruit soldiers. There must be good material in the German gun shells to make a private go to captain after being hit by one of them. It is, therefore, not strange that many join the army to try their luck. I wonder if the enemy gun shells have the same influence on the Germans."

Olav and Albert had been on their home-steads since March. There was plenty of carpenter work available and many other jobs, as well. Olav wrote that he had done well in the last few months.

They were shocked to receive news of the death of their cousin Anders in early June. Olav wrote that there were thousands of workers who lost their lives like Anders. In bad times, when jobs were hard to get, unemployed workers would jump on a freight train and hide there. Then they travelled from place to place looking for jobs. They believed that Anders and his friend travelled this way. His family in Norway wondered if Anders had some money somewhere that they didn't know about. *"As the times are here, I don't think he had any more money or clothes than what he was carrying with him when he died. There are thousands of people who have nothing more than what they can cover their body with."*

After a bumper crop in 1915, Olav was optimistic for another good crop in 1916. There had been adequate rain in the spring, so farmers were hopeful. The weather was not very warm until June, but then it heated up and everything seemed to be growing and turning green. And they had a little more rain.

They had not had any mail from Norway recently, and they were longing to hear from their family. Germany had set up a naval blockade in the North Sea and they suspected that some of their mail was not getting through. Earlier letters had sections censored. *"Parts were blacked out because they might contain news the authorities do not want us to get. American newspapers are still banned here because of that."*

■ ■ ■

Britain, Germany and the United States were involved in a deadly war at sea. As a neutral nation, the United States could trade with belligerents on both sides, but her sympathies and trade were largely with the Allies. The American economy had received a jump-start with the outbreak of the war. America was doing a brisk trade with the Allies, and was willing to trade with the neutral countries as well. With the naval blockade, Britain hoped to strangle shipments of food and war supplies to Germany, and to neutral countries such as Holland and Denmark, to prevent reinforcements from finding their way to the enemy. Early in 1915, Germany had introduced a new weapon, the submarine, and sunk a number of American ships indiscriminately. The Americans protested, but ultimately, this issue would draw the United States into the war.

■ ■ ■

The promising summer had turned into a wet summer. *"First, in August, we got a few hailstorms. That destroyed thousands of acres, and a couple of weeks later came a night of cold weather, so most of the wheat that was not thrashed by the hail, froze. And most of the wheat has a coat of a kind of rust, so it is not worth to thresh it."* Stem rust on wheat is a fungus that grows under cool and moist conditions, damaging the wheat, when mildly affected, by giving it a strong unpleasant taste and, when badly infected, by destroying the whole kernel of wheat. In 1916, farmers lost millions of bushels of wheat to stem rust.

Prairie farmers originally planted Red Fife wheat, which took longer to mature than prairie weather permitted. In 1911, Dominion government scientists introduced Marquis, a new variety of wheat that matured a week earlier than Red Fife. Its popularity quickly spread across the western prairies. But, with the unpredictability of the weather, even wheat that matured more quickly was not enough to ensure a wheat crop.

The homesteaders were farming in a high desert region, which extends north from Mexico to Canada. At an elevation of about 3,000 feet, this area was carved by coulees and rivers. In simple terms, rain occurs when the cool winds from the north meet with warm moist air from the south or the west. Over the relatively flat prairies, weather can travel quickly from all directions. Conditions have to combine perfectly to produce rain, but there are many variables, such as dry air from the south, freezing air from the north, or warm air from the west. With these many variable circumstances, extreme weather conditions can rise rapidly, capable of destroying a crop in minutes or hours.

Olav wrote, *"What I have left of the wheat is not enough to cover the expenses for sowing and harvesting . . . . I make good money as a carpenter. So, I made some money this summer. I have worked in town for a while now, and I will maybe work here all winter."*

■ ■ ■

The weather in the fall had been in flux, with a lot of frost, so their wheat was of a poor quality. Although wheat prices were high, the price they got for their wheat was low. *"Farmers who got good crops this year made good money."* Some pockets of land in this dry desert region enjoyed better growing conditions, better than in the rest of the area. And hailstorms, frost and rain could hit randomly in little pockets, or regions within the entire area. At times when most farmers had a reasonable crop, other farmers lost their entire crop. Success depended on hard work and a great deal of good luck.

Olav was interested in his sister's description of conditions in Norway. *"I must say that much has changed since I left home. Sure enough, it costs you more to make a living these days, but we feel the same. There isn't any more work or better wages here than in Norway."* The wages had gone up in Canada and the cost of living had gone up as well. Inflation reached 17 per cent annually in 1917. They paid as much now for a sack of flour as they paid for room and board for a week in 1914.

"It costs Canada $2 million each day, and then the loss of men who die. A lot of Canadians have died who have to pay these expenses." Canada was losing its taxpayers while taxes were rising. The national debt had risen dramatically, so the government announced an income tax to cover the cost of the war. Gustav believed that most of the taxes would be paid by farmers, but he didn't want to say more because *"Who reads the mail these days?"* He didn't think that they touched the mail from Norway, but one never knew. All the mail from the United States was opened and read, and U.S. newspapers were forbidden. *"Anyone found with a forbidden paper must pay a fine. Yes, it is an awful war. It must look awful in the countries where the war is on."*

■ ■ ■

Their sister reported more news on the death of their cousin Anders. The earlier information had given the incorrect reason as to the cause of his death. He had not died while "riding the rails," but had been killed in an industrial accident. Gustav wrote, *"Poor Anders, we are sorry to hear what happened to him. I understand that you will not hear much more about him. There are many that die like that, here in America. There is nothing you can do about it. These big companies have their own laws and a man, or a thousand men, are not worth more than a creature."*

■ ■ ■

They sent their family Christmas greetings. Olav wrote," *It is a disappointment for me, and also a disappointment for you, that I am not coming home this year . . . . We will live in the hope that I will see you all at Christmas in 1917 . . . and then we will shake hands with each other, when we see each other again."* As usual, Gustav apologized for not answering his sister's letters. *"The spirit I need to write is not there, and that is why you do not hear from us. But we haven't forgotten you, and we think of you all the time."* They sent greetings to all their friends and relatives in Norway.

■ ■ ■

Late in 1916, Olav took a portrait of the whole family seated at the kitchen table in the sod house. There were no flash attachments for cameras in those days. To photograph indoors, Olav arranged the people and the setting, set up his camera on a tripod, and then lit the correct amount of magnesium to give off a flash of light. As soon as the magnesium

Albert's homestead

was lit, he ran to get into the picture before it flashed. Well, on this one occasion he stumbled and fell while running to get into the photo. All hands went in the air, and everyone was laughing when the flash went off, but Olav wasn't in the picture because he was on the floor. Albert also described two other photos that he sent home to Norway, taken on his homestead during threshing time.

The Battle of Verdun, which had commenced in February 1916, finally ended on December 19, 1916. The Germans battled the French and British over a French fortress on a tiny piece of territory, and 600,000 men were lost, killed, or injured. Neither side could claim victory.

The war was in crisis in early 1917. French morale was slipping, and in Russia, Tsar Nicholas was

Family portrait 1916. Left to right: Olav, Gustav holding Arnold, Hildur, Anna, Magnhild, Gudrun, Faye, and Albert holding Agnes

coerced into renouncing the throne, as the country slipped into anarchy. In Great Britain there was conflict over management of the war, and a new prime minister took power in December 1916. The new prime minister, David Lloyd George, summoned the leaders of the Dominions to London in February. Prime Minister Borden returned to Canada convinced that it was necessary to introduce conscription in Canada, to bring the recruitments to the army up to the desired level. Recruitments had fallen off badly in late 1916, and with the heavy losses of life in battle, Borden deemed it essential to strengthen the army, so that the war would not be lost.

Early in 1917, submarine warfare reached a peak of intensity, and after the Germans sank several American ships, the United States entered the war in April. The Americans mobilized, but it was not until 1918 that their military strength began to help turn the tide of the war. With the collapse of the Russians on the eastern front, the Germans used the full strength of their army for a renewed offensive on the western front.

In May 1917, Borden announced to his cabinet the introduction of conscription legislation. The issue was divisive and Borden was uncertain whether he could get the necessary support of Parliament, so he introduced two other controversial pieces of legislation that tampered with voters' franchise. Several Liberal members joined the Conservatives to form the Union Party, and won a smashing victory for Prime Minister Borden in December 1917. Support for conscription came mainly from the articulate, urban middle class. Opposition came from Quebec, farmers, non-British immigrants, and the working class. Able men in Canada would all have to be registered, and if they were told they had to go into the army and go to war, they had no choice.

■ ■ ■

Olav and Albert did not want to go to war. At thirty-seven and twenty-six years of age, they were Norwegian by birth and sentiment, and were appalled by the war. They did not have the spirit of nationalism that drew those of British origins to support the British against the Germans. In mid-1917, they still did not have the deed to their land, the land into which they had poured their labour for five years, and their reason for remaining in Canada. They re-applied for the deed, or patent, to their land in the late summer of 1917. The deed on Albert's property was approved in October 1917, subject to payment of liens charged against him

Olav and Albert in trapper's cabin in B.C., 1918

under the Seed Grain Act. The deed for Olav's property was transferred to him in December 1917.

It is not clear exactly when Olav and Albert left Alberta, but it was probably in the summer of 1917. They spent the winter of 1917-18 high up in the mountains on the west coast, between Prince George and Prince Rupert, trapping animals for furs. Together with a Norwegian friend they had met in Burlington, North Dakota, they had acquired a fur-trapping licence, which gave them the right to trap furs in an area that stretched for 30 miles along a rugged stretch of mountains. They were safely hunkered down, high in the coastal mountains of British Columbia for the remainder of the war, as far away from Canadian officialdom as they could get at the time.

Chapter 11
"Full of hope and ambition"

OLAV AND ALBERT had visited Gustav and Anna frequently, often staying overnight, and they doted on their nieces. So the Roseland girls missed their uncles when they left. Olav had sometimes read to the girls and told them stories. Albert was more playful. Faye later remembered the day that the girls tied Albert's hair up in rags to give him curls, when neighbours dropped in unexpectedly for a visit. Albert was embarrassed.

The whole family loved music and singing. Albert and Uncle George (Juergen) each played the accordion, and Magnhild and Gudrun played the organ. Magnhild also had a strong, clear voice and Gudrun had a good ear for music. Gustav and Anna had taught the girls a little about harmony, and the family often sang together. Uncle George later acquired a Victrola gramophone, with a large curved horn that played after it was wound up. The girls loved to visit Uncle George and he, too, was very fond of his nieces.

The family visited back and forth with the Tibbetts and Johnson families. The women assisted each other with tasks of canning and preserving, and shared their sewing experiences, making clothes for the children, and household items. They ordered their fabrics from the Eaton's catalogue, and used clothing was never thrown away. The last

Five sisters 1916.
Left to right: Hildur, Agnes, Faye, Gudrun, Magnhild

use made of clothing, when it had worn out, was to cut out the usable pieces of fabric and sew them together to make a quilt. The ladies did hand mending and needlework in their rare moments of relaxation, but did their other sewing on the reliable Singer treadle sewing machine.

The men helped each other at threshing time, but one of their major co-operative efforts with their neighbours was the "beef ring." A group of about eight households took turns slaughtering a cow or a pig, butchered the meat and shared it with the others, taking turns so that they shared equally.

By co-operating this way, they had less fresh meat to store than if they had to kill an animal for just one family. These smaller amounts they could keep safely in a cool, specially built dug-out in the ground. They also cured their own bacon and made pickled pork, a specialty served at Christmas.

The children loved Christmas. They left cookies out for Santa and he always came, leaving each a gift, such as a new hair bow and perhaps a small toy, and of course he filled their stocking with candies, nuts and an orange. No evergreen trees grew in the area, so they decorated the only kind available, a small leafless poplar from near the creek, for which they saved small items to fashion into decorations, and strung popcorn around the tree. Particularly prized for making decorations was the shiny tinfoil on the inside of fancy envelopes from Christmas cards. On Christmas Day, Gustav and Anna always read from their well-worn Bibles, and the family sang Christmas carols. Anna made special Norwegian cookies and *yulekage*, a sweet-bread with raisins and cardamom seeds that the children loved. For Christmas dinner they had chicken, with pickled pork as a special treat. Later Faye told of being heartbroken when she learned at school that there was no Santa Claus.

In 1917, Gustav and Anna's second son was born, Ernest Gustav. Families were not planned in those days; babies just arrived whenever deter-mined by Mother Nature. Pregnancy, childbirth and the care of an infant were very demanding on a woman who was already working very hard, and mothers and babies did not always live through a crisis in childbirth, when frequently no medical help was available. However, Anna survived all her pregnancies, as did her babies.

Anna fussed over her five daughters. Her girls always wore the trademark Roseland white dresses for special occasions, white hair bows, and little black dress-shoes from the Eaton's catalogue. Gustav and Anna were especially proud of their eldest daughter, who was a confident and independent child. At fourteen, Magnhild drove herself daily by horse and buggy, six miles each way, over the open prairie to the high school in Youngstown. Gustav and Anna were committed to having their children get as much education as possible, in an era when few children went to high school. Gudrun was an excellent student and skipped a grade in school, and she and Faye were bosom buddies. Agnes had a little game she played as a pre-school child: in her red fuzzy coat and bonnet, she would flap her arms like wings and cry out, "I am going to the moon!" She had a lively imagination and everyone got a great kick out of her. Hildur, as the youngest daughter, was her father's favourite. Years later Hildur wrote,

"There never were such pals as my Dad and I,
He shared all my secrets as the years rolled by."

In the long, dark evenings of winter, Gustav or Anna would read to the children by the light of a coal-oil lamp, or Gustav would tell the children stories about his life as a sailor and his travels around the world—climbing Table Mountain in Cape Town, or discovering ports in South America, Australia or other faraway places. Later, Hildur wrote:

"We'd sit by the fire at night while Dad read,
And then he would tenderly tuck us in bed.
If we were in trouble, or hurt any way,
Our Mother would kiss all our worries away."

Anna kept their home clean and cozy. In the summer she grew geraniums in the window boxes of the two kitchen-living room windows. At the door to their home was an enclosed porch for protection from the weather. On the deep, lace-covered window ledges inside, Anna kept a variety of foliage plants year-round. The wooden floor she scrubbed until the wood was white.

■ ■ ■

The main articles of furniture in the kitchen-living room were a large wood-coal range, with a water-warmer on the side, and a small round heater at the other end of the room for use when winter weather became bitterly cold. Anna stored and prepared her food from a free-standing kitchen cupboard unit from the Eaton's catalogue, about four feet wide. It held dishes, pots and pans, dry foods and a flour bin. A flat counter top at waist height, below the upper cupboards, was her kitchen counter. The kitchen table was the heart of the room where everyone gathered. One corner had a bench against the smoothly plastered wall, and there were several more chairs. Each person had their own place at the table. Above the table hung three large framed portraits, a wedding photo of Gustav and Anna, a photo of Magnhild as a baby, and one with Anna and

Magnhild, the latter two taken in Norway when Gustav and Anna were separated for three years after their marriage. Family portraits were always taken with the family seated at the kitchen table. On the opposite wall stood the Singer treadle machine and the organ.

Gustav added a room to the sod house, the full length of the original sixteen feet by twenty feet, and divided it into two bedrooms. The doors to the bedrooms were curtained off from the living room. Gustav and Anna had one bedroom with a mattress and box spring, and a cradle for the baby, and the other girls shared the second bedroom. In this room Gustav hung a second bed from the ceiling, over a double bed. Although their home was humble, it was similar to all the other homes in the area. Anna kept the home clean and tidy, and it was filled with love.

Doing the laundry for a family of nine was a huge task for Anna. She had to carry pails of water in from a nearby well to heat on the stove in a large oval, galvanized Beatty tub. For many years she scrubbed her laundry by hand on a scrub board, and wrung everything out by hand. Sheets, towels and men's clothing were a particularly laborious task. Only in later years did she acquire a washing machine that she agitated by hand, by pushing a long handle back and forth, and then put the clothes through a wringer, which she again turned by hand. Anna made her own laundry soap, with rendered fat and glycerine, but Gustav bought soap from the store for personal washing. Anna also carried the rinse waters in and out, and when the washing was done, she threw the rinse waters on the garden and the soapy water she threw out behind the barn. The clothes dried well outside in the dry climate, but in freezing weather had to be brought in. The vivid memory of drying clothes indoors in the winter was the image of a pair of frozen long-johns standing up alone in the corner, unaided. For ironing she used two flat-irons heated on the stove, alternating them as the irons cooled, an onerous task when a hot fire was required in the stove, while temperatures soared outside in the summer heat. Saturday night was the legendary bath night, and the same galvanized tub accommodated them all, one at a time.

Gustav and Anna shared the outdoor duties of caring for the vegetable garden and caring for the animals. It was the Norwegian tradition for the woman of the house to milk the cows, and the chickens and pigs had to be fed and cared for as well. They lived largely on what they produced on the land. The vegetable garden was a problem as the soil was sandy and dry, and the gardens struggled. Dry foods they kept in the house, but vegetables, meats, butter and milk were kept in a cool dug-out in the yard outside. They had quite a good water supply on the homestead as Gustav had built a deep well, which never froze over in the winter. The bathroom was an outhouse, with a pot under the bed for night use.

Gustav made a trip or two in the fall to the Sheerness mine to bring home a wagonload of coal for winter use. Line-ups waiting for coal were a possibility, so it was often an overnight trip and Gustav slept under the wagon. If Anna thought Gustav might be home late, she left a coal-oil lantern lit on the window ledge, but she didn't have to worry, as the horses always found their way home. The family usually found enough kindling near Sounding Creek for lighting the fire. Gustav also did the shopping at Youngstown, but occasionally Anna was able to go with him. On one occasion Anna went to town with Gustav and he surprised her with a gift. He bought her a winter coat, of a black velvety fabric, with a collar that she could pull up to frame her face in the cold weather. She loved the coat and treasured it for years.

Anna had learned to speak English in the backwoods of Kentucky and on the barren Canadian prairie. After leaving the homestead, Anna later reflected on the years they spent there:

"The memories of yesterday still linger so near,
How oft I recall the happy days so dear.
When we were both young and everything bright,
Full of hope and ambition, and burdens light.
The children were little, and the sorrows were small.
Oh, how we were planning and cared for them all.
We worked and we toiled, and gave them our best.
Oh happy days of old, with these my memories rest."

■ ■ ■

In the spring of 1918, the German army went on a renewed offensive on the western front in Europe, and land prices back home remained good with the prospect of a continued wartime demand for wheat. Gustav and Anna decided to sell their homestead and move to a property south of Youngstown. The CNR had announced plans to construct a new railroad line south to the Red Deer River, connecting with the existing one that passed through Youngstown. This made the area to the south look more attractive. Gustav had received the patent, or deed, to his property in February 1916, and in 1918 it seemed the right time to sell, while prices appeared strong. Their property was transferred to a new owner, a veterinarian, in May 1918 for the price of $3,250. After years of hard work, this was a nice little nest-egg Gustav could put in the bank awaiting another opportunity.

The Roselands moved to a property thirty miles south of Youngstown, on the route south to the Red Deer River. Their new home was located just a mile or two west of the road allowance that ran due south from Youngstown. Families who had suffered bad crop years were already leaving this area, financially unable to carry on, and one farmer had enough cash to buy out some properties from those who were in desperate financial circumstances, and eager to leave. From this man Gustav and Anna rented a small, wood-frame house on a 160-acre homestead property. They brought with them their cows, horses, chickens and pigs, and whatever farm equipment they owned, as they would be farming again at the new location. Their democrat buggy filled with the family of nine, including Anna still nursing her infant son, would have been a sight to see. Gustav probably made several trips over the grassy trail to bring their household belongings and farming equipment down to their new location.

For the first year the family lived in the
Cobblestone area, there was no school nearby for
the children to attend. Magnhild remained in
Youngstown, where she boarded and attended high
school. She worked at the creamery in the summer
and on weekends during the school year, and
worked full-time as their bookkeeper after she completed high school. That first year at Cobblestone
the parents did home-schooling, just as they had
experienced in Norway. Gustav spearheaded a drive
to get a school in the area and the children were all
in school again at Cobblestone by the second year.
Gustav acted as secretary-treasurer for the school
board. In 1920, Magnhild was sixteen, Gudrun was
twelve, Faye was ten, Agnes was eight, Hildur was
six, Arnold was five, and Ernest was three years old.
Anna just had two boys at home in the fall of 1920,
but in December their third son was born, Erling
Arthur, and the Roseland family was complete.
Anna was then forty-two years old, and Gustav was
forty-six.

■ ■ ■

To Olav and Albert, returning to Norway had
remained a dream, dependent on obtaining the title
to their homesteads. In 1917, they secured the title,
and by 1920 they were both back in Norway. Olav
later told the story of their experiences in British
Columbia. Their trapping area was about thirty
miles, in rough terrain high up in the mountains,
and 300 miles from the west coast. From the mountain tops Olav claimed that they could clearly see
the strip of British Columbia coast. The three

Norwegians found the high mountain air quite difficult to endure and took aspirin regularly, which seemed to help relieve their symptoms. It was probably in the summer of 1917 that they began building six timber cabins in the mountains, about a day trip between each. When winter came they hunted bear, lynx, marten, ermine and beaver. The snow was frequently six feet deep, or more, and was difficult to travel through. However, they used snowshoes, on which they could travel easily, even in loose snow. The only food supplies they had were what they had packed, so for most of the winter they lived on moose meat. Bread, or bannock, was their only other food staple. They did their shopping and delivered their furs at Fort George. Olav said they did quite well financially, mentioning that they had received $2,000 for their last load of skins delivered. Along with their Norwegian friend from Kostel, near Rosseland in Norway, they left Fort George by train in June 1919, and arrived back at Kristiansand in October 1919.

Before Olav left the homestead area in 1917, he had given Gustav power of attorney over the sale of his property. Late in 1920, Olav's property sold for $1,600. Land prices had declined since the war ended, with the reduced demand for wheat.

Albert had liens on his property from loans made under the Seed Grain Act, which could have been cleared when payment was made. However, for whatever reason, the liens were never cleared and the property was never sold. Albert's dream of $1,000 a year for the work on his land never materialized. He made nothing. Upon his return to Norway, Albert met the sister of his hunting companion in British Columbia, and they immediately formed an enduring relationship. Albert had found the beautiful Norwegian girl of whom he had dreamed for many years. He had apparently returned to Norway after acquiring a sufficient nest-egg from his hunting days to emerge as a proud "wealthy American." The now thirty-year-old Albert and his bride quickly voyaged to the New York City that had so dazzled Albert as a sixteen-year-old in 1907. Neither Olav nor Albert ever returned to Alberta.

■ ■ ■

The Roselands soon made friends in the Cobblestone area. Magnhild came down to visit her family one weekend, driven there by a young woman friend who had a small roadster, a two-door, open-air car, following the grassy trail down the road

Inga Roseland, Albert's wife, and their firstborn child

allowance. When they left the Roseland home to return to Youngstown, they had only driven two or three miles when the little car gave up the ghost. They pushed it onto the property of the Berild family, and the two young women met the family and had a great visit with Mrs. Berild. She was Swedish and her husband was Norwegian, and they had the same large family that the Roselands had. Before Magnhild left the Berilds' home, she insisted that her mother and Mrs. Berild had to get acquainted, as she was sure they would become friends. The two young women found another ride back to Youngstown, and the next week a friend towed the little car back to the city.

The Roseland and the Berild families did meet soon after and the families became fast friends, often visiting back and forth and celebrating Christmas together, with one family sometimes sleeping over on Christmas Eve at the home of the other. In this area to the south of Youngstown poplar trees were even scarcer, so there were times when the Roselands had no Christmas tree. The families played games together and sang, thoroughly enjoying their visit together. Some settlers even resorted to catching a Russian thistle as it rolled over the prairie on a windy day, and taking it home to be decorated as a Christmas tree, a large prickly ball of weed. It didn't matter that it was a thistle—it looked beautiful to them.

Schools closed in December after the Christmas concert. Fierce prairie winds, blizzards and bitter cold determined that the school year

should be from April to December. The school was
the heart of local social life. When residents wished
to form a school district, they could petition the
provincial government, and then follow the guide-
lines of the Department of Education in order to
meet requirements to have the district approved.
Local residents elected their chairperson and secretary-treasurer and hired a teacher, supported by
provincial grants and local taxes. Gustav was elected
secretary-treasurer for the Cobblestone School
while the family lived in that area. Local residents
held meetings, parties and picnics at the school,
which also served as a place of worship when student ministers travelled through the homestead
areas. If there was a death in the region, the funeral
might also be held at the school. The major annual
event at the school was the Christmas Party, when
Santa Claus and the whole family attended, and
were entertained by the school children.

The operation of the school was a challenge
to local residents. They had to find a teacher, equip
the school, and provide room and board for the
teacher, or build a teacherage. Other problems they
had to cope with were managing the finances, digging a well, building an outhouse, and providing
heating in the cold months. In 1921, when the
Cobblestone School was formed, the board was fortunate to obtain the services of a local married
woman, Mrs. Sydney Grey, a respected teacher who
was long remembered by her students.

Students attended the local school from age
six to sixteen, or until they completed grade eight.

Most students never went beyond grade eight, but Gustav and Anna intended to see their children educated. Magnhild completed high school, and then Gudrun left for Youngstown in 1924 to attend high school, followed by Faye in 1925. Faye boarded with a Mr. and Mrs. Martin who operated a grocery store on the main street. The Martins came to Youngstown in 1919 from Philadelphia and had one little girl born in January 1924 who was eight months old when Faye moved to Youngstown. To earn her board, Faye took the little girl for a walk after school in her baby buggy, and she also helped Mrs. Martin with household chores on Saturday. The family lived upstairs above the store, where Faye had a room to herself that looked down on the main street. From there she could watch all of the action in town. Although Youngstown was a small town, it looked like a big city to Faye after living on the open prairie. When the girls went home to visit the family, Mr. Martin sometimes drove them down in his car, an open-air model with a steering wheel and windshield, and no roof. They would bump along over the grassy trail south from Youngstown to Cobblestone.

When the older girls left for Youngstown, there was more room for the family in their small wood-frame house. By the mid '20s, all five girls had reached their teens, and no doubt wanted more space and privacy. They shared a bedroom, and they had the usual outhouse, and water from the outside well. Years later, when shown a photo of the Cobblestone house, Faye said, *"Yes, I have seen that before,"* and turned her face to the wall. She had spoken fondly of her days in the sod house on the original homestead, and she had happy memories of the next house they moved to. But she could not bring herself to speak about the Cobblestone house. It was too small to offer the privacy that teenagers need. The five or six years that they spent at Cobblestone she dismissed almost as if they had never happened.

The Roselands were a closely knit and loving family. Gustav often gave Anna a hug, or he would pull her down on his lap and call her "my little girl." Magnhild visited often from Youngstown, bringing a girlfriend or boyfriend, usually a friend with a car. Gudrun and Faye were bosom buddies and were helpful to Anna. Agnes was a defiant child. She loved riding horses and reading, but wanted nothing to do with housework. Agnes chummed with Hildur, and got along well with Arnold, who was three years younger than she. Hildur was frail, a quiet and thoughtful child who loved to read and enjoyed spending time with her mother, and caring for Ernest and Erling, her two youngest brothers. The boys played softball, rode horses, swam in sloughs, caught gophers and generally found amusement in the outdoors. The Roseland girls became known for their singing at social events.

The post-war decade of the '20s saw a greatly increased number of musical and variety entertainments. Hoagie Carmichael and George Gershwin, among many others, rose to national prominence as songwriters. Gramophone players and sheet music brought the latest hits to even the most remote areas. Crystal sets were common for radio reception in the early '20s, but picked up very little. By the end of the '20s, new radio stations transmitted the latest popular music, picked up by tube and electric radios, which were becoming more popular each year. A whole host of bouncy, happy songs of the era became well known and well loved for decades, and many of them remained popular throughout the 20th century—"Yes Sir! That's My Baby," "When You're Smiling," and "Five Foot Two, Eyes of Blue . . . ." In the homestead area, singing was a popular pastime. The Roseland girls knew all of the old favourites and learned the latest songs, and were frequently asked to perform.

Each summer, the entire family would pile into their democrat for the one-and-a- half-hour ride down to the Red Deer River to attend a picnic, which attracted families from the whole region. The Roseland horse-drawn democrat would have been quite full with the whole family in it. In this era, the democrat was the usual family vehicle, until a family owned an automobile.

After having eight children Anna was considered well qualified to act as a midwife, which she did occasionally. One time, Anna used her small remuneration to treat herself to something special. From the Eaton's catalogue she ordered linoleum to cover the wooden floor in the kitchen-living room. The children came home from school one day to find the floor newly covered with bright, clean linoleum. In this sandy country it was so much easier to keep clean than sweeping and scrubbing bare wood. Anna was very pleased with her new flooring.

In 1923, Anna acted as midwife for her friend Mrs. Berild when the Berilds' son Johnny was born. The Women's Institute in Youngstown had built a small two-room dwelling that could be used as a resting place for women who came to town from their homesteads. Mrs. Berild had booked the dwelling for about two weeks, near her expected due date. The ladies stayed in this little dwelling along with another Berild toddler. Magnhild also came over and spent a few days with them. Anna prepared the cottage for the delivery and called Dr. W. W. Cross in time to attend the birth. When mother and baby were well enough, they returned home.

Dr. Cross had come to the area in 1914 but left in 1916 to go to Europe during the First World War. He returned in 1919 after serving overseas. He was held in high esteem in the region, as he always responded to requests for medical assistance. He travelled many miles over the prairie with his horse and buggy, more reliable than the automobile, which required gasoline (which was not readily available), and often the services of scarce mechanics. Dr. Cross had answered a call to the Roseland home once when Hildur was acutely ill with pneumonia. The doctor thought she might not survive the night. However, under his supervision, Anna nursed Hildur through the illness, and she did survive. Dr. Cross later became a well-known public figure, serving as a minister of health in the Social Credit government of Alberta.

■ ■ ■

After the bumper crop of 1915, settlers north of the Red Deer River complained bitterly of the forty- to fifty-mile drive to the grain elevators in Youngstown and Hanna, so the CNR constructed the rail line south to Steveville, completing it in 1919. Several small towns sprang up almost immediately, and it was Cessford and Pollockville that proved to be the closest to the Roselands. Further north on the line was Sheerness. Gustav could deliver grain and do his shopping without the regular trip to Youngstown, but he still had to make the long trip north in his wagon to get his supply of coal.

For Gustav, and all the wheat farmers, farming was a year-round job. New rocks were pushed up from the soil with the winter frost, and each spring the glacial rocks had to be cleared away before ploughing, or after. After the ploughing and seeding, the fields required cultivating to keep the weeds down, especially after badly needed rain when Russian thistle, or tumbleweed, germinated and grew very quickly in the summer heat. In late summer the wheat had to be cut and stacked, then later threshed and taken to market. The theory of summer-fallow recommended that the stubble left after the wheat was cut should be ploughed and turned over into the soil in the fall. A loose surface allowed winter moisture to be sucked into the soil and retained for the next crop, and stubble added roughage to the soil. The theory also recommended that portions of the wheat fields should be left uncultivated every two or three years, so that more moisture could concentrate in the soil below. Ploughing and cultivating the soil also cut back the weeds whose roots sucked the moisture from the ground. The theory advocated that the farmer who practised these methods could produce a crop regularly, regardless of the rainfall.

However, the farmer could not control the weather and natural pests. Precipitation in the area was light, and its timing was critical. The rain had to fall at just the right time to produce a good crop, as it had in 1915. If the rain fell too early before seeding, or too late after seeding, the crop was lost. Not only rain fell from the clouds; at times giant hailstones fell, which could completely flatten a mature wheat crop, wiping it out in minutes. In the late summer and fall, early night frosts sometimes ravaged the crops. The erratic weather of this region could produce dry snow at any season, except not usually in mid-summer. With scarcely a forewarning, an intense wind could swirl dry snow above the ground, creating blinding blizzards. Temperatures could also change within an hour or two, from a bitter cold to a balmy warm. During a cold spell in the winter, the clouds over the mountains on the western horizon could be seen to lift, creating a "chinook arch." A balmy chinook wind from the Pacific travelled through the arch, causing the thermometer to rapidly jump upwards. The only thing consistent about the weather was its inconsistency.

Throughout the year, homesteaders prayed that rain would come at just the right time for their crops to mature. They watched the clouds as they floated across the big open sky, waiting to see where they would drop their bounty. On one occasion the Berild children were visiting the Roseland home when large, black clouds dropped an abundance of rain on the Roseland wheat fields. Gustav joyously gathered all the children on a knoll not far from the house, and led them in a rousing hymn of thanks, as a rainbow formed its brilliant arc across the sky.

If the wheat crops struggled to produce, the pests did not. A wide variety of pests multiplied in abundance. After a rain, mosquitoes bred and formed dark clouds that attacked any living being, human or animal. The seeds of Russian thistle germinated rapidly after a rainfall, their glowing, tender green shoots choking out the wheat. After the thistle died in the fall, winds rolled it across the prairies, spreading its seeds bountifully on the way. In a prairie fire, the rolling tumbleweeds carried the flames quickly through the dry fields. If the wheat wasn't choked by the thistle, it might be eaten by cutworms that feasted on the stems at ground level. The multitude of grasshoppers, gophers and rabbits that thrived on the open prairie was legendary. They devoured the crops. The government sponsored contests, offering prizes to those who produced the most gopher tails, paying children a few cents for each. This was one of the few ways that children had to earn money, and catching gophers became a recreational pastime. Flies, too, were everywhere, prolific and bothersome, a reason for putting the barn well away from the house. Farmers had few defences against pests.

■ ■ ■

Wheat farmers had much to discourage them in the years after the First World War. From 1917 to 1919, very little rain fell and the region was teeming with grasshoppers. During the same years, until 1920, the cutworm feasted on the stems of a good portion of the crop. But the overall yield in 1920 was fair. The crop was dried out again in 1921 and 1922, with the yields in 1923 to 1926 fair to average.

But even more devastating to the wheat farmers was the collapse of wheat prices after the First World War. The world economy changed after the wartime demand for wheat diminished, ushering in a whole new set of problems.

Chapter 12
"We closed the doors and left"

BY 1920, THE FARMERS in Europe had begun to recover from the war and were growing wheat crops again. Within three years of the war ending, the price paid for wheat in the world market dropped by half. The Canadian government had encouraged increased wheat growing early in the war, and with the optimism after the 1915 crop, farmers purchased and cultivated more land, much of it poor agricultural land. On the strength of the demand for wheat and the attractive prices, farmers had also extended themselves by purchasing farm equipment and other items on credit. Combined with their seed grain debts, many farmers were carrying a very high debt load by 1920. Until then, mortgage lenders, equipment dealers and banks had fuelled the optimism by providing generous credit to the farmers. But after three dry years, farmers could not get out from under their debt load. Land prices had fallen, and they received a deflated price for their small wheat crops. Many signed away everything they owned as security for outstanding loans. The economic world of the farmer collapsed in an ocean of red ink.

By 1920, 600 families had already left the southeast corner of Alberta, and by 1926 it was almost a mass exodus. Many farmers faced a great dilemma. If they left the land they would walk away with nothing, but if they remained on the land and their debtors received a judgement against them, they would also lose everything. The Alberta and federal governments brought in legislation intended to solve some of the problems. In 1922, the Alberta government enacted legislation determining that land under tax arrears would default to the government rather than to the mortgage holders. Mortgage lenders were not happy with this. In 1923, the Alberta government brought in legislation that provided for mediation to assist in determining who was eligible for collecting on the assets of the farmers. In most cases the various laws enacted in the early '20s still left farmers with nothing in the end. The minority who were not struggling under debt load were able to purchase items at many auctions. The auctions offered, at give-away prices, the possessions of those who were abandoning the area. Children benefited from the auctions because homesteaders leaving, and schools closing, offered boxes of books at bargain prices.

■ ■ ■

During their years at Cobblestone, Gustav and Anna considered options for the future. A major consideration would have been a larger house, education for the children and their future economic security. Should they gamble on their future in wheat farming? What other choices did they have? There is no record of Gustav's financial status at that time, but assumptions can be made. One is that Gustav was cautiously using funds from the sale of his homestead property to keep himself out of debt.

Another assumption has to do with a land transaction on the Rosseland farm in Norway. When Olav returned to Norway in 1920, he still intended to look for an occupation elsewhere, but in 1923 he undertook to purchase the Rosseland farm from his parents with a contract to provide for them as long as they should live. Olav had always proven himself fair-minded in his attitude towards money transactions within the family. As part of the transaction, Olav likely sent money to Gustav to compensate for the money that Gustav had sent to his father over many years. In later years, Gustav's children stated that they understood Gustav had "signed away" his rights to the Rosseland farm, which further supports this assumption. The cash that Gustav received for his homestead, and the cash from Gustav's investment in the Rosseland farm, is likely what carried the family financially for a number of years.

■ ■ ■

In 1924, Gustav entered into a contract with Thomas and Andy Hogarth to purchase their property a few miles south of their Cobblestone home. The Hogarth property included a large wood-frame, two-storey house. Gustav paid $750 cash, and assumed two mortgages. The Hogarth brothers intended to return to Scotland to find themselves wives, and in the meantime they would retain a bedroom in the Roseland home. Financially, this was probably a desirable arrangement for both families. Gustav was not in debt, or he would not have qualified to assume the mortgages.

228 From Sailing Ships to Spitfires

The Hogarth house stood on a knoll with an expansive view of the gently rolling prairie. The house was constructed on a concrete foundation, with a crawl space high enough to stand in. On the main floor were the kitchen, living room and bedroom, with three more bedrooms upstairs, including one large one that spanned the length of the house. This was the girls' bedroom and the boys shared one of the others. There was also a wood frame barn on the property, well away from the house. As testimony to the house's solid construction, it was still standing, unoccupied but structurally intact, in the year 2000.

The family was now living about eight miles further south of Cobblestone in an area known as Cabin Lake, with the Blood Indian School about a mile away. Gudrun had started grade nine at Youngstown in 1924, so Faye, Agnes, Hildur, Arnold and Ernest attended Blood Indian School, while four-year-old Erling was still at home with Anna for two more years. The 1924 school term was the first time that Youngstown offered grade nine, and the following year they also offered grade ten. Meanwhile, the Cobblestone school closed once the Roselands left. Because of declining enrolment, two other schools in the area amalgamated. The parents from the newly amalgamated school purchased the old Roseland home, relocated it and used it as a home for the teacher. They also purchased blackboards and other equipment from the school. In this way those who remained on the land did benefit from those who left.

In the fall of 1924 the weather was again a disappointment to the farmers, as drenching rain fell in mid-September during threshing season. The problem with rain in September was that dampness could degrade the quality of the grain, cause mould, or if the weather turned warm again, the dampened wheat kernels could sprout, rendering the crop useless for the grain market.

In December, a major snowfall dumped three inches of snow, followed by high winds and drifting snow that persisted for two days. A relatively small amount of snow could seem like much more when swirled by high winds that caused it to drift in places that impaired traffic and work on the farm. Temperatures dropped to minus 50 degrees Fahrenheit and lower, below the lowest measurement registered on thermometers. *The Youngstown Plaindealer* noted that Magnhild and Gudrun Roseland had left early on the day of the storm, a Sunday, to spend the holidays at their home at Cabin Lake. Blizzard conditions struck in the late afternoon. They probably made it home just before the worst of the storm hit.

As long as the weather remained cold, the skating rink and curling rinks were open for business, and the men's hockey team played regular games at Youngstown. *The Plaindealer* noted that the town of Hanna had hosted a men's bonspiel the previous week, and Youngstown had hosted a ladies' curling bonspiel that current week. Magnhild was now a young working woman in Youngstown, doing office work and bookkeeping at the local creamery.

She participated in town social activities, including becoming an active member of the Ladies Curling Club. *The Plaindealer* also noted another winter and spring recreation—hunting and trapping antelope, rabbits, badgers, coyotes and weasels.

Automobiles were becoming much more common in Alberta, with 42,000 licensed automobiles in 1924, and 10,000 more licensed in 1925. *The Plaindealer* noted in May 1925 that the Calgary Good Roads Association had proposed the construction of a highway from Calgary to Winnipeg, and most of the towns along the Goose Lake line agreed to affiliate with the movement. In May 1925, the Youngstown Council sided with the suggestion of the Good Roads Committee that Youngstown " . . . undertake the blazing of the trail from Youngstown to the Saskatchewan border." It was hoped that this would become the main auto route from Winnipeg to the Rocky Mountains. Some early trails and unimproved roads already existed through to the mountains. In the summer of 1925, *The Plaindealer* revealed that Gudrun Roseland had joined friends on a motor trip to the Rockies. The increasing number of automobiles and improved roads meant that the Roseland girls were now beginning to travel beyond the small world that they had known on their homestead.

The Chautauqua came to Youngstown in August 1925, and *The Youngstown Plaindealer* reported the event in some detail. This travelling show consisted of groups of varied and currently popular entertainers, who gave their performances in a very large brown tent. These shows travelled

widely throughout North America and were particularly popular in rural areas where other
entertainment was less accessible. The theme of
the 1925 show was the promotion of better citizenship and better training for youth, with a program
that included a wide variety of vocal and musical
entertainment, dances, comedy and character
sketches. One highlighted speaker gave a lecture on
"the training of children and imparting knowledge
on sex relations and morality." In another lecture
she spoke of her international experience, noting
that " . . . it is a crime in China for a child to be inso-
lent to elders. In that way the Chinese are 5,000
years ahead of us."

On the Friday evening the featured performance was Gilbert and Sullivan's *Mikado*. The
audience had no sooner got seated in the tent when
a heavy wind storm arose, which continued through
the evening, causing a terrible flapping of the tent.
However, "the fine voices of the company" were
able to rise above the storm and "performed
admirably." The week's program continued with a
variety of other entertainment and lectures on citizenship. The Chautauqua remained popular
throughout rural North America until improved
roads, increased mobility and the Depression
brought an end to the once popular show.

■ ■ ■

In mid-August 1925, harvesting of the wheat crop
was in full swing but, on the 1st of October, a snowfall of about six inches halted threshing. The snow
was followed by rain. Again, the farmers feared that

a spell of warm weather in October would ruin their crop. This was a dry region with a low annual rainfall, but a problem almost greater than the scant rainfall was the timing of the rain. A spring planting might not germinate without a rainfall, and a fall crop could be ruined by untimely rain.

According to *The Plaindealer*, continent-wide telephone service from Alberta began in late October 1925. The first long-distance phone call from Alberta was made from Edmonton to Minneapolis. The first telephone service in Youngstown started from the bakeshop in 1914. By 1920, AGT had installed telephone lines to a distance of 15 miles south of Youngstown, which connected with the service in town. However, farmers had begun installing phone lines between neighbours earlier, as soon as they had constructed barbed-wire fences. A group of neighbours communicated with each other by running a phone line along the barbed-wire fence and raising the line above gates by means of high poles. These phones were not connected to the central exchange. However, many farmers were without telephones because of lack of adequate fencing or willing neighbours, or from lack of funds to install the lines and phones. The Roselands were forty miles south of Youngstown and did not have a telephone.

■ ■ ■

Prior to Christmas, advertisements featured new tube radios run on battery power. Previously some had owned crystal sets, which operated due to the unique quality of crystals that could absorb radio transmissions. With these sets the family shared a headset, passing it from one to the other, to hear voices or music coming through the airwaves. In the early '20s, both Calgary and Edmonton initiated new radio stations. Radio brought great relief from isolation for farm families, bringing to them news, music and culture with much greater immediacy.

They also read newspapers, such as the weekly *Youngstown Plaindealer*, *The Grain Growers' Guide* and *The Winnipeg Free Press*, which was a very popular newspaper with special sections for children. The Roselands also read Norwegian-American newspapers. The most valuable reading material for those learning to speak English was the Eaton's catalogue. Each item was pictured, named and briefly described, a wonderful resource for learning a vocabulary.

■ ■ ■

Wallace Auld, who established the first hardware store in Youngstown in 1912, in a tent, engineered the first electrical service to Youngstown in 1917. He had purchased a generator from Calgary, and found that he had more power than he required, so he began taking on customers. The original plant and store burned down in 1924, when the company had 102 customers, and several streetlights. The plant provided service until 1930, when a large company bought out many electrical generating businesses in small towns, combining them to provide a more extensive service.

The highlight of weekend entertainment in this era was the movie presented at the Rex Theatre on Fridays and Saturday evenings. The theatre was owned by a Mr. Sterling, who owned and operated an adjoining hardware and grocery store, and also acted as the local undertaker. He hired a "barker" who walked up and down the main street with a megaphone prior to the evening movies, drawing customers like magnets. With only one projector, the customers waited while the projectionist changed the films several times during the presentation. This was an era of silent films, so it was also the duty of the projectionist to add or provide sound effects when necessary.

The first motion picture to win the Academy Award for Best Picture was *Wings*, for 1927-28. It came first to Youngstown as a silent picture, returning later with a sound track. On the first run, a young man came along with the movie and added sound effects such as whistles, bells, airplane motors and shotguns. *Wings* was a story of two First World War fighter pilots caught in a love triangle, and featured dramatic sequences of early aerial warfare.

Fighter pilots who returned from the First World War were highly enthusiastic about their flying skills and had purchased surplus aircraft, which they used to travel the country. Their aircraft were two-seater biplanes with an open cockpit. They visited agricultural fairs for a fee, or created their own fair when visiting different communities. Once established at a location, they would mingle with the crowd and sell tickets for a fee, for a ride in their aircraft. They often used farmers' fields for take-off and landing, earning them the name of "barnstormers." Their performances featured such feats as wing-walking, and changing from one aircraft to

another while in flight. Immediately following the war
the public was wildly enthusiastic for these feats, as the
whole notion of flying seemed an unbelievable possibility. The practice of offering rides in aircraft continued at
country fairs through the '20s and '30s. There is later
evidence that Arnold Roseland flew in one of these aircraft as an older teenager, or young man.

■ ■ ■

The weather in the growing season of 1926 followed
another unique and unpredictable pattern. *The
Plaindealer* reported a good start to spring work in
April with warm and dry weather, which left the surface of the fields in good shape for harrowing and
disking. Farmers began the season with general
optimism because, in addition to the dry surfaces,
there was more moisture in the ground than usual.
The sloughs were filled with water "standing in
places where old-timers had never seen water
before." Then, in the middle of May, a storm came
up suddenly late one afternoon and raged with great
force for about half an hour, accompanied by sand
and dust that greatly reduced visibility. "Tumbling
mustard (weed) came rolling along with the wind
like an army." The surface dust blown off the
recently seeded crops did considerable damage.
The wind was so strong that it blew down fences,
damaged rooftops, and caused storekeepers to fear
that their windows would be blown in. In mid-July
came a spell of scorching weather. The paper
reported that it had "wrought immense damage to
crops throughout the district, and lessened the
yields considerably." What crops were left seemed

to be ripening early and the farmers feared that they might have to undertake an early harvest.

The same edition of the newspaper reported excitement over last-minute planning of the Agricultural Fair. In addition to an increased number of exhibit entries, the baseball diamond had been prepared for games, and basketball and football games were scheduled. The committee reported that there would be a good supply of ice cream, pop and hot dogs along with a variety of other snack foods and cigarettes.

In early September 1926, the newspaper featured a front-page essay by grade ten student Faye Roseland, entitled "Alberta as a Province." The essay examined the natural resources of Alberta and the development of agriculture in the province, and it was written to mark the occasion of the twenty-first year since Alberta had become a province. The school literary society had recently elected their officers, with Faye Roseland on the refreshment committee. In late September, the society held a "jolly party" in the recreation hall of the United Church. Everyone dressed as children, and all new members had to wear their clothes backwards. After a short business meeting they read aloud the recent issue of their newspaper, the *Literary Echo*, which was enjoyed by all.

The school board had discussed again the possibility of installing electric lights in the school building. Windows were being broken occasionally by children, and were expensive to replace. Before deciding whether to install electric lights, they voted to reduce the size of the glass panes by half, and await a report by a special committee.

In early October, the weather again wrought havoc with the wheat crop. Threshing was halted when a storm came up quickly in the forenoon, with sleet and two inches of snow falling through the afternoon. Recorded temperatures noted several degrees of frost every night that week. A few weeks after the snowfall, railway section men burning the weeds off the railway right-of-way accidentally started a grassfire near Cessford. Blazing tumble-weeds were caught by gusts of wind and rolled across the dry, grassy fields. The fire headed east from Cessford, in the direction of the Roseland home, but flames did not reach that far.

Auction sales throughout the fall were plentiful. Advertisements noted the date, time and the property where the auction would be held, and included a list of items such as horses, cattle, pigs, hens, machinery, household furniture and "other items too numerous to mention." The terms were cash—no reserves. The families who were leaving took very little with them.

In early December 1926, the area was hit again by the worst snowstorm in years, with three persons losing their lives. A mother and child froze to death when they could not find their way back to the house from the barn. Another man could not move his wagon and team of horses in the storm. He cut loose his horses and tried to ride one of them home, but froze to death before making it.

■ ■ ■

By late 1926, Gustav and Anna had to make a decision about their future. Many farmers had already
left. The 1926 census indicated that there were
10,000 abandoned farms in Alberta, most within the
dry area. Although some farmers had been relatively
successful within the dry region, most had problems.
The land within the Palliser's Triangle varied greatly,
from excellent to submarginal and poor. The triangle
was a large area of the western prairies that extended
across the 49th parallel in southeastern Alberta and
southwestern Saskatchewan, and north to a point
near the border that separated the two provinces.
Palliser had made his cursory evaluation during dry
years, declaring the area unfit for agriculture. Later,
Canadian botanist John Macoun examined the area
more extensively during wet years and gave a more
positive opinion of the suitability of the land for agriculture. There seemed to have been some truth in
both opinions, in that success or failure of a crop
depended not only on the land, but on the amount of
rain that fell and, more importantly, on how the timing of the precipitation corresponded with the needs
of the crops. Recent dust storms had also been an
ominous sign of future problems for the region. The
frequent cultivation of the soil, as advocated by summer-fallow, had led to depletion of fibre in the soil,
causing drifting and dust storms. What prospects
were there for a future in this area?

     Since making the critical decision in the
spring of 1924 to remain in the area and gamble on
their future as wheat farmers, Gustav and Anna had
experienced repeated disappointments. The

weather had been disastrously unkind, as had the economy. While eastern Canada had bounced back from a brief recession in 1921-22, farmers in the west faced declining wheat prices and crop failures. Gustav had gambled a significant amount of his cash when purchasing the Hogarth property, but his wheat crop had not provided enough return to cover his mortgage payments. Lack of income from the farm clearly demanded a decision about their future. But in December 1926, the Roselands set aside their worries about the future and celebrated the marriage of their eldest daughter.

By 1926, the now twenty-three-year-old Magnhild had been living and working in Youngstown since finishing school. She had a vivacious, bubbly personality and led an active social life, with a steady boyfriend. But, when a new young CNR station agent came to town, Magnhild determined that her future would be with Paul Eberly. She married Paul on December 27, 1926; a reception was held at the home of friends in Youngstown. Paul's relatives came over from Okotoks, a small town thirty miles south of Calgary, for the occasion. The families got along well together, and it was a happy occasion. Magnhild and Paul settled in Youngstown.

Rather than risking the loss of any more of their financial resources, Gustav and Anna decided to leave the area. At Magnhild's wedding they learned from Paul's relatives about a farm near Okotoks that would be available in the spring. Gustav and Anna later reached an agreement to take over this farm. An advantage in making the move to Okotoks was that they would be closer to social life in town, and could give the children better education opportunities.

The economic failure of their farming experience, and their decision to purchase their last home south of Youngstown, were pivotal events in the lives of Gustav and Anna. Although Gustav's original intention was to return to Norway as soon as he met his financial goals, his inability to earn enough money inadvertently made Canadians of the Roseland family.

There was no hope of selling the large house they had lived in for only two years. They packed their belongings and shipped their animals and farm equipment to Okotoks. Then they closed the doors of the house and left to catch the train at Cessford, twenty miles to the east. From there they took the "Peavine Line" to Youngstown. They made the connection there to the "Goose Lake Line" that would take them west to Calgary.

Home the family abandoned at Cabin Lake, Alberta in 1927, as it still stood in June 2000

PART FOUR
"We Thought It Couldn't Get Worse"
(Canada 1927-1939)

Chapter 13
"It once was so cheerful,
that place we called home"

FROM THE TRAIN, the low rolling hills behind them blurred to a brown nothingness on the horizon. As the train chugged its way westward the land looked much the same, but the hills were higher and the valleys deeper. In the distance they caught glimpses of the jagged snow-capped peaks of the Rocky Mountains that formed a north-south corridor along the western horizon. The train snaked its way into Calgary, where they changed to a CPR train. In the thirty miles south from Calgary the train lowered into the valley, following the Sheep River to their destination, the small town of Okotoks. There they saw the same winter-brown landscape, but also the tall stands of trees that lined Sheep River on either side, and a silhouette of trees on high rolling hills on the horizon. The CPR Station was located at the east end of town, on the north side of the river. From there they found their way to their new home less than two miles southwest of town.

From Okotoks, glimpses of the Rockies could be seen on a clear day, in the far distance to the west. Over thousands of years the melting ice and snow of the mountains had carved creeks and rivers that flowed towards the South Saskatchewan River, through verdant and wooded valleys. With the melting snow from the Rockies in the springtime, these gentle creeks and rivers became raging torrents. From the eastern edge of the foothills of the Rockies, to the region east of Okotoks, the country gradually flattened to the low mounding of the dry homesteading region. To the west of Okotoks some flat areas were suitable for wheat farming, but much of the land was low, undulating mountains, exposed to winds, with grasses suitable for cattle or horses.

Soon after the CPR brought its transcontinental route through the southern part of the country in the 1880s, Calgary was established as the main city of the south. The attractive countryside caught the attention of the privileged classes of the United Kingdom and eastern Canada, and in a short time the whole region was claimed for cattle ranching. Some former North-West Mounted Police became ranchers, and their influence, along with that of the privileged class of British settlers, created a society that was essentially law-abiding, with a strong interest in arts and culture. Some areas suitable for wheat farming did fall to the homesteaders, and other early settlers turned to raising horses, often pedigreed. In general, the economy of the region became less dependent on wheat farming than in the eastern portions of the province. Just south of Calgary, Okotoks became a commercial and cultural centre for much of the ranching community. Nestled in the valley of Sheep River, Okotoks is protected from the harsh winter weather that sweeps over the plateaus and rolling hills of the surrounding countryside.

The proximity of the Roselands' new home to the town made life simpler for the whole family. From the farm the children could walk to and from the town. Their house was a comfortable wood-frame dwelling on a perfectly flat, open acreage. The previous owners of the property had engaged in wheat farming, and Gustav intended to do the same. He planted his first crop shortly after getting settled on the farm. When he threshed his wheat in the fall, Gustav would have only a short trip by wagon to deliver his wheat to the grain elevator. Okotoks boasted four grain elevators, a fact that made the emphatic statement that wheat farmers also contributed to the local economy.

The horse-lovers in the family—Agnes and Arnold—were particularly happy with the move to Okotoks. On one occasion, Faye and Agnes each selected a horse to ride, from the horses that they had brought with them from their homestead. Faye took a familiar old favourite, while Agnes chose "Cyclone," a horse that had never been ridden before. Fifteen-year-old Agnes soon left Faye in the dust as she made a wide circle on the flat region south of the river. She returned, smiling broadly and utterly pleased with herself for bringing her horse home under perfect control. In foothills country, expertise in horsemanship garnered respect and prestige.

One day the family became alarmed when seven-year-old Erling did not return home from school. After a frantic search, the family was relieved to find Erling sound asleep in the afternoon sun, on a warm sandy hillside. He had stopped to watch ants in an anthill scurrying about, tidying their nests and bringing provisions for their young.

■ ■ ■

In the late summer of 1927, Gustav was cutting his wheat crop when his leg got caught in the teeth of the cutting-blades of the binder, creating a deep, jagged flesh wound. It became severely infected. The older girls, who had gone to visit Magnhild and Paul at Hanna, were called home because it appeared that Gustav might die. Although their father did recover, he was left in a much weakened state, with a heart condition. Gustav, now fifty-three years old, would never be able to engage in strenuous physical labour again. The family had no choice but to make yet another move.

They found a home in town east of the CPR Station, on the north side of Sheep River, close to the school and all the social activities in the town. From the town, seventy-four steps took the children up to the new school, a solitary building on the bench above. Faye had completed grade eleven in 1927. Alberta offered grade twelve to high school students for the first time in 1929, and Agnes was one of about 1,400 students in Alberta who graduated from grade twelve that year. Also in 1929, Hildur and Arnold completed grade nine, and Ernest and Erling completed grade four.

Arnold won academic prestige in 1928, and again in 1929, when he was awarded a $5 gold coin and a certificate for graduating first in his class in grade eight, and then again in grade nine. The local

Family Group 1928: Hildur, Faye, Gudrun, Anna, Gustav, Arnold, Ernest, Erling (missing – Magnhild and Agnes)

Knights of Pythias gave awards annually to students who excelled academically.

Gudrun started working for the Royal Bank upon arrival at Okotoks, and after completing high school Faye clerked and worked on the soda fountain at the drug store. Gudrun and Faye soon knew most people in town. The Elks Hall on Elizabeth Street was the site of many social functions and dances. The two oldest sisters who remained at home, Gudrun and Faye, often had dates who took them to dances there. They dressed in their late '20s flapper dresses, Faye in green and Gudrun in pink.

■ ■ ■

The family's new home was a few blocks from the two main streets, Elizabeth and Elma, named after the daughters of John Lineham, who constructed a logging mill in 1890. Mr. Lineham had obtained the rights to logging higher up on Sheep Creek, and when the waters ran high, he floated his logs down the creek. The mill had been a major employer in Okotoks over many years. The town thrived through the boom years prior to the First World War, but suffered greatly with the Depression in western Canada in the '20s, when the population declined to about 400. By 1925, the economy started to improve. By 1929, the population had risen again to about 700.

With a healthier economy in the late '20s, provincial and town finances improved. Prohibition had been proclaimed in Alberta from 1916 until 1923, when the government decided that prohibition was unenforceable. After that time the government engaged in the selling of liquor, with liquor taxes adding to the public funds. The great increase of automobiles also added revenue, from gasoline taxes and the sale of licences. Governments were pushed into extending highways, with growth in service stations and motels, which bolstered employment and tourism. Increased property values and property taxes enhanced the financial health of the Town of Okotoks.

In the late '20s the hitching posts were removed from the streets, sidewalks were paved, and the streets graded and re-gravelled. Council passed a motion to have the Picture Hall stuccoed and upgraded to provide for the new sound movies. The old rink, constructed prior to the First World War, collapsed under a heavy snowfall in 1925, and

Okotoks Main Street circa 1929
Photo courtesy Glenbow Archives, Calgary, Alberta

in September 1929 a town plebiscite approved construction of a new rink. At home, many were setting
aside their old crystal sets with headphones, and
acquiring the new electric console radios, which
could pick up the new stations transmitting from
Calgary.

■ ■ ■

The family did not live long in the house by the
river. Because Gustav was limited in his physical
capabilities, fifty-year-old Anna became the bread-
winner of the family.

Another prolific oil producer began operating at the Turner Valley Oilfields in 1929, six miles
away. With the influx of workers, Gustav and Anna
could see the need for boarding accommodation and
providing meals for day workers. They found a large
home of solid construction on Elma Street, and sank
their last resources into acquiring it. The house had

Okotoks-Roseland boarding house, lower left corner
Photo courtesy Glenbow Archives, Calgary, Alberta

several large rooms on the main floor, an upstairs, and a lean-to addition for boarders. The family moved into the boarding house in the spring of 1929. Gustav was able to assist Anna, but she now carried the burden of providing for the family.

■ ■ ■

Then, on October 29, 1929, the stock market crashed and ushered in the Great Depression. At first, Prime Minister William Lyon Mackenzie King did not believe that this was a serious economic crisis and allowed the country to drift.

■ ■ ■

The boarding home venture started out well. During the summer of 1929 they had as many as seventeen boarders—three or four who had rooms, and the rest day boarders who took their meals there. The older children in the family began to spread their wings. Faye moved to Hanna, where she helped Magnhild with her children and found a clerking job. Gudrun married a young man she met at a dance at Lethbridge, and they moved to Coutts, where their first child was born. Agnes met a young man who came to Okotoks from Pincher Creek. They married and left for Creston and then Trail, B.C.

In town the three boys were able to take part in many more social and sports activities. They skated and played hockey in the winter, and took in movies at the Picture Hall. For street hockey, two rocks marked the goal posts, and shin pads were made of sections of old catalogues. When snow was on the ground, they made skis out of staves from an old barrel and caught rides on the back of runners on horse-drawn sleds. In summer they swam in the river, and when the water was high, dove off one of the bridges. Ernest, in particular, was a very good swimmer, a robust and physically active child. Erling was a better student, a sensitive and frail child.

In September 1930, Hildur and the boys all returned to school. Hildur and Arnold were in grade ten, Arnold having caught up with Hildur by skipping a grade. Erling had done the same and caught up with Ernest. The two youngest boys both enrolled in grade five. All four attended the Okotoks School, on the bench above the town.

■ ■ ■

The country experienced a rapid economic crisis after the Crash of '29. Still not recognizing the severity of the economic problems, Mackenzie King left the provinces with the sole responsibility of financially assisting the unemployed. But the voters of Canada made a strong statement to Mr. King when, in the summer of 1930, they elected a Conservative government with R.B. Bennett as prime minister.

Mr. Bennett faced daunting problems. Western Canada was reliant on export markets, but Canada had a surplus of wheat, and wheat had fallen to the ruinously low price of thirty-two cents a bushel, not enough to cover the cost of production, nor the freight. The new Conservative government brought in the Unemployment Act and the Farm Relief Act, and finally began sending funds to aid the cash-hungry provinces. The Bennett government spent on relief projects, such as the construction of a Trans-Canada Highway, and on airports across the country. But the Depression deepened, and money that Ottawa spent, and the money it sent to the provinces, was never enough.

The most pressing problems at all levels of governments were the high cost of relief, and where to allocate their sparse resources. The town council was obliged to pay a portion of relief cost, and often had the responsibility of selecting who were eligible recipients. With so many unemployed, revenue from property taxes fell into arrears, causing town revenues to drop sharply.

The Okotoks council did not wish to grant financial assistance to non-residents for relief or medical care. This included "sojourners" who were drifting around looking for work. In order to protect local businesses, council also attempted to make itinerant peddlers unwelcome. The council even attempted to "deport" residents after they made a request for assistance, if council believed they had not lived in town long enough to qualify. For qualified, established residents of the town, arrangements were made to allow them to collect direct relief. Recipients were given credit at local businesses where they could collect minimal amounts of items essential for living. The Okotoks council passed a motion that before being approved for direct relief, applicants had to show statements of their accounts at local businesses. Before their applications could be approved, the local constable had to check the adequacy of the supplies in their cupboards at home.

The town council was faced with tough decisions. In 1931, a councillor moved that teachers' salaries be cut by 15 per cent. Arguments were advanced that it would create uncertainty among teachers, which would be reflected in their work, thereby hurting the children. The motion was defeated. However, a year later salaries were reduced, "based on the District's capacity to pay."

■ ■ ■

The Honourable George Hoadley had represented Okotoks in the provincial legislature since 1912, and he happened to be the minister of health in the provincial government. Okotoks-High River was one of two areas in Alberta selected to participate in a cost-sharing arrangement in the establishment of a permanent health department. The new health department would introduce such programs as communicable disease control, maternal and child health care, medical inspections of school children, and the testing and inspection of various food handling and dairy establishments. In 1930, the Okotoks town council approved their participation in this health unit.

The provincial Health Act provided that an indigent person could seek health care and the town was obliged to pay a portion of the hospital fee, only if it was a case of "urgent or sudden necessity" in the opinion of the medical officer of the hospital. These criteria left the door open for interpretations, which often required other medical and legal opinions. When an amendment was proposed making the health minister the final judge concerning "urgent or sudden necessity," the legislature was deeply divided.

The high rate of tuberculosis and the inadequacy of facilities to treat and care for the patients was a major health concern. In 1931, *The Edmonton Journal* reported that an immediate objective of the government was "to have at least one bed to accommodate a tuberculosis patient for every annual death from the disease." Based on current figures, the number of treatment beds in Alberta would have to be doubled. Infectious cases of the disease were waiting weeks and often months before being admitted to hospital for treatment, during a time when the patient was dangerously infectious to others.

■ ■ ■

Many houses in Okotoks were in tax arrears and the town was desperately short of money. There were no welfare departments, and the town was obliged by law to contribute to the destitute through a few provincial programs of limited assistance.

■ ■ ■

However, in spite of the cash shortage, weekly reports in the *Okotoks Review* revealed a town of 760 inhabitants with a surprisingly rich social and cultural life. The ranching community in the area participated in Okotoks's social and cultural activities. Their two major interests were church and sporting events.

The United Church in Okotoks had the largest congregation by far, but the Anglican Church had sufficient members to support a resident priest, who also served groups of adherents throughout the area. A Catholic Church served mainly a small number of parishioners in the rural areas. The Roselands belonged to the Okotoks Gospel Chapel, a group of about sixty faithful followers led by lay pastor Helmer Jacobsen, who managed a local lumberyard. The Jacobsens had immigrated from Arendal, Norway, the town where Anna worked before she was married. The members of this church formed a small but strongly bonded sub-culture within the town.

The Roselands lived within two or three blocks of all the social venues in town. The new arena was home ice to the Okotoks Hockey Club as well as one from Turner Valley. Fans travelled twenty miles by train to High River for games there, and High River and Calgary fans came for games in Okotoks. When Okotoks advanced to the provincial hockey playoffs, the newspaper reported, "It was a smashing display of hockey that Okotoks gave the fans."

Gustav and Anna's church in Okotoks

The Curling Club sponsored local bonspiels with eighteen competing rinks. The Tennis Club had two tennis courts, and softball and baseball teams had regular scheduled games. The horse races at Millarville, twenty miles away, had been an annual event for Okotoks and Calgary society since the 1890s, and in 1933 drew a record crowd, one of the most successful events ever.

The older Roseland children enjoyed the dances and eagerly attended the social events in

*Pastor Jacobsen and his family, showing the Okotoks school
on the hill behind.*

town. Arnold's good friend Maurice Ardeil was a
member of the Anglican Young People's Group,
which sponsored a Rose Ball each spring. For the
occasion, the walls of the Elks Hall were decorated
with paper roses up to the ceiling. The event was
the highlight of the season for Okotoks's young people, and it also attracted guests from other small
towns in this south Calgary area.

Arnold and Maurice Ardiel circa 1932

The Okotoks Dramatic Society put on regular performances in the Elks Hall, where they "filled the hall to the doors." The Anglican Church Young People's put on plays and participated in drama festivals in towns throughout that region. The Chautauqua came to town annually in November, and moving pictures came from Calgary to the Picture Hall every Monday evening. Children ran to the Picture Hall after school on Mondays in an attempt to be the first there for the matinee, and gain free admission by becoming the ticket taker.

The newspaper reported large attendance at a wide range of service clubs and lodges: The Agricultural Society, Royal Purple Lodge, I.O.D.E., Country Club, Masonic Lodge, Elks' Club, Eastern Star, and the Women's Christian Temperance Movement.

For such a small town of 760, the Board of Trade was remarkably active. In November 1933, Magistrate H.G. Scott from Calgary gave a talk, with sixty-two members present. Recently returned from a trip to Europe, he spoke of Hitler and the political situation in Germany. "He embodies and expresses the German resentment under their defeat . . . . His one theme is that Germany has been ill-treated and must secure restoration of her past glory . . . . The Jews, by their superior intelligence, had made themselves a very powerful factor in Germany . . . . Some, especially the Nazis, claimed that their influence was not healthy . . . . The young men of the country are preparing for war. They are itching to recover

their lost lands, the Rhineland, the Ruhr Valley . . ."
The speech was filled with such interesting detail
that the *Review* continued its lengthy coverage into
the next issue of the paper. Events in Europe were
foreshadowing the coming of a world war, but like
the period prior to the First World War, Canadians
were preoccupied with domestic problems.

■ ■ ■

In 1933, in the depths of the Depression, Arnold
graduated from high school. He had done very well
on his matriculation exams, but job and education
opportunities were virtually non-existent. At the
same time, Gustav and Anna were experiencing
severe financial problems. Taxes on their boarding
home had fallen into arrears. Fewer and fewer men
had jobs, or money to pay for meals or board. A good
many other houses in Okotoks were in tax arrears
and the town was threatening to take possession of
the properties and then rent them out, in an attempt
to recoup money to pay for the increasing costs of
relief. Arnold made a trip out to Trail, B.C. to look
for work, but when he found none, he returned
home, perhaps hoping to be of some assistance to
his parents.

Gudrun and her husband Francis had moved
to a job at Coutts, Alberta in 1930, where a boom in
exploration for oil had taken off in the '20s. Oil companies constructed refineries there, turning a tiny
commercial hamlet on the U.S. border into a busy oil
town. Francis' job in Coutts lasted only two years, as
the company let him go after he took a company car
to Lethbridge and used it for private business.

While Gudrun was a tall, poised young woman with a steady temperament, Francis was a tall, lean, quick-minded Irishman, an inveterate storyteller who never tired of parties and socializing. In later years Francis told stories of his "rum-running" days at Coutts. Prohibition was on in the United States, and this grassy and gently mounded countryside offered great opportunities for selling Canadian liquor south of the border. The sister city to Coutts was Sweetgrass, Montana, less than a mile away, with a ready market for Canadian liquor. Rum-runners from Canada could drive their trucks to the American border where the booze was picked up by purchasers waiting on the other side. Workers and homesteaders short of cash drove their booty across the open prairie at night in cars that had all lighting removed, always finding a ready market and a waiting buyer.

By 1933, both Gudrun and Agnes were living in Trail with their families. The Consolidated Mining and Smelting Company in Trail had a major construction project under way when the recession hit in 1929, but they carried the project to completion. Jobs were more readily available there than in most places in Western Canada.

Faye worked in Hanna until 1933, and while there she met Lewis Derby, the son of a minister. That summer, Faye and Lew and another couple drove Lew's mother back to Nova Scotia in a Model T Ford. In 1933 a camping trip with five persons, on gravel roads, from Alberta to Nova Scotia and back, was a very long drive. After returning to Alberta,

Trail, B.C., 1933: Francis, friend, Gudrun, Agnes, Bill with Shirley; front row, Donna and Ted.

Lew found work in Coutts, at the new British-American Oil Company refinery there. Faye left Okotoks in November 1933 for a quiet wedding in Sweetgrass, Montana, and she and Lew settled in Coutts.

Just before Christmas, the Town took possession of Gustav and Anna's house, and seized all their possessions "not essential for daily living." The city granted them possession of another, smaller house just east of the CPR Station, one that had been boarded up after being foreclosed by the Town. They removed the boards from the windows, and Anna set about making the house as comfortable and as cheerful as possible, as they still had Hildur and the three boys at home. Arnold was doing casual work at a service station in town, and also working for a farm implement dealer, and that may have been the only income they had at that time.

On a Saturday evening, January 13, 1934, Gustav had his first heart attack. There was no hospital in Okotoks, so he remained at home, cared for by Anna. Dr. Ardeil, the Okotoks physician, visited him on Sunday after he experienced a second heart attack. On Sunday afternoon when he visited with his wife, Pastor Jacobsen said prayers with Gustav and Anna. Just after the children left for school on Monday morning, Gustav suffered a third and fatal heart attack. Mr. and Mrs. Jacobsen rushed over, perhaps called by Arnold. Mr. Jacobsen assisted Anna writing telegrams to notify the children, and called the undertaker. He conducted a prayer meeting at the home on the evening before the funeral, the 18th of January. Gustav was buried on a cold, wintry day. Faye said later that his children believed that Gustav had died "of a broken heart."

Later, Anna wrote:

"So oft in the night time when all are asleep,
I turn on my pillow and in loneliness weep.
And often the heartache is hid by a smile,
With unbidden teardrops kept back all the while."

Gustav's funeral, January 1934

Chapter 14
"Often the heartache is hid by a smile"

GUSTAV AND ANNA had barely settled in the older, unpainted house across from the CPR section house when Gustav died. Now Anna was alone with Hildur, Arnold, Ernest and Erling. The week after the funeral, fifteen-year-old Erling was excluded from school temporarily, quarantined with chicken pox. Life went on.

Anna was very short of money. She received $15 per month Mothers' Allowance and it is not clear whether this was matched by the provincial government. Welfare did not exist, and whatever help they received was very little. The two older boys, nineteen-year-old Arnold and seventeen-year-old Ernest, learned to pump gas and change oil and they worked occasionally at local garages. But the garages were not very busy. Few purchased new cars, and many who had purchased cars earlier were now using them as "Bennett Buggies," named after Prime Minister Bennett, mocking him for his failure to provide any solutions for the Depression. Owners removed the engines from their cars and hitched a horse up to the vehicle, as a means of powering it. Few could afford to buy gasoline, so it meant that Arnold and Ernest did not have steady work.

■ ■ ■

Hildur had not been well since her father died. In late February she was in bed for several days with a bad cold. On the 10th of April, Mrs. Jacobsen served a birthday cake to the Ladies' Group from the church to celebrate Anna's fifty-eighth birthday. Two days later, a devastated Anna told these same friends that Dr. Ardeil had just delivered the bad news that Hildur had tuberculosis.

It was common knowledge in the town that three other young women had been diagnosed with tuberculosis in the past year. Just six months previously, Dr. Ardeil had attended the meeting of the town council to plead on behalf of a twenty-one-year-old woman. Council approved a request to pay her portion of sanatorium care, as she was dangerously ill with consumption. Her only slight hope for improvement would be as a patient in a sanatorium. One month later the newspaper reported " . . . a largely attended funeral (for Christine), testifying to the regret for the loss of a bright, and young, life thus untimely cut off."

That same month another young woman from Okotoks was admitted to the sanatorium with tuberculosis, and her sister entered for a two-month period with a milder case of TB. These young women were close in age to Hildur, and in contact with each other at school and social events. Tuberculosis is highly contagious to susceptible persons through breathing air contaminated by coughing, and through ingesting the germ via contaminated hands and food. Throughout the '30s, tuberculosis was the leading killer of persons in the fifteen to forty age group.

Hildur was admitted to the Central Alberta Sanatorium (CAS) in northwest Calgary, across the river from Bowness Park. About the turn of the century, the high and dry climate of this region had been touted as suitable in the treatment of TB. This attracted patients to the area when there were no treatment facilities.

During the First World War a sanatorium had been established at Frank, Alberta in an old CPR hotel, for the purpose of treating soldiers who had the disease. From 1914-1918 tuberculosis killed almost as many Canadians as were killed in the war. The CAS in Calgary was constructed, and opened after the war ended. Hospital costs were split three ways, between two levels of government and the patient, but if the patient had no money, the town had to pay. During the Depression, towns were so short of money that they could not always make the payments.

The CAS was located on the other side of the river from the end of the streetcar line, not easily accessible for visitors without a car. Although the sanatorium was originally intended to house and educate ambulatory patients, and to integrate them back into the community, the reality was that there were so many critically ill that they kept the institution filled, with long wait lists. General hospitals did not wish to care for infectious tuberculosis patients. Patients in the sanatorium were often referred to as "inmates."

Treatment had not changed much since the turn of the century. The main aim was to build the body up so that it could fight the disease. This included good food, adequate rest and fresh air, and as much exercise as an individual patient could tolerate. About one-third of patients had treatments that involved the collapse of a lung. A common method was "pneumothorax," a method of introducing gas or air into the pleural cavity about once a week, the purpose being to allow the lung a more restful state, so that it might heal more readily. The biggest problem in treatment was to fill in the long patient days for those who were excluded from broader society for often one, two or three years.

Anna visited Hildur as often as she could, as did Magnhild and Faye and her brothers. Hildur wrote poetry during the long weeks and months that she spent in bed. She wrote for Anna:

> *"TO MY MOTHER*
> *If I had strayed far, far from home*
> *Without a friend and all alone*
> *I know who'd pray for me and pine*
> *You, dear little mother of mine*
>
> *Or if I disgraced for the world to see*
> *I know whose love would follow me*
> *If in this world I had no other*
> *I could still count on you, dear mother.*
>
> *If I were bound for the blackest cell*
> *Or were so sick I couldn't get well*
> *I know whose heart would breaking be*
> *I know whose tears would fall for me!*

I know who's waiting there alone
With open arms, to welcome me home.
I know whose eyes for me will shine
Yours, dear little mother of mine!"

Faye and Lew were still living in Coutts, and it was a 200-mile trip for Faye to visit Hildur. Faye had to take a bus from Coutts to Lethbridge, and another one to Okotoks. Then a friend would drive Faye and Anna up to the CAS, usually Mr. and Mrs. Jacobsen. Faye did visit Hildur several times, wrote her frequently and sent small gifts. One stanza of a poem she wrote for Faye reads as follows:

"I can't repay your kindnesses
While in this San I stay
But in my heart's a great big place
For you, dear sister Fay!"

She wrote of her recollections of her family and her childhood:

"HOME
It once was so cheerful, that place we called home.
But now it is lonely with mother alone.
Oh! Those pleasant memories of days I recall,
When we were so happy, the family all.
But that's long ago, now we've drifted apart.
My mother's alone with a broken heart.
Since my dad has been taken, she's left there to pine.
And wait for her children to drop her a line.
My sisters are married and I'm in the San.

But I'm going back home just as soon as I can.

I like to dream of those days long ago.
When we were all children and didn't know
The troubles and hardships we'd find in this life.
Before we had learned of the sorrows and strife.
We'd sit by the fire at night while dad read.
And then he would tenderly tuck us in bed.
If we were in trouble or hurt any way
Our mother would kiss all our worries away.

There were never such pals as my dad and I.
He shared all my secrets as years rolled by.
Oh! How I shall cherish those memories forever!
I'd like to go back to then—but I can never.
For everything's changed so with everyone gone.
Just a little old mother still carrying on,
I know that for me she will patiently wait.
Oh! How I pray I shall not be too late!"

For her nurses she wrote:

"TO OUR NURSES
This world keeps going round year by year
But all our nurses in their little sphere
Put on their aprons, tie up the strings
And keep on doing the same old things.

Taking our temperatures, giving out pills
Hearing complaints of our numerous ills
Hiding their heartaches and all the while
Cheering us up with their pleasant smile.

Continually answering the ringing of bells
Being polite with a heart that rebels.
They may be weary, longing for home
Sharing our troubles—hiding their own.

Taking the blame for other's mistakes
Taking it cheerful, expecting no breaks.
Hearing the dying draw their last breath
Closing the eyes that are stilled in death.
Is it a wonder the nurses we love?
I'm sure it is recorded in Heaven above."

The patients were surrounded by death. Hildur underwent "pneumo" treatment for some months until early January when she developed pneumonia, a complication of the pneumothorax treatment. In January 1935, nine months after entering the sanatorium, Hildur died of pneumonia, at the age of twenty years and nine months.

■ ■ ■

Deep bonds of affection united the family. They grieved for the loss of their daughter and sister, but it was not only grief that they shared, but fear. Tuberculosis was a disease that could creep up silently. On top of her grief, Anna had more financial problems. The town council minutes in February 1935 indicate that Anna was no longer eligible for Mothers' Allowance, as her children had all turned fifteen years of age. However, the council did vote her a stipend of $7.50 per month.

In 1935, voters retired both the sitting federal government and the provincial government, at that time led by the United Farmers of Alberta. The federal Conservatives had run out of ideas on how to deal with the Depression, so the voters of Canada brought the Liberals back to power, although they had no solutions either. In Alberta, people could see the stores filled with goods, and few had money to purchase the goods, so the voters bought the "funny money" theory of Social Credit. The new party came in with a landslide victory.

The election of the Social Credit government became particularly pertinent to the problem of tuberculosis control. In October 1935, L. C. Matthews from Calgary wrote to the new premier, William Aberhart, as follows: " . . . Tuberculosis patients are being fought in the courts by cities and towns, seeking to force some unfortunate relative to pay for the monthly sanatorium charge for those who are the nearest next of kin. What is worse, TB cases of two, three or four years standing are facing a slow death rather than have their relatives hounded by some dime-pinching rural municipalities, towns and cities that are chasing the nearest relatives to the ends of the earth for their pound of flesh . . . "

Comments in the *Okotoks Review* in 1935 further highlight the complexity and futility of chasing private individuals for payment of fees. The parents of one of the young women from Okotoks who developed tuberculosis were divorced. The town sought legal opinion and believed that the father should pay, even though the mother was receiving support and had custody of the girl. Later, the father attended a council meeting. He said he had never been asked for money. The complexity of the problem was further highlighted by an explanation in the *Review:* " . . . the law puts the primary responsibility for a patient on the municipality and not the parent. The San claimed that the town of Okotoks was primarily responsible . . . which the council disputed, and claimed that the municipal district was responsible. The town could not pay the account and let the father pay them, as by doing so the town would be admitting liability, and the San refused to collect from the father . . . ." The father requested that, if there were any more accounts received, that they be sent directly to him and he would pay them.

On the 1st of June, 1936, the new Alberta Social Credit government announced that tuberculosis care would be free to all residents of Alberta. Applications for admission to tuberculosis hospitals went up by eighty-eight per cent.

■ ■ ■

Anna had been in the old house just over a year when Hildur died. Always a competent gardener, she started growing potatoes and vegetables, and she kept chickens. She canned some vegetables for winter, and kept potatoes in cool storage under the house. In the boarding house she had had running water in the kitchen by means of a pump, but in the old house where she now lived her water pump was in the back yard. Okotoks did not have a city water supply or sewer until after the Second World War. Because residents obtained water from wells, they

could not dig pits for their outhouses. The city
employed a scavenger who came around weekly to
empty buckets in the outhouses. In some ways,
Anna's circumstances had not improved since leaving Norway. In other ways, she was worse off than
she had been in Norway. The home that she had
left on the Rosseland farm compared favourably
with any of the finest homes in Okotoks. But Anna
accepted her poverty with grace. She recalled her
childhood in Norway, when she had cared for the
younger children in the family as her mother was
dying of tuberculosis.

> *"ARE ALL THE CHILDREN IN?*
> *I think of times as the night draws nigh*
> *Of an old house on the hill.*
> *Of a yard all wide and blossom starred*
> *Where the children played at will.*
> *And when at last the night came down,*
> *Hushing the merry din.*
> *Mother would look around and ask*
> *"Are all the children in?"*
>
> *'Tis many and many a year since then,*
> *And the old house on the hill*
> *No longer echoes with childish feet,*
> *And the yard is still, so still.*
> *But I see it all as the shadows creep*
> *And though many the years have been,*
> *Even now I can hear my mother ask,*
> *"Are all the children in?"*

I wonder if, when the shadows fall
On the last short earthly day,
When we say goodbye to the world outside,
All tired of our childish play.

When we step out into that Other Land
Where mother so long has been,
Will we hear her ask, as we did of old,
"Are all the children in?"

And I wonder too, what the Lord will say,
To us older children of His.
Have we cared for the lambs?
Have we showed them the fold?
A joyful privilege it is.
And I wonder too, what our answer will be
When His loving questions begin:
"Have you heeded my voice?
Have you told of my love?
Have you brought my children in?"

During the years spent in the Appalachian Mountains and in the western prairies, Anna had mastered the English language well. Her daughters described her as the perfect lady, soft-spoken and kind. Gustav and Anna had never allowed their children to say "gosh" and "darn," as it was too close to saying "God" and "damn." Now, in a very sad time in her life, Anna found solace in words.

Only two of Anna's poems have survived, found in her possessions after she died, but she also gave handwritten copies to neighbours who lived next door to her, the Camerons. They belonged to the same church as Anna, and they were good friends and good neigbours. Anna must have written many poems before she wrote these two, but perhaps they were in scribblers, not recognized and thrown out. In the second poem she reflects on her married life, her husband and children. Since childhood, religion had been an important part of Anna's life, and now, in her later years, she became more deeply religious.

Anna's world was changing. Her older daughters had married and left home. She had six grandchildren, whom she saw occasionally. She had lost her husband and youngest daughter. But there were also changes in her family in Norway, those she loved dearly, whom she had left behind when she sailed for North America in 1907.

In late May 1907, just after arriving at Stearns, she had written to Gustav's sister Anna, "I am thinking about you all the time. I wish I could hug all of you and thank you so much for all you did for us when we were home with you. I couldn't say much when I left. I cried inside and couldn't say a word." In late 1935, Anna received word that the sister-in-law she had loved dearly had died suddenly. As she probably feared in 1907, she had never seen her again.

Gustav's sister Anna had remained at home caring for her elderly parents. Gustav's father had died in 1931, at the age of eighty-three. His mother was still alive at age eighty-five, frail and with poor eyesight, but still mobile. These were the parents

Rosseland family in Norway circa 1930. Left to right: Gustav's sister Anna, Andreas, Gunhilde and other family members. Olav second from right.

that Gustav had so much compassion for, worrying that they had worn themselves out with such hard work. Each lived a much longer life than Gustav.

Gustav's father had wanted so badly to sell his farm to one of his sons. Of the three sons who came to North America intending to earn money and return to Norway, Olav was the only one to return and remain there. As he had feared, all the girls were married when he returned at the age of thirty-nine. Olav never married. Albert lived in New York and kept in touch by mail. After Olav and Albert ran away to the mountains in British Columbia in 1917, Anna never saw either of them again.

Anna's younger sister Elizabeth was still living in Arendal with her husband Knut, their four sons and one daughter. Anna corresponded with her, but they never saw each other again. She never met her sister's husband, nor did she see their children. Her brother Juergen, or Uncle George as he was fondly called by the Roseland children, worked at Red Deer in the coal mines, only a few hours away from Okotoks. He died at Red Deer, in 1963, at the age of eighty-one. Like Olav, Uncle George never married. But he kept in touch with Anna, and always came for family events such as weddings and funerals.

Anna's world now was her family and friends in Okotoks. The Jacobsens, with whom she shared her Norwegian heritage, sometimes took Anna for a drive to Calgary, and they visited her regularly at her home. Anna was fortunate to have electricity and had been given a console radio as a gift. The Camerons next door did not have electricity, so the family had to share a headset from a crystal radio. This was awkward and not much fun, so sometimes the two families all gathered around the Roseland radio to listen to special programs. Years later, next-door neighbour Ralph Cameron remembered an exciting evening listening to a Joe Lewis boxing match there, on the rare occasion that the fight went for fifteen rounds, and was won only by the decision of a referee. Anna became an enthusiastic fan of *Hockey Night in Canada*, the NHL hockey games on Saturday evening that commenced on Canadian radio in the early '30s. Her eyes would sparkle, and she smiled broadly when she mimicked Foster Hewitt announcing in the game, "He shoots! He scores!!"

■ ■ ■

In 1936, after Lew lost his job when the refinery closed at Coutts, Faye and Lew moved back to Okotoks to live with Anna. From there Lew could commute to Calgary to look for work. Their first child, a son, was over a year old, and he loved the attention he got from eight-year-old Ralph Cameron next door. Arnold was still working at Wilson's Garage and Ernest was at Waldron's. Arnold also found other odd jobs. The house was full with a family of seven. In the spring of 1937, when Faye was due to have her second child, the three brothers went out to Trail to look for work, as they could stay there with either Gudrun or Agnes. Anna delivered her seventh grandchild, a second son for Faye and Lew, in May 1937. While in Trail in 1937, the brothers became acquainted with friends of Gudrun and Agnes and their husbands. They also found a little work and took part in social events in the area.

■ ■ ■

Tragedy struck the family again in 1937, at Trail, when twenty-nine-year-old Gudrun and seventeen-year-old Erling were both diagnosed with tuberculosis. They were admitted to the sanatorium at Tranquille, near Kamloops, B.C. Unhappily, Gudrun was separated from her two daughters, aged five and seven. After Gudrun's hospitalization, the girls spent time between Trail and North Vancouver, where their father's parents now lived. Although Kamloops was serviced east-west by both national railways, travel between Trail and

Kamloops was by a circuitous and time-consuming route. Francis did visit Gudrun at Tranquille, and on one occasion brought with him their eldest daughter. One consolation for Gudrun and Erling was that they could visit each other in the hospital on occasion.

Donna and Frances 1936 (Gudrun and Francis' daughters)

Francis and Gudrun at Tranquille, B.C. 1937

■ ■ ■

In the dry, desert-like valley of the North Thompson River, Tranquille was located eight miles west of Kamloops. The sanatorium was located on an extensive property on the north side of the valley, where it overlooked Lake Kamloops, a widening of the river. The location gave the property maximum southern exposure to the sun, and the mountains behind the institution protected the property from north winds. Despite fear and protests from Kamloops residents, the sanatorium was developed in 1907, when TB was the leading cause of death in British Columbia. The provincial government assumed the administration following the First World War. An elaborate irrigation system had been developed on the property, which allowed production of most of the produce and meat required, so the sanatorium was largely self-supporting. By the 1930s, the buildings were surrounded by beautiful park-like grounds.

In April 1938, Erling wrote to Agnes, *"It is sure lovely here right now. The flowers are all starting to bloom, trees and grass are all green and boy! The weather is lovely. If a person could be out walking around now, it would be nice. I should be out walking before the summer is over, I think."* He had been going over to visit Gudrun but fluid developed in his lungs and he had been put on bed rest. In January, the doctor told him he was over the critical stage and there was little danger of complications. *"Then three weeks ago fluid formed, so you can see that it is hard for them to state anything definite. However, staying here a year or longer doesn't worry me as time sure flies."*

Patients were entertained with a wide range of activities. Hallowe'en and Christmas parties were special occasions, in addition to the regular social programs. Movies were presented weekly and ambulatory patients gathered to listen to radio dramas. *The Tranquillian* was published regularly to keep patients amused and informed. As well, church and service clubs from Kamloops took patients for drives and picnics, and brought entertainment to the institution.

One difficulty for Erling when he was confined to bed was that he could no longer visit Gudrun, but they did get messages back and forth to each other. Gudrun was feeling better, although she was still "*. . . darn sick. She has certainly had tough luck since she came here. She would have been better off if they had never tried to give her pneumo to collapse her lung.*" Complications had developed with her pneumo treatment.

Faye and Lew were still with Anna at Okotoks. Faye wrote regularly to Erling. Lew still hadn't found work. Arnold had been hospitalized in Calgary with a sore throat, so he hadn't been working. Ernest had not had much work either, so he thought they were having a pretty tough time.

Erling was looking forward to a visit from Magnhild. Magnhild and Paul were taking their holidays and driving to Jasper, and from there Magnhild planned to take the train to Kamloops. Faye reported that Anna was looking very well and hadn't aged much at all, although now, at age sixty, her hair had started to turn grey: "*. . . a little salt and* *pepper.*" Because of the cost of travel, Anna was unable to visit her children at the San.

Erling had become a keen hockey fan. He had followed hockey in Okotoks and attended a few games in Trail, where hockey was strongly supported by the community. He wrote, "*I suppose they made a big fuss over the Smoke Eaters when they arrived back in Trail. They sure must be some team. We listened to all the games on the radio. One of the fellows I'm in with right now has his own radio, so it made it pretty nice.*" In the spring of 1938, the Trail Smoke Eaters won the national senior trophy, the Allen Cup. The next season they would travel to Europe, where they lost only one game and won the World Championship.

Gudrun did not recover from the complications of her pneumo treatment. Just two weeks after Erling wrote his letter, in May 1938, Gudrun died. When the telegram arrived announcing Gudrun's death, Faye was shattered. She and Gudrun had been close, went to social events together, slept together and shared all their secrets. In her grief, Faye went to bed. It was her youngest son's first birthday on the 16th of May, but she could barely get herself up. And it was raining. When Faye said she had no raincoat to wear to the funeral, Francis, who had just arrived, went to a shop in town and purchased one for her. Then, on the evening of the 18th, Agnes arrived accompanying the body.

Gudrun's funeral happened to be on Faye's twenty-eighth birthday. For her birthday, Mrs. Jacobsen made an angel-food cake and some cookies. She brought these over before the funeral, ready to serve at the family gathering after the funeral at 2:30 p.m. Anna had written the obituary describing Gudrun as a " . . . very sweet and love-able girl . . . quietly laid to rest beside her father." In addition to grieving for Gudrun, the family was concerned for the welfare of her two little girls. The girls spent a little time with Anna, with Agnes in Trail, and also with their father's parents in North Vancouver. They spent most of their school years in Trail.

After the funeral, when everyone from out of town had returned to their homes, Faye discovered that the raincoat that Francis had "purchased" for her had been charged to the family account at the store in Okotoks. As Lew was still not working, they could not afford an extra expense, but they had no choice but to pay for it. Francis had borrowed money from his parents and the family understood that he was paying the account for the funeral. However, the funeral home later sought payment from the family in Okotoks. Some time later, when Lew was working again, Faye and Lew paid the funeral account. Their grief was compounded by unpleasantness related to finances. Francis always enjoyed the socializing, but he never paid his way. This would later be the source of many problems when he failed to take financial responsibility for the care of his daughters.

■ ■ ■

The tuberculosis problem was always a mystery to the family, and after the death of Hildur, a source of great fear and worry. Faye reported that they were all "scared stiff." Anna believed that Gudrun may have contracted the disease from the lady that she boarded with while attending high school in Youngstown, as the lady was sickly. On the other hand, it is possible that the original contact was with one of the cases in Okotoks. In spite of her extensive contact with tuberculosis when she was young, and contact with her children, Anna never contracted the disease. Family members in Okotoks had skin tests and X-rays arranged through the local health unit to make certain that none of them had the disease. Faye remembered having many tests done before being told that she required no further testing. But, if Gudrun and Erling contracted the disease from Hildur, or at the same time, it is a mystery why their cases were not diagnosed earlier. However, this was an era when health units and diagnostic facilities were just becoming established, and the necessary testing may not have been adequately performed. Or, a cold or a bad case of "flu" could cause an early, undiagnosed case of tuberculosis to progress rapidly, and perhaps that is the reason that Erling and Gudrun were diagnosed at the same time. The sources of tuberculosis infection in the family would never be known.

Anna was very aware of the importance of good hygiene in the prevention of tuberculosis and she was a clean housekeeper. This may have been a factor in others in the family remaining free of the disease. An incident in 1916, before Olav and Albert left their homesteads, indicates the family's attitudes. Anna had made a pot of soup and young Magnhild was serving soup to Olav. The soup was hot, so she unthinkingly blew on it. Olav became distressed and said, "You might as well have spit in it!"

■ ■ ■

By 1935, across Canada, the economy had begun a slow recovery from the depths of the Depression, but the prairie west was yet to experience the extremes of the drought. Hot, dry winds whipped across the prairies in the summer, followed by fierce cold and blizzards in the winter of 1935-36. The summer that followed was again hot, with record-breaking temperatures. By 1937, the winds blew away the topsoil, which drifted and reshaped the landscape, covered fences and banked up against buildings. In some places roads were covered and impassable. Lakes dried up. Black clouds of grasshoppers devoured everything green that found its way out of the ground. Then, late in 1937, after the growing season had ended, the rains came. When the dreaded Russian thistle grew in the spring, the farmers cut it and fed it to their starving cattle. In 1938, the prairies were lavished with adequate rain and the land began a slow recovery from the drought.

After their election in 1935, the Social Credit government of Alberta had established a resettlement program and gave incentives to farmers from the dry region to relocate. Many joined the ranks of the jobless in the cities and others went north, farming or pioneering in the northern woods. In southeast Alberta, 5,000 farmers abandoned their farms. The small towns that had served the farming population dwindled in size, abandoned by merchants and other service people. In 1935, the federal government had established the Prairie Farm Rehabilitation Authority, which would provide leadership in projects that were of great benefit to agriculture in the region. But those benefits did not appear until a few years into the future.

In 1938, soon after Gudrun's death, Lew was hired by British-American Oil Company in Calgary, and Faye and Lew and the children left Okotoks for Calgary. Arnold and Ernest both remained at home to help Anna financially. By this time, the brothers were well known to employers in Okotoks, and they took whatever jobs they could get. Arnold was now twenty-three years old, and Ernest was twenty-one. Nineteen-year-old Erling was still in the sanatorium at Tranquille. Anna was deeply concerned for him and appreciated having Arnold and Ernest for companionship during her period of grief and worry. More work was available in 1938, and the local economy started to improve.

■ ■ ■

In the spring of 1939, as Western Canada was beginning to feel the effects of the economic recovery, Canada celebrated the first official visit of King George VI and Queen Elizabeth. Prime Minister Mackenzie King accompanied the royals across Canada on their train tour, and shared the spotlight in all activities. The Royal Tour visited Calgary and Edmonton in late May 1939. The mood was jubilant and celebratory.

The purpose of the tour was twofold. The King and Queen, newly crowned in 1937, wished to become acquainted with the subjects of one of the largest Dominions in the Empire. The other purpose was more sinister. Fearing that another European war was forthcoming, the British wished to cement the bonds of affection in Canada that tied them to the Empire. Hitler had been increasingly flexing the might of Germany in the late '30s. In March 1938, Germany annexed Austria. In 1939, Germany dismembered Czechoslovakia. Great Britain and France were becoming increasingly concerned that their policy of "appeasement" to Germany would not prevent war.

In 1939, following the visit of the King and Queen, Soviet Russia and Nazi Germany signed a mutual non-aggression pact, with a secret clause agreeing to the division of Poland. On September 1, 1939, Germany invaded Poland. Two days later, Great Britain and France declared war on Germany. On the 10th of September, King George VI declared a state of war between Canada and the Third Reich. After only twenty-one years of peace, Canadians would again participate in another European war.

PART FIVE
"I Hope the Lord Will Protect Them"
(Second World War, 1940-45)

Chapter 15
"It makes you just itch to get over there"

ON DECEMBER 17, 1939, Prime Minister Mackenzie King announced to Canadians, by radio, the formation of the British Commonwealth Air Training Program (BCATP). In the late 1930s, when war with Germany appeared imminent, Great Britain realized that her weakest line of defence against Germany was in the air. She had recognized an urgent need to train more air crew, and the need to relieve pressure on the limited air space and crowded skies over Great Britain. The decision had been made, in the fall of 1939, to locate the program in Canada and to commence preparations immediately.

Once the program was announced, thousands of young men rushed to recruitment centres to join the Royal Canadian Air Force (RCAF). During the '30s, the futures for many young men had seemed bleak, but the air training program brought the opportunity for training and travel, and above all, the opportunity to learn to fly. In January 1940, Arnold Roseland kept his appointment at the recruitment centre in Calgary, where he had the first of several in-depth assessments by Air Force personnel. Physically, he was rated a "first class risk," and personally rated as an officer type, suitable for commission. However, there was still a massive amount of work to be done in Canada to

293

establish the training schools, before training could begin. Along with thousands of others, Arnold was placed on a reserve list to be called up later.

Prime Minister Mackenzie King announced that the BCATP would "... establish Canada as the site of one of the greatest air training programs of the world." By late January 1940, the Department of Transport (DOT) had selected sites for 120 training schools, and for eighty new landing fields. Other existing landing fields would require upgrading. Infrastructure needed on the sites included hangers, offices, education facilities and barracks. Training aircraft were also required, along with parts and other supplies. The RCAF and DOT also faced the monumental task of finding qualified staff with the wide range of specialized skills necessary to operate the schools—in particular, finding qualified instructors. To do so, the RCAF tapped into civilian resources, such as trained civilian pilots and private airfields. The planning and organization for the program was a massive undertaking.

■ ■ ■

The first winter of the war, up to the spring of 1940, was known as the "Phoney War." German and French armies had made no advances against each other over the winter. On the 9th of April, Germany invaded Norway and Denmark, followed by Belgium, Luxembourg, Holland and France. The German army forced the withdrawal of 338,000 French, Belgium and British troops from France to Great Britain at the end of May, at the Battle of Dunkirk. The British government then recognized

General Charles de Gaulle as leader of a French government-in-exile, in Great Britain. The southern portion of France had surrendered to the Germans. In early July 1940, the German air force commenced its devastating aerial assault of Great Britain, known as the Battle of Britain. The whole world was shocked by rapid advances of the German military machines.

■ ■ ■

Arnold Roseland was twenty-four years old in June 1940 when he was called up for active duty with the RCAF. On July 2, 1940, Arnold reported to Manning Pool in Toronto.

Manning Pool had been hastily set up in the Canadian National Exhibition grounds, where all existing facilities were being used, including bull pens converted into living quarters. He had entered a world of line-ups and rigorous testing—medicals, needles, interviews and marches. At the end of a month the recruits were designated to the line of work they would initially follow. Most wanted to be pilots. Arnold was selected for air crew and proceeded a few miles down the road to Initial Training School (ITS) at the Eglinton Hunt Club.

"The Eglinton Hunt Club is a very nice place, much better than at Manning Pool . . . . We eat off china and have waiters. You would hardly think we were in the army. We have a lot of extras on our menus, such as catsup, sauces, etc." Arnold reported that they were studying hard. He had joined up to become a pilot, but he was facing rigid screening procedures. He had many qualifications to pass before being

accepted, including an altitude test, which many failed. He passed his exams with good marks, and was evaluated as "good commission material—splendid type." Just as he had hoped, he was selected for pilot training.

Arnold remained in Toronto until the new Elementary Training School at Cap-de-la-Madeleine in Quebec was ready for its first class of students. While in Toronto, he attended a social reception at "Little Norway." When the Germans occupied Norway, many young Norwegians fled in open boats over the North Sea and found their way to Canada. The Norwegian government-in-exile purchased land at the foot of Bathurst Street in Toronto and set up a flying training school, known as Little Norway, to train these young men as pilots. The Norwegians were very popular on the social scene in Toronto and attracted large numbers to their socials. At one of these socials, Arnold met an attractive young brunette recently returned from New York. Both were from a rural setting, and both were from a family of eight. While Arnold was somewhat reserved, Audrey was mischievous and fun-loving, and he delighted in her company. He left for Elementary Flying Training School (EFTS) in mid-October, but was determined to maintain contact with this stunning young woman.

■ ■ ■

After more than three years at the sanatorium at Tranquille, twenty-one-year-old Erling wrote that in her letters Anna seemed to be quite happy, although she missed Arnold an awful lot at first. She was get-

ting only a $15 monthly allowance from the govern-
ment for herself, and Arnold was sending her half his
pay. She intended to put Arnold's money in the bank
for him for when he returned. Erling hoped to get
out of the San before Arnold went overseas, but did-
n't know if that would happen. *"I would try to get out
right away if I was able to work, but can't as long as I am
taking pneumo. I will never be able to do any heavy work
again, anyway. One of the biggest problems is finding
something suitable to do. It sure has me stumped."*

■ ■ ■

At EFTS, Arnold began the actual business of
learning to fly. Quebec Airways operated the No. 11
School at Cap-de-la-Madeleine, east of Quebec
City. The civilian schools were usually smaller,
more informal and well supported by local communities. The RCAF, however, set the curriculum and
provided some of the instructors.

Their training aircraft at Cap-de-la-
Madeleine was the Fleet Finch, a biplane with a
wingspan of 28 feet and a 125 hp motor. Like all
training aircraft, it was painted bright yellow. This
frail-looking structure had two cockpits with a slid-
ing canopy and a cruising speed of about 85 mph,
but it was exceptionally responsive and pleasant to
fly. Novice pilots began with an instructor behind
them in the cockpit, and graduated eight weeks
later with formation flying. Upon completion of this
course, they had learned to fly by relying solely on
the data they observed on rudimentary instruments,
rather than flying by visual observations and their
instinctive "feel of the plane."

They were being pushed hard and put in long days. The weather was bad, which made flying strenuous. Because they kept their schedule free in the daytime to get in as much flying time as possible, classes were held in the evening. The coming exams had everyone worried. *"They wash us pilots out if we fail even one ground subject."* They had their flying test after fifty hours in the air, and had to be able to do all elementary flying tests *"almost perfect."*

"Don't breathe a word of this to Mother— she would positively worry herself sick . . . . I cracked up my first ship after two hours solo." He was practising a forced landing, descending from 4,000 feet into a little farmer's field, when his motor conked out. He started to spin, then got straightened out—but it was too late, and the aircraft dove into the ground at about 45 degrees, at 75 miles per hour. He went end-over-end a few times, and then walked away without a scratch. There was a court of enquiry about it, but he was absolved of all blame. *"I went up and practised forced landings in the same field the next day, much to the surprise of some of the other boys. However, it did teach me a lesson, i.e., be very careful close to the ground."*

Arnold wrote that just before exams, he cut a wisdom tooth and his cheek abscessed quite badly. He wrote his exams and then reported to the medical officer, who put him in the hospital and lanced the abscess.

"I have been classified as a fighter pilot, just what I wanted. I was afraid for a while that due to the fact that they usually prefer real young fellows as fighters, that I would be classified as a bomber." Most fighter pilots

Arnold's crash in a Fleet Finch, November 1940

were four to five years younger than Arnold. He wrote that the officer who tested the class said Arnold had done very well in aerobatics.

As the BCATP expanded, there was a great need for more instructors, and frequently instructors' positions were offered to the top students in each class. Arnold wrote that he declined the offer for instructor's training, as he wished to further his pilot training. He added that he had been recommended for a promotion to Pilot Officer.

He added a note at the end of his letter. *"By the way, Aggie, another fellow and I, each in a shift, went to Quebec the other day. On seeing the Quebec bridge, we flew under and then proceeded to loop around it. As luck would have it, some squadron leader was on the bridge, reported us and we were called up by the C.O. yesterday. Everything is okay."* This was a very serious offence for a training pilot. Perhaps Arnold was lucky he was in a civilian training school with tolerant supervisors, or the course of his pilot training could have taken a sharp curve in another direction.

■ ■ ■

Arnold was posted to the next level of training at Service Flying Training School (SFTS) No. 2, at Uplands, near Ottawa. This was a larger and more formal setting with stricter discipline. More advanced training included night flying, emergency procedures, reconnaissance missions and simulated bombing runs. The students were allowed more leeway in their flying practice, to increase their skill in flying manoeuvres. But strict regulations forbade unsafe procedures, such as low-altitude flying and participation in "dogfights." Arnold wrote in January 1940, *"Two fellows were killed yesterday morning from getting reckless and diving fast enough to take the wings off."* Sometimes the skill of young pilots didn't match their daring, or the capabilities of the machine.

Their learning machine at SFTS was the Harvard, one of the outstanding training aircraft of the Second World War. The complex instrument panel was similar to that of most fighter planes,

Arnold after he received his "Wings," February 1941

preparing pilots to fly the more advanced fighter aircraft. The Harvard had a 42-foot wingspan, a 600 hp engine and a cruising speed of 140 mph. It was a sensitive machine that could be tricky to handle, especially on landing. Arnold wrote, *"In a Harvard there is nothing that can't be done!"*

He was glad he had turned down the instructor's job, because the Air Force had spent another $10,000 on his training since then. He thought it was a wonderful course, but it would be a relief when it was finished. *"After all, we are trained for a definite purpose, and that is what we are looking forward to. I don't know what it is about this training, but it does something to you. It just makes you itch to get over there."* He was looking forward to getting his "wings" in another four to five weeks.

In February 1940, the weather had been nasty and freakish: winds, snow and icy runways. On the day Arnold was to receive his wings at a "Wings Parade," he was on a navigation trip, and got caught in a snowstorm near Kingston. He landed there and waited out the storm, missing the ceremony, so he had his own personal little parade the following morning.

Meanwhile, Magnhild wrote to Erling's doctor at the San, asking if there was any chance that Erling could be discharged home in time to see Arnold, before he went overseas.

■ ■ ■

Arnold was posted next to No. 1 Flying Instructors' School at Trenton. Teaching involved long hours sharing the cockpit of a learning aircraft with a beginning pilot, and repeating the same lessons for days and weeks on end. Arnold had other aspirations, and he wasn't happy instructing. He had been studying a training manual that taught them to co-ordinate each sequence of flying. They had to memorize the manual, which was quite boring. He had flown a twin motor a few days previously and did get a bit of a thrill out of that, but they were even easier to fly than a Harvard. *"I hope I do not get stuck in a twin school to instruct. About all you ever do with them is fly straight and level. It is a real safe job instructing on them, but it isn't exactly the type of flying I prefer."*

A friend had come back from Toronto with a newspaper featuring photos of Arnold and two friends, side by side. *"We have palled around ever since we started. We were grimy and sweaty and had just come in off a drill. Why we were picked for the pictures, I don't know. Perhaps, because the three of us were more or less screwballs, and all granted commissions."*

He had received a letter from Erling recently, who mentioned a new $8-million plant in Trail. The CM&S Company in Trail was constructing a new plant that would ultimately provide the heavy water for the atomic bomb. Contrary to conditions in the '30s, there was now an extreme labour shortage. Arnold thought he could probably get a job there now, but he wouldn't make the money he was making in the Air Force. He was making $6.25 a day, soon to be increased to $8.00 a day, for every day of the month.)

■ ■ ■

To Anna's great joy, the day after her sixty-third birthday, twenty-one-year-old Erling arrived home to Okotoks after four years in the sanatorium. But Erling would have to continue attending the tuberculosis clinic in Calgary for pneumo treatments. Anna rented two rooms on 12th Avenue West so that Erling would be closer to the TB clinic. The Jacobsens and other friends in Okotoks had several farewell parties for Anna, and presented her with gifts before she left for her new home in Calgary. The Jacobsens continued to visit with Anna in Calgary, and maintained their friendship.

Just a few months earlier, in October 1940, Anna had sent a request through the Canadian Red Cross seeking information about her sister Elizabeth in Norway. Anna had heard nothing from her relatives in Norway since the German invasion the previous spring. Anna named two persons who could be contacted for information: Gustav's brother Olav at Rosseland, and Arnt Stensvand at Arendal, who was Gustav's uncle by marriage. Stensvand was now almost 100 years old and had been retired for twenty-one years, after a sixty-year career as a teacher and school administrator. The Red Cross in Norway made contact with Anna's sister Elizabeth. Her husband Knut had died suddenly of a heart attack the previous April, the day that the Germans invaded Norway. The rest of the family were well, and she thanked Anna for her note.

In May 1941, just after Anna and Erling settled in their new home at Calgary, Arnold sent Anna a Mother's Day telegram. *"More than ever, now that*

*we are separated by many miles, I appreciate how good
and dear my Mother is. All my love, Arnold"*

■ ■ ■

Arnold also made a move in May 1941. He had two
flying tests at Trenton, which should have qualified
him as an instructor. His report found him unsuit-
able instructor material. His flying was rough and
inaccurate and various tests yielded poor results.
However, they found him very keen and recommended him as a service pilot or staff pilot at a
bombing and gunnery school. This was the only
negative report Arnold was given, so it appears that
he blew his exams deliberately in order to avoid
instructing. The recourse for a deliberate failure
was posting to a mundane position. Arnold reported
to the Bombing and Gunnery School No. 3 at
Macdonald, Manitoba, on May 13, 1941.

■ ■ ■

Arnold's life brightened considerably in June when
he travelled to Toronto with another officer from
the base. Arnold and Audrey acted as witnesses for
the wedding of Arnold's friend. Then, the following
day, the newly married couple returned the favour
and witnessed Arnold and Audrey's marriage.
Arnold promised a photo that had been taken the
evening before their wedding. The two couples
returned to the base at Macdonald immediately
after the weddings.

■ ■ ■

In the summer of 1941, the families from Alberta
drove out to Trail for a reunion, bringing with them
Anna, Erling and Ernest for a few days of happy vis-

Family picnic at Kootenay Lake, B.C. 1941. Back row, left to right: Ernest, Paul, Erling, Lew, Bill. Middle row: Thelma, Magnhild, Faye, Agnes, Anna and friend. Third row: Donald, Frances, Shirley, Marion, Jim and Ted. Front row: Duane, Ken, friend and friend.

iting. Family picnics were common in the era, and the Roseland family took numerous photographs on their family picnic at Kootenay Lake. Erling, a tall, lean, and handsome Nordic, was smiling in every photo.

Later that summer, while on leave, Arnold took Audrey back to Calgary to meet Anna and the rest of the family who lived in Calgary. Erling and Arnold did have their long-awaited visit. Later, Audrey wrote, *"We really had a marvellous vacation. Your mother is so sweet and loveable, and that goes for the whole family. They made me feel so at home."* Arnold was hoping for an Alberta posting but they weren't too hopeful. Arnold wrote that he had a grand trip home. *"But there aren't many of the old gang left around there."*

Arnold and Audrey were living on the base at Macdonald, but in the early fall they found two beautifully furnished rooms in a private house in town. *"It is really lovely and the folks are grand. We cook and eat together and get along swell."* He had bragged about Agnes' Italian spaghetti and asked her for her recipe—enough for six to eight.

Arnold had started with night bombing practice, so he was now flying mainly from 6 p.m. to midnight. He was taking student observers out for night bombing exercises. The previous night they had dropped twelve bombs.

Audrey had been busy knitting, and had been remarkably well, with never a sick day. He expected to be working on Christmas Day, but he had five days off at New Year's. They were planning to spend a quiet time at home.

■ ■ ■

On December 7, 1941, the Japanese bombed the American base at Pearl Harbour, a devastating attack that changed the course of the war. The following day the Japanese army invaded Hong Kong, and during the month of December attacked Singapore, the Philippines, Wake Island, Guam, Thailand, Shanghai and Midway. The surprise attack by the Japanese on Hong Kong ended tragically, on December 25, 1941, for the newly arrived Canadian troops. Seventeen hundred either died or were taken prisoner by the Japanese and forced to work as labourers in dreadful conditions, under which many more succumbed. Immediately after the attack on Pearl Harbour, Great Britain and the United States declared war on Japan. China declared war on Japan, Germany and Italy.

■ ■ ■

A few days after the United States declared war on Japan, Germany declared war on the United States. In December 1941, the reluctant and neutral Americans were brought into the war on both the European and Pacific fronts. By 1942, the major powers of the world were bound in a network of complex alliances that defined the combatants of the Second World War, namely the Allied and the Axis powers.

Chapter 16
"Nothing but rain, rain, rain"

ARNOLD AND AUDREY'S PLANS for Christmas and New Year's were changed with the outbreak of war in the Pacific. Arnold reported to Rockcliffe, near Ottawa, on Jan. 1, 1942 for the formation of Number 14 Fighter Squadron (F).

Squadron Leader (S/L) Dal Russel, a veteran of the Battle of Britain, was sent home to Canada to lead the newly formed fighter squadron. Russel had been one of the first three Canadian officers to receive the DFC in the Second World War, and he had just completed a tour of duty in the European theatre. His task now was to train the pilots of No. 14(F) in the Kittyhawk MkII. The aircraft was manufactured in the United States, where it was known as the Curtiss P-40. Arnold wrote that they were about the same speed as a Spitfire and a little faster than a Hurricane, with a top speed of about 400 m.p.h. *"It is nice to get into something hot, after this long time. I like the squadron fine. It is what I have wanted all this time."* The top speed of the Kittyhawk was actually 360 mph.

■ ■ ■

"Congratulations are in order! It's a boy!" Arnold wrote in February 1942. When he got word that Audrey was in labour, *"I did manage to get there in time, even though I did have to catch a train in twenty minutes and leave AWOL (absent without leave).*

Everything did turn out okay though." After travelling 2,000 miles by train between Christmas and New Year's, Arnold had left Audrey in Toronto with friends for the last month of her pregnancy. She had a hard labour, which the doctor attributed to fatigue from all the travel. But mother and baby were doing well, as was the new father.

■ ■ ■

In March, the squadron was posted to Sea Island near Vancouver, a trip that took three weeks. They had stopovers at Toronto, Detroit, Chicago, Milwaukee, St. Paul, Winnipeg, Regina and Lethbridge. Arnold managed to arrange an overnight flight for Audrey, to avoid a four-night trip on the train with the baby. He took a one-week leave and flew back to Calgary to meet her. *"We had a very pleasant and quiet visit."* Erling was now driving a cab on a part-time basis. Ernest had just joined the Canadian army, where he was taking courses to become a motor mechanic. Anna lived close enough to visit Faye regularly, and she still saw her friends in Okotoks.

Ernest 1942

■ ■ ■

Upon their return to Vancouver in late April, Arnold and Audrey took up temporary residence at the Sylvia Court Hotel on English Bay. Housing was scarce, but they soon found a suite in a home on Dunbar Street, near the waterfront in Point Grey. The population of Vancouver had ballooned after the Japanese attack on Pearl Harbour. The military presence had increased dramatically, and American and Canadian construction workers moved to the West Coast to work on the upgrading of defence infrastructure.

After Pearl Harbour, the Japanese had advanced throughout the Pacific with breath-taking speed. Within weeks they had advanced as far south as New Guinea, just north of Australia. Their rapid advance made their victories seem even more dramatic. They were known as brutal victors. Tales of Japanese brutality in China in the late '30s were seared into the memory of Canadians, leaving them deeply shocked when Hong Kong fell and 1,700 Canadians were killed or taken prisoner. The thought of going to war with the Japanese was abhorrent.

On the west coast of British Columbia lived 23,000 Japanese-Canadians. Although they had suffered discrimination over the years, they had lived peacefully and contributed to the Canadian economy. Many Japanese men owned fishing boats and travelled coastal waters. Some owned radios, and the fear was that, among the Japanese fishermen, there might be spies. The other fear was that there might be some among them prepared to sabotage such critical structures as railway bridges and harbours.

Following the attack on Pearl Harbour, the Canadian government seized Japanese homes and fishing boats, and swiftly started an evacuation program to remove their owners and families from coastal areas. The government offered these Japanese-owned homes and fishing boats for sale to the general public. While awaiting transfer to internment camps, the families were detained at the Pacific National Exhibition grounds in Vancouver. Such facilities were commonly transformed into living quarters in Canada during the Second World War. The Japanese were sent to internment camps scattered in remote mountainous country in the west and on the prairies.

After Japan invaded China in 1937, the United States and western countries had growing fears of Japanese aggression. When the United States placed an oil embargo on Japan in 1940, the Japanese were dismayed. With a growing mutual concern for the aggression of both the Japanese and the Germans, President Franklin D. Roosevelt and Prime Minister Mackenzie King had signed a plan for the joint defence of North America. After Pearl Harbour, the Permanent Board of Joint Defence came into operation, based on the agreement that laid the groundwork for co-operation between the two countries.

■ ■ ■

In March 1942, fear of Japanese invasion reached near hysterical heights. *The Vancouver Sun* ran a series of inflammatory front-page editorials, condemning Canadian military and political leaders for their lack of initiative in planning for West Coast defence. The first editorial, on March 13, accused the politicians and military in Canada of inertia "almost beyond belief," and of hiding behind a screen of censorship and propaganda. The newspaper accused the politicians and military of having prepared no defence against the Japanese. But military and political leaders, including the Allied Supreme Command, did not believe the Japanese capable of invading North America.

The second editorial was headed "Total Defence Means Total Determination." The editorial advocated that citizens should be determined to die and to wreck their homes, towns and cities rather than surrender to the Japanese. They should "make the enemy pay in lives, hardship and starvation for every foot he advances." Shortly after came another editorial in which was stated, "The *Vancouver Sun*'s recent analysis of preparations has caused a good deal of discussion in Ottawa, and in certain quarters this newspaper has been condemned for alarming the public . . . "

Bias in the press and reports of the treatment of Canadian prisoners of war heightened emotions on the West Coast. In May, the *Sun* reported that the Japanese were employing Canadian and Chinese prisoners of war in the docks at Hong Kong, where damaged Japanese ships were being repaired. The same day, the *Toronto Star* noted that Canadian prisoners and Chinese labourers were

employed by the Japanese in the construction of
Kai Tak airdrome. Indignation at the treatment of
Canadian war prisoners served to escalate racial dis-
crimination against Japanese-Canadians.

In May, another *Vancouver Sun* headline
reported the "Japs Plan to Fight Real Estate Sales."
A *Sun* editorial followed: " . . . It is nothing short of
shocking to witness the continued activity of
Japanese in this province trying to thwart the proper
and well-considered designs of authorities regarding their affairs and properties . . . . These examples
of Japanese effrontery are pretty hard to explain.
Perhaps not so hard, in view of some of the despica-
ble occurrences recently in Tokyo. They have gall
enough for anything."

In June the *Sun* reported that "all but 325 of
the 1,250 Jap fishing boats impounded at the outbreak of war in the Pacific have been sold to
fisherman of other nationalities, to fishing companies, or turned over to the army, navy or air force . . ."

Later, a *Sun* editorial commented, "Mean-
time, for the benefit of all concerned, the *Sun* is glad
to record the fact that British Columbia is getting
along very well without Japanese assistance or inter-
ference or domination in certain industrial fields."

■ ■ ■

American defence of its Aleutian Islands near
Alaska required transit through northwest Canada
and Canadian coastal waters. In 1942, Canadians
granted the United States the right to construct a
highway through Canadian territory to Alaska, with
an agreement that it would revert to Canadian own-

ership after the war ended. Canada had commenced work in 1935 on a string of airstrips from Edmonton to Alaska, and in 1942 granted the Americans the right to upgrade them to their standards. Ultimately, the most important route to Alaska during the war proved to be the rail-sea route via the Canadian National Railway to Prince Rupert, where the port facilities were also upgraded by the Americans. The Canadian government designated Prince Rupert a "port of embarkation" for the Americans to facilitate their transit through the port. The Alaska Highway was pushed through wilderness country at an amazing rate between the spring and fall of 1942, and the staging route of airstrips was upgraded during the same period.

The number of Americans working in the Canadian Northwest increased rapidly after Pearl Harbour. By December 1942, there were 15,000 Americans working in the Pacific Northwest, and six months later, in June 1943, there were 33,000. This was of great concern to the Canadian government, which feared that Canada would lose sovereignty over her lands when Americans claimed a vested interest in the developments after the war. To the credit of both countries, a great deal was accomplished and relations remained co-operative.

■ ■ ■

In the late spring of 1942, the war in Europe was at its lowest point. Most of Europe was under occupation by Germany and Italy. Several eastern European countries declared war on Russia, while Russia and Great Britain signed a non-aggression pact. German and Italian armies invaded Greece, Yugoslavia, Egypt and other North African countries. The German army moved relentlessly deep into the heart of Russia. The rapid enemy advances in the world war were shocking to Canadians, with memories of the First World War still fresh in their minds. This gave rise to a general feeling of fear and disbelief that such a tragedy might happen again, this time with the Japanese bringing war to Canadian territory.

All across Canada, homes were hushed each evening as a young Lorne Greene delivered the latest war news on CBC Radio. His deep, baritone voice became familiar to all Canadians and earned him the title of the "Voice of Doom." From overseas, Matthew Halton delivered radio reports from the front lines, complete with booming explosions, whistling shells and chattering machine guns. The immediacy of radio news reports ushered in a new era for listeners, many of whom had come to own their first radio within the past ten years.

■ ■ ■

Once settled in Vancouver, the pilots of No. 14 Fighter Squadron rotated on "forty-eight-hour readiness," and continued their training in the Kittyhawk. Pilots were kept on standby, prepared to investigate any sightings of Japanese ships or aircrafts in the coastal region. Practice in the Kittyhawk included flying to the 27,000-foot level with oxygen, air-to-air firing practice and wing formation flying.

In mid-May 1942, the United States intercepted a coded Japanese message revealing a planned attack on Midway Island in the Pacific and on Dutch Harbour, the American air base under construction in the Aleutian Islands. Because the Americans had been at war for only six months, they had a limited number of experienced pilots. The American government made an urgent appeal to Canada for aerial assistance in Alaska, for the anticipated bombing of Dutch Harbour. In response, West Coast Command sent several RCAF squadrons to American air bases, including Annette Island near Prince Rupert and various air bases in Alaska. No. 111(F) advanced to Alaska, while No. 14(F) remained at Vancouver on West Coast defence.

The Japanese first bombed Dutch Harbour on June 3-4 as a diversion, and then attacked Midway on June 3-7. The American forces won a decisive victory at Midway, a victory that proved to be a turning point in the war in the Pacific. Following their defeat at Midway, the Japanese occupied two of the most westerly of the American Aleutian Islands. In order to save face with the Japanese public, their occupation forces established bases on Kiska and Attu, only 650 miles northwest of Japan. The alarmed Canadian and American public feared that the Japanese might use these islands as a base from which they could attack the west coast of North America.

On June 7, 1942, a Japanese submarine torpedoed and sank an American merchant ship, SS *Coast Trader*, at the southwest entrance to the Straits of Juan de Fuca. In the early hours of the 20th of June, a Japanese submarine torpedoed and badly damaged the British SS *Fort Camosun*, and later that night shelled the lighthouse and radio station at Estevan Point, on the west coast of Vancouver Island. Although there were no further incidents of this type during the war, these events inflamed suspicions and fears.

■ ■ ■

"The weather has been horrible here, nothing but rain, rain, rain," Audrey wrote to Agnes in July. *"But, regardless of the rain, we are having a very gay time here in Vancouver—partying, dancing and so on. It has been very exciting. But, oh boy, one gets rather tired after three or four nights of outing."* Audrey lit up a room when she entered, with her engaging and sparkling smile, and her devilish and fun-loving personality. She was also very poised. She had a fertile mind for dreaming up antics, all in the aid of fun and laughter. But Audrey was also a deeply religious Roman Catholic and took her personal responsibilities seriously.

She wrote that Arnold had more patience than she did, and that father and son got along well together. *"He sure is a chip off the old block. Blue eyes like Arnold . . . he coos and laughs most of the time . . . ."* They had tried to get in touch with Gudrun's two daughters when they visited with their grandparents in North Vancouver. They had managed to visit with the older daughter, and hoped to see the younger one when she came for a visit that summer.

Magnhild and Faye and their families drove out from Alberta to Trail again in the summer of 1942, bringing with them Anna and Erling. Ernest

Audrey, Gary Lee and Arnold

was not there in 1942, because he had joined the army. They had several days of visiting and the usual picnics.

■ ■ ■

" . . . *Even with the wet weather we like the city fine. We have enjoyed our stay out here very much,*" Arnold wrote. Their social life was lively. Parties were a favourite pastime, but there were some limitations on parties. Each adult had a coupon for a monthly liquor ration, and liquor consumption was carefully planned in advance. Bootleggers snapped up any coupons they could locate and sold liquor at inflated prices. All liquor establishments were restricted in their hours of operation. Crocks used for making illegal home-made beer sold in large numbers. A *Vancouver Sun* headline blazed, "Unguarded Liquor Rolls Through the City." The mayor of New Westminster wanted trucking companies, rather than the city, to pay the cost of police escorts for liquor in transit through the city. He said it was cheap insurance for the company against possible hijacking.

The Canadian government had enacted legislation under the War Measures Act to establish the Wartime Prices and Trade Board. The purpose was to prevent prices and wages from spiralling out of control. Scarce food items were strictly rationed. These included tea and coffee, meat, butter and sugar. Gasoline for cars was also rationed.

In early August, a shopkeeper in Vancouver heard the announcement of tea rationing on the radio. He proceeded to move eleven pounds of tea from his store shelves into the living quarters at the rear of the shop. An investigator from the Wartime Prices and Trade Board brought a charge against him, that he had accumulated tea beyond a reasonable amount required for a household. Because the shopkeeper was a disabled war veteran, the judge fined him only $5 and costs. Investigators also watched for any inflated prices, and brought charges against any who were charging more than the usual cost prior to the legislation being enacted.

In late September, Arnold wrote, *"We are fully settled in our new home and like it very much. It is handier for me to go to my work also."* Their new home was in the exclusive Shaugnessy district, just a block off Granville Street in a large, stately home.

Like many homes in Vancouver, it had been divided into suites in response to the housing shortage. Arnold could catch a streetcar south on Granville Street, towards the Sea Island airport where he was stationed. Very likely, it was Audrey who found their accommodation in this lovely residential area. With her outgoing personality, Audrey established social connections with great ease.

"It is almost impossible to get a place to live, and some of the rents they are asking, in spite of the rent controls, are outrageous. In our last apartment we were paying $90 per month, paying extra for gas, light, phone, fuel and telephone. It wasn't a speck nicer than this place either." In October 1942, *The Sun* reported that Vancouver was facing the greatest shortage of housing in its history, with unprecedented overcrowding of homes, apartments and rooming houses. The *Sun* later reported that a "For Rent" sign was a "Signal for Mad Stampede . . . People learning of housing accommodation, be it ever so meagre, flock to the scene . . . . Any bedroom with a clothes closet converted for use as a kitchenette, with a gas or electric hot plate installed therein, is readily rentable . . . . Sharing the bath, having no running water in the room, these and a dozen other inconveniences are willingly endured for the sake of shelter."

In September 1942, Arnold purchased his first car, a 1929 Plymouth. The squadron had a farewell party for one of the pilots who had been transferred east: *" . . . he sold it to me at the party for $75. Cheap enough and it is in good running condition, licence and all. He bought it for $150 and had it only two months."*

■ ■ ■

On September 29, Group Captain G. R. McGregor, DFC, gave a lecture to the squadron on "the situation in Alaska." McGregor had returned from Great Britain after being awarded the DFC the previous year for his role in the Battle of Britain. When Western Air Command sent several RCAF squadrons to Alaska in May and June, he was placed in command of these squadrons under a newly formed "X-Wing." These RCAF squadrons flew under the operational command of the United States Army Air Force (USAAF) and McGregor co-operated with the USAAF in coordinating their duties.

In November, a rumour went around that the squadron would be moving to Alaska. The squadron diary noted that all pilots were granted two weeks leave " . . . to dispose of their wives." Squadron Leader B. D. Dal Russel was posted back to duty in Europe, and was leaving at the end of November. The squadron diary notes that a "highly successful" farewell party was held for Russel at the home of Pilot Officer (P/O) Roseland. At the end of November, Squadron Leader (S/L) Brad Walker took command of the squadron at Sea Island.

In December, P/O Roseland accompanied S/L Walker to a meeting of the Kiwanis Club of Vancouver, where Walker gave an address. In December, the squadron took part in a search for a missing Canadian Pacific Airlines plane, carrying ten passengers and three crew members. The aircraft had disappeared just fifteen minutes from Vancouver on a trip from Whitehorse.

On January 1, 1943, the squadron celebrated the first anniversary of the formation of No. 14 Fighter Squadron. Arnold and Audrey hosted the party at their home. Dignitaries in attendance included Air Vice Marshal L. F. Stevenson and Mrs. Stevenson, and Group Captain G. R. McGregor and Mrs. McGregor. The squadron diary noted, "A very delightful time was spent."

■ ■ ■

In early January, Ernest wrote to his sister Agnes, thanking her for his Christmas present. He wrote, *"Mother was sure surprised when I walked in the house before Christmas . . . . I was sure tired when I got back in camp after the long trip."* Ernest had travelled out to Calgary and back again, from London, Ontario, to spend Christmas with Anna and Erling. Train travel was always crowded at holiday times during the war, and he may not have had very much sleep. He had started a diesel course as soon as he got back and was finding it most interesting. After the course was finished he expected to go to Camp Borden for more practice in work. Then, in the spring, he thought he might be going overseas with large group of maintenance men, who were due for overseas posting.

■ ■ ■

In Vancouver, the *Sun* was full of news about the new "dim out" regulations that would take effect on the 31st of January. "Homes, places of business, industries and institutions must all be dimmed out daily from one-half hour after sunset, to one-half hour before sunrise." Stores in the Vancouver area were swamped with orders for blinds. Lighting in store windows was strictly limited, lighted neon signs were forbidden and the city's 8,000 street lights were dimmed. The top seven inches of the globe of the street lights was to be first dipped inside and out in white paint and then given black caps on the exterior, to eliminate "sky-glare." Every second street light was to be extinguished at midnight. Cars would be restricted to 20 to 25 miles per hour after dark, but because of the safety factor, headlights would not be dimmed.

In September 1942, the Provincial Civilian Protection Committee began distributing thousands of gas masks and respirators. "The masks are of the simplest design . . . but they are effective protection against war gas. In a 100 per cent concentration of poison gas, the civilian respirator will continue to filter out gas and permit only fresh air to reach the wearer for nearly three hours . . . " The Vancouver ARP (Air Raid Patrol) Committee recommended that a basement room of sufficient size for a family be chosen and prepared, in case of an enemy air raid attack. Two weeks later, the provincial ARP declared this recommendation invalid. "Basement rooms are not suitable, since some gases sink to the lowest level." But many Vancouver homeowners had already prepared emergency rooms in their basements.

The ARP was a body of civilians who assumed responsibilities for defence. Their tasks had to do with educating the public, planning for emergency situations and disaster planning. In early January 1943, Vancouver had its first city-wide ARP rehearsal. The rehearsal had plenty of flaws. Eight empty ambulances showed up at St. Paul's Hospital instead of reporting to the points where the "casualties" occurred. The ARP recruited and trained 2,500 messengers. Children as young as twelve were trained as runners " . . . to keep an unbroken line of communication, so that if the telephone service should go out of operations, messages would be able to get through . . . "

On the 20th of January, the *Sun* reported, "Censorship restrictions placed upon newspaper weather reports and forecasts as a result of the war were lifted today." The province had suffered blizzards and record low temperatures for several days. City transportation systems were barely operable, and major highways and rail lines were closed from snowdrifts. Weather news was censored so that the enemy could not take any strategic advantage of adverse weather.

"Cold Snap Adds Beef Shortage to Fuel and Milk Famine," the *Sun* reported. Even before the cold spell, fuel had been in short supply. On the 13th of January the *Sun* had reported that "No Trespassing" signs were lifted from city-owned lots to permit citizens to help themselves to any fuel they could find. A later article was headlined, "10 Ways to Keep Warm Despite Fuel Shortage."

■ ■ ■

On the 25th of January, all leaves for the pilots were cancelled. The squadron diary noted, "All personnel preparing for the move. We don't know where we are going, but we hope to see some action soon."

On February 8, 1943, a light snowstorm delayed the planned departure of No. 14 Fighter Squadron from the Sea Island Airport. That night Arnold wrote his sister that he was leaving Vancouver in the morning, and he couldn't write much because he had a lot to do. *"Have quite a trip ahead of us—over 2,500 miles, which will take us west of Dutch Harbour. We will be under U.S. command, and they're so secretive that we don't know our own address as yet."* Audrey would let her know the new address and to please write her, as he knew she would be lonesome. He would appreciate a line, too, but *"Don't expect to hear from me very regularly though, as the mail service is pretty grim."* The squadron departed on February 11, 1943 for Dutch Harbour in the Aleutian Islands.

Number 14 Fighter Squadron RCAF, leaving for Alaska February 1943. Arnold is second from right.
Photo: Department of National Defence and Mr. David McDuff

Chapter 17
"It was a terrible place to live"

Early in 1943, Canada and the United States had a force of 40,000 in Alaska, defending against 7,500 Japanese on the islands of Kiska and Attu. The Japanese believed this was an effective use of their troops, because the Americans and Canadians had a force five times larger defending the islands against the smaller number of Japanese. The Allied Supreme Command decided that the islands should be taken back, to release manpower badly needed for other theatres of war. In the fall of 1942, the commander of the Eleventh Air Force had requested the posting of a second RCAF fighter squadron to Alaska. Finally, in January, Group Captain G. C. McGregor notified Alaska Defence Command that Western Air Command had approved the transfer of No. 14(F) to Alaska, to be under the command of the USAAF.

■ ■ ■

Upon hearing of the approval, Colonel W. O Butler invited McGregor and his Wing Commander, W.E.E. Morrow, to join a tour of inspection of Alaska defence bases. They travelled first to the new base at Fort Glenn, on Umnak Island, off the tip of the Alaska Peninsula. Because of the rugged terrain on the islands, the naval facilities were 75 miles northeast at Dutch Harbour. Barges ran back and forth to transport supplies and staff. When the

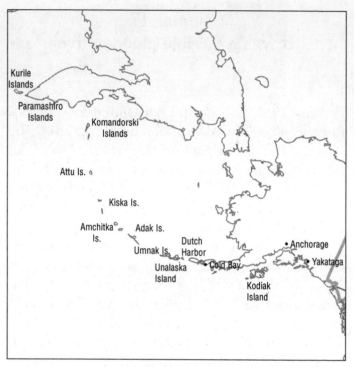

Alaska and the Aleutian Islands

Japanese bombed Dutch Harbour the previous June, the airstrip at Fort Glenn was still under construction and barely operable. In January, the inspection tour found many new buildings and a greatly improved airstrip.

Their next stop was at Adak, the second largest island in the chain, which the Americans had occupied just four months previously. It now had an airstrip and a harbour and resembled a small city. After diking and draining a tidal flat, engineers had constructed the airstrip and covered it with interlocking steel matting; this was accomplished in just eleven days. The steel matting was an invention of the Americans and became widely used in the Second World War.

They continued west to Amchitka, just sixty miles from the Japanese base on Kiska. The island had been occupied just three weeks previously in a roaring storm. Conditions there couldn't have been worse. The southeast half of the island was little better than a swamp. A huge amount of work was necessary to make the base operable, but it was only a short distance from Kiska, which was desirable because of the short range of fighter aircraft.

When the inspection tour ended, McGregor proceeded south to brief No. 14(F) on their impending trip.

■ ■ ■

The bad weather that delayed No. 14(F) on the trip north from Sea Island was an ominous sign of what was ahead. They were fogged in for four days at Port Hardy, on the northern tip of Vancouver Island, after which they flew to the American base at Annette Island, just off Prince Rupert.

McGregor had decided to fly the coastal route to avoid the intense cold of the interior. But coastal waters were poorly charted. There were stories of earlier flights using road maps to chart their course along the coast. They followed a limited number of radio beams stationed along the coast, but the Kittyhawks did not have beam-receivers, although the Canso accompanying them did. There was no radar, and weather reports were not available during flight. Weather changes in this northern region could be dramatic, swift and dangerous.

At Annette Island they waited eight days for rain, low clouds and mist to clear, before taking off in a clear blue sky for Yakutat, Alaska. To their right was the beautiful Coastal Mountain range. On their arrival at Yakutat, the base was completely socked in with dense cloud. After circling several times they flew another 125 miles on near-empty gas tanks, to Yakataga. In the next four days the Canso made trips to Anchorage to bring gasoline back to the thirsty Kittyhawks.

■ ■ ■

Several weather systems meet in the North Pacific: frigid water and air from the Bering Sea north of the Aleutian Islands encounter the temperate Japanese Current south of the islands. These two systems are churned by strong, cold winds that blow eastward from Siberia. Winds and fog move quickly in all directions along the uncharted rugged and rocky coastlines of the islands, often shrouding their many volcanic peaks. The predominant weather pattern, moving from Japan eastward, favoured a Japanese advance up the islands, with a break in the weather. When flying down the Alaska Peninsula and across the North Pacific towards Japan, the Americans and Canadians had to fly into unknown advancing weather with no meteorological information.

McGregor had led a tragic trip from Anchorage to Fort Glenn the previous July. When the flight ran into advancing bad weather, McGregor ordered the Kittyhawks to turn back, but five had crashed into an unseen peak, with the loss of all pilots. A devastated McGregor returned to Cold Bay alone.

■ ■ ■

No. 14(F) was delayed two weeks again at the Elmendorf base near Anchorage, and detained again at Naknek, when heavy winds from across the Gulf of Alaska buffeted their small aircraft. When the squadron finally reached their airfield, after a five-week journey, the whole ground crew rushed out to meet the fifteen Kittyhawks flying in, in formation. The ground crew had arrived earlier and commenced setting up their new base at Berry Field, a satellite of Fort Glenn.

■ ■ ■

Living conditions in the Aleutians were grim, as was the mail service. The men slept in metal Quonset huts and other prefab huts, and on Amchitka they slept in tents. At Berry Field they had electricity, but as they moved forward they relied on candles or Coleman lanterns in their living quarters. Heating in their living units consisted of a small stove with a limited ration of coal or oil. The ground was boggy and muddy underfoot. The closer they got to the Japanese, the more primitive their living conditions became.

The squadron was hit with a spell of very cold weather after arrival at Berry Field. Flying Officer C. F. Griffin later wrote of their experiences with the RCAF in Alaska: " . . . *only those who have lived in the mud, the williwaws, the penetrating cold, the rain and sudden fog, can fully appreciate the loneliness and hardship of existence in that bleak region."* Williwaws are winds that seem to come from all directions at once, and were known to lift and carry items to new locations—even aircraft.

In late March, the squadron was split into two echelons that would alternate on operations at Amchitka. The first echelon of twelve pilots advanced westward to Adak in a Douglas Dakota, on the last day of March. Because of a shortage of space, Alaska Defence Command had agreed that the Canadians should rotate on operations with the American pilots and fly the American P-40K1s (or the Kittyhawk, as it was known to the Canadians.) The pilots bunked in with the American pilots for two nights, until they got their own huts.

At Adak they were hit again with another two weeks of very bad weather, with snow and strong winds. When the winds hit 105 miles per hour, the wind-measuring anemometer broke. How much harder it blew after that was not known. The pilots kept busy for the duration of the storm, plugging the cracks in their huts that let in cold draughts.

By mid-April, the new Adak base was well developed, with a busy harbour. The radio station at Adak had instant communication with Kodiak on mainland Alaska, and with ships and aircraft throughout the chain. Adak was becoming more heavily populated with the stepped-up preparations for the forthcoming invasions of Kiska and Attu.

In mid-April, the pilots moved further west to Amchitka, where they relieved the RCAF squadron,

No. 111(F), whose pilots were going on a rest. After arriving, they spent the remainder of the day getting settled in their tents and procuring high boots needed for walking in the mud. In the evening, the pilots of No. 14(F) met with the pilots of the USAAF No. 11 Fighter Squadron, and arranged their rotation schedules. The rotation was for four days—operations, alert, defence and a day of rest.

■ ■ ■

To take back the two islands, the strategy was to invade Attu first, the one furthest away. This would isolate the occupation force on Kiska. The P-40s could not fly the distance to Attu, so their task was to keep up a constant bombing and strafing barrage on Kiska. The U.S. navy also was setting up a barricade around the islands, to interfere with any reinforcements that the Japanese might be sending to their occupation forces.

The Japanese never got their airstrip in full operation because it was constantly bombed. One thing the Japanese did have on Kiska was a radar installation, which they had salvaged from the SS *Prince of Wales,* a British ship that they had sunk off Singapore in December 1941. When the Kittyhawks rose in the air to begin their trips to Kiska, the Japanese knew they were coming and prepared a barrage of flak and anti-aircraft fire to greet them. Amchitka was so close to Kiska that at night the lights of Kiska could sometimes be seen from the north tip of Amchitka.

On the trip to Kiska, the usual routine was to look for a break in the clouds, at about 1,000 metres, and then head down at about a 45-degree angle to drop their bombs. Bombing from a P-40 was not accurate, but they did do considerable constant damage to the runway, and also damaged other important enemy defences. The P-40s were not designed as a bomber, but they were fitted with racks to carry bombs to Kiska. After dropping their bombs they flew up, and then down again, to shoot up selected targets on the land. The Japanese had constructed many of their buildings and living quarters underground in volcanic caves.

When asked if he wasn't frightened when he flew over Kiska, one pilot responded, "I got scared, but not because of flak. I'm scared every time I get over to Kiska because I don't know whether I will find a place to land when I get back." They might leave their base in flying weather, only to find it completely socked in with clouds and fog on their return.

The squadron flew on bombing operations to Kiska for a month before they were relieved again in mid-May. On May 6th, they were briefed on the upcoming invasion of Attu, which would primarily be a land attack from the sea. Arnold flew back to Berry Field with the rest of the squadron on May 13.

■ ■ ■

Arnold was very fortunate to be granted a leave to Vancouver for a visit with Audrey, who was then five months pregnant. He and a flight lieutenant from the squadron arrived in Vancouver on May 22nd. He reported on his son: *"He is growing like a weed, and was running around talking and jabbering incessantly . . . . It certainly was grand to get back to the family . . . . Audrey and I spent one weekend in Victoria.*" Just prior to their return to Alaska, Arnold and his officer companion spent four days together with their wives in Seattle. From there they made their return flight to Alaska to rejoin the squadron.

■ ■ ■   *

Ernest visited Anna in Calgary in May. He expected to be posted overseas soon, but he found it hard to tell Anna, which he didn't do until he was leaving. He had some trouble socially while in Calgary.

"*I spent seven hours in the city jail in Calgary the first night I was there, on account of another guy's doings . . . .*" Ernest had been drinking beer with several of his friends when someone picked a fight with a Chinese man. Ernest said that he interfered to stop the fight, but got blamed for starting the confrontation. He phoned the MPs from the jail and they came to his rescue. As soon as the MPs got to the jail they sorted out the problem and then drove Ernest back to the hotel. "*It sure made me mad, as it was the first time I have been run in. Don't tell the folks about it . . . . I had a good time in Calgary and also had a very enjoyable trip back as far as Toronto.*"

Ernest wrote again in mid-June from Nova Scotia. "*We are sadly disappointed that we are still in Canada. Of all places to land, we hit this place!*" He didn't know how long he would be there, but he thought he had been pretty lucky as he'd been back to Calgary three times in the past year.

■ ■ ■

Arnold and his travelling companion arrived back at Elmendorf Field at Anchorage about the 10th of June, and awaited transport to Berry Field. In the interim, they stopped over at the Officers' Quarters of the USAAF, where they socialized and played bridge.

On the Saturday night, about sixty people gathered for a party. The RCAF officers were drinking beer and some were rolling dice for small amounts of money. Arnold's companion went upstairs about midnight, followed about an hour later by Arnold and a couple of U.S. officers. While the three were chatting in the hallway they heard a gun go off. Arnold's companion and roommate had taken Arnold's gun and shot himself through the head. Although the man had a few beers through the evening, no one thought that he had enough beer to make him drunk. He left a note saying, "This would not have happened if I had been sent overseas." He died a few hours later in hospital.

A Court of Inquiry, from June 24th to the 29th, could find no reason for his suicide. Arnold's testimony indicated the he and Audrey had found the man and his wife on excellent terms while they vacationed together in Seattle. The only reason that could be determined for his suicide was that he couldn't tolerate the idea of returning to the difficult conditions at Amchitka. News of such tragedies was never circulated within the groups where the person was known. When news of the officer's death was reported to the squadron, Arnold could not reveal that his death was a suicide, nor any details of the tragic circumstances.

■ ■ ■

Arnold arrived back at Berry Field on the 20th of June, where he received word that he had been promoted to Flight Lieutenant. The next day, in the absence of the squadron leader, Arnold managed the weekly Squadron Parade and took temporary command of the squadron. He wrote that he had a lot of letters to respond to when he got back to the base, and had been very busy. *"There was a bit of good news awaiting me on my return—a promotion. So now I am a Flight Lieutenant. . . . A little more work but also a few more dollars—so I am not kicking."* On the 3rd of July S/L Walker, Arnold and eight others left again for Amchitka. They were held up again by bad weather at Adak, and then flew the final leg to Amchitka to relieve No. 111(F).

■ ■ ■

The invasion of Attu took place when Arnold went on leave to Vancouver. On May 11, 1942, American forces began their assault on Attu. A force of 11,000 army troops, supported by the U.S. Navy, landed on Attu on for a battle that was expected to last only a few days. However, the weather and geography were more difficult than expected. The turbulent waters and rugged coastline of the island, which was hemmed in with dense fog, made for a difficult landing. The terrain was mountainous and icy, with narrow valleys. The Japanese had dug themselves into fortifications high in the mountains, and shot down through the fog at the landing forces. The battle was concluded on May 29, with 549 Americans dead, and all of the 2,400 Japanese dead, except for 28 prisoners of war. Historian C. P. Stacey described The Battle of Attu as "a thoroughly nasty little campaign."

■ ■ ■

As a result of the Attu experience, and the knowledge that the Japanese had a greater number in the occupying force on Kiska, the invasion force was doubled to 34,000. Fifty-three hundred Canadians from the Thirteenth Infantry Brigade participated, along with another 500 from the highly skilled First Special Service Force, a joint Canadian and American force trained in commando tactics. In preparation for the occupation planned for August, Kiska was subjected to a near constant barrage of bombing and the U.S. navy encircled the island in a near complete blockade.

Once back on Amchitka in early July, the squadron met with bad weather again. For three days in late July, a spell of unusually fine weather permitted the squadron to participate in the frequent assaults on Kiska. By this time the runway was well cratered. On the 27th of July the weather again turned bad, and the flight that Arnold led was the only one that got through to the island that day, during a break in the clouds. Several days of heavy clouds followed. Once the weather cleared, the bombing resumed again.

In early August, Arnold, as the most senior pilot, returned to Berry Field to take temporary command of the squadron, while S/L Walker went on detached duty. Arnold was at Berry Field for the two weeks prior to, and during, the invasion of Kiska.

■ ■ ■

The period leading up to the invasion was again cloudy and foggy. Only a few flights got through from Amchitka to Kiska. On the 3rd of August, No. 14(F) participated in a bombing and strafing attack on anti-aircraft battery positions, but only one pilot had noticed any flak. A week later no flak was seen. Questions were raised about the lack of activity, but no one in command seriously believed that the Japanese had evacuated. When the troops landed at Attu, the Japanese had been lodged in fortifications in the mountains. Who could tell what they might be up to on Kiska? Through dense clouds and fog there was no way to know.

On the 15th of August, the invasion of Kiska began. In the fog, at midnight, the First Special Service Force landed. At 0630 the main landing force waded in, tensed for battle and waiting for a response from the enemy. All was still on the island, but they feared that the Japs might be up in the hills ready to ambush. The landing force of 34,000 stalked the fog-shrouded hillsides of the Japanese encampment area. In the thick fog, the troops shot at anything that moved, including their own troops. After four days, it was apparent there were no Japanese on the island. In the end, twenty-eight soldiers were dead and fifty injured, including four Canadians dead and four wounded. No. 14(F) had been briefed prior to the invasion, but bad flying weather precluded their participation. The "Alaska Escapade" was over.

■ ■ ■

Japanese submarines and a ship had stolen into the bay on Kiska on the 28th of July. In a mere fifty-five minutes the 5,400 troops stationed on the island were loaded into the waiting vessels. They made their spectacular escape under cover of dense fog. The island had been unoccupied for over two weeks while being bombed by the American and Canadian air force.

For weeks, the Canadian and United States governments had negotiated how they would release favourable news of their successes against the Japanese at Kiska. With the discovery of the evacuation of the Japanese garrison, American enthusiasm quickly evaporated. The Americans had sent all news correspondents home in 1942, while they were secretly preparing their advance bases of Adak and Amchitka. With no news correspondents in the Aleutians, the occupation received sparse attention in the media. The Kiska operation was tagged as a "fiasco" and the U.S. government did not see fit to make much of it in the press. The war in the Aleutians became one of the lesser-known fronts of the Second World War.

■ ■ ■

Meanwhile, on the home front, family members worried about the events of the war. Audrey moved into a little rented house on West Second Avenue, near Jericho Beach. She and Edith Stiles, the wife of one of the other No. 14(F) officers, had kept busy redecorating the house and visiting second-hand and antique stores. But Edith's husband was posted back east for a course, a problem for Audrey, because Edith had planned to stay with her in the last weeks of her pregnancy. Now it looked as if she might be alone during that period. *"Daddy (Arnold) is so worried, but I am sure something will turn up . . . . You should see Gary Lee. He really is the picture of health. We are only two blocks from the beach and he just loves it there. So we simply have to go to the beach every day if the weather permits. This last week . . . if I scold him he puts his fingers in his ears. I am sure I don't know where he picked that up at eighteen months."*

■ ■ ■

Ernest had finally travelled from the holding location in Nova Scotia to an overseas location. *"I am doing pretty well and I think the work is going to be pretty interesting . . . . We are in the field now, and accommodations aren't very good, but we don't mind putting up with it when we know it can't be helped. The boys all get along swell together, so that is the main thing."*

■ ■ ■

"This is my fifth letter tonight and I am in rather a daze," Arnold wrote to Agnes from Berry Field on the 20th of August. *"I just received the news about Erling— a week after it happened. I feel very shocked, helpless and hopeless at present."* Arnold had just received a telegram notifying him of Erling's death the previous week. While driving a cab for a limited number of hours each day, Erling attended the tuberculosis clinic in Calgary for regular pneumo treatments. He also had a girlfriend and was enjoying his limited freedom after years in the tuberculosis sanatorium.

On the 13th of August, Erling had attended the clinic for his treatment, but they didn't do the treatment, because they noted an abnormality in his

X-ray. After leaving the clinic he stopped in to visit his sister Faye. While they were chatting, Erling commenced to cough, and as his cough got more out of control he started to bleed from the mouth. He went into the bathroom. Faye became terribly upset and ran to a neighbour's home asking them to call for help on the telephone. When she returned, Erling had collapsed on the floor in front of the toilet, and the toilet was full of blood. He died before any help could arrive.

Faye was nine months pregnant, due at any time. Except for Arnold and Ernest, all the family gathered in Calgary for Erling's funeral. The next day Faye had her baby. Later, Faye stated that after Erling died she just couldn't face having the baby. She felt too sad. However, the birth of the baby became a day of rejoicing, because, after two boys, Faye delivered a little girl, a child that she had wanted. The whole family was very happy for her. She named her little girl Sandra, after Erling's girlfriend.

■ ■ ■

Arnold continued, *"However, I will do my best to drop you a few lines just to let you know that I am okay—at least . . . . I don't know any of the particulars naturally. A telegram is so damned indefinite. I have a great mania against them! I heard from Magnhild a while ago that Erling had pneumonia and was apparently well over it, and was merely resting up. So I imagine that complications set in. It happens so often!"*

He wrote that he had sent a telegram to Anna immediately on receipt of the news, and then he wrote her a letter as well. *"Now, along with every-thing else, I'm worried about Faye and Audrey both. It will be a great shock to both of them. I hope Faye is okay. I wrote to her and Magnhild also tonight. Faye's time is about up—and for all I know may be over. Audrey should have about a month yet."*

"But poor old mother! I really feel sorry for her! I am certain she's taking this very badly. She has had so much sorrow, poor creature. We just must see that she is taken—not only care of—but that she is not left by herself. I believe that we perhaps fail to realize that mother is well on in years, and quite possibly has a numbered few ahead of her. Let's all try and make those quite as liveable as possible for her! Well folks, I will just have to sign off for this time. I can hardly control my pen any more. Hoping this finds you all well."

■ ■ ■

Audrey wrote that she was terribly upset when she heard the news. She was so glad that Faye had a little girl. It gave her a little encouragement, because that is what Arnold wanted. She said that she had written to Anna and asked her to come out to Vancouver for a visit in the fall, when Arnold returned home. She asked Agnes to encourage Anna to include a visit to the West Coast with her planned visit to Trail.

■ ■ ■

By the end of August all pilots from No. 14(F) had returned to Berry Field from Amchitka, and then they received word of their possible return to Canada. On the 14th of September, seven members of the squadron were awarded American Air Medals for their service in Alaska. The squadron diary noted, "At 1300 hours, Brigadier-General J. A. Ladd, Commander General, Fort Glenn, presented the Air Medal to seven pilots (including Arnold Roseland) . . . . The presentation took place with the squadron formed in a hollow square, after which General Ladd took the salute as the squadron marched past." At the end of the ceremony the band played the national anthems for both countries. Apparently the Americans were impressed with the military formalities of the Canadians, and would sometimes come over to watch the weekly Squadron Parade at Berry Field.

■ ■ ■

The air party, with eighteen aircraft, left Fort Glenn on the 21st of September. They followed the inland route back to Boundary Bay, via Whitehorse, Fort Nelson and Prince George, and arrived at Boundary Bay on Oct. 6, 1943.

■ ■ ■

Back in Vancouver, Audrey came home from hospital with their newborn son three days after Arnold arrived home, and he started on a 21-day leave. *"It certainly is wonderful to be back . . . . Of course there wasn't a great deal for us to stay up there for, and we were all very pleased when we got our moving orders. We are all quite satisfied to settle down for a few months again, now that we are home."*

Arnold bought a 1940 "Morris 8," a small English car in "wonderful condition." He needed it for the twenty-mile drive from his house out to the Boundary Bay Airport because public transportation out that way was very difficult. *"Vancouver certainly is a different city from peace time—and if it weren't for the liquor and gasoline rationing, it would be quite a place. It succeeds in being pretty lively in spite of all that, and a person often wonders where all the cars come from. With all the 'AA' cards, a person doesn't expect to see so many around. I guess where gas rationing is noticed most is in the rural districts and on the highways."*

He had received a letter recently from Anna, and she seemed to be in slightly better spirits. He wrote that Erling's girlfriend, Sandra, had called to visit and that she had seemed very nice.

■ ■ ■

In early December, Arnold wrote that Anna had arrived for her visit and that they were tickled to see her. She was looking well and had a good trip out on the train. *"We haven't had a chance to show Mother around Vancouver at all yet. We have been having some terribly foggy weather and a person can hardly get around in a car, let alone see anything."* At that time coal, as well as wood and sawdust, were used as heating fuels, and in industry. They were dirty-burning fuels, bringing dense particles into the air, especially noticeable at times when there was little wind. Coupled with moist air from the ocean and the mixture of warm and cold air, the fog could reduce visibility to ten, twenty or thirty feet, after which nothing could be seen. During such weather foghorns moaned incessantly, and traffic was sometimes slowed to a crawl.

Arnold urged Agnes in Trail to come for a few days during Christmas week, so that they could have a visit and Anna could travel back to Trail with her. *"I'm supposed to be going overseas with the rest of the fellows early in the New Year, so goodness knows when we will get a chance to see each other again."* Also, Audrey was looking forward to meeting Agnes. *"When I go overseas Audrey is going east with me—to stay until I return so you may not have a chance to see her again for some time either . . . . Think it over and let us know. We have lots of room and would love to have you."* Agnes, however, was unable to travel to Vancouver for the visit. Arnold added that Anna had received a letter from Ernest and that he was getting along well.

"Yes, I was decorated by the Americans—the Air Medal. I made twenty missions or so over Kiska before the Japs left. It was a terrible country to live in— especially after the excitement was over. I had the honour of leading the last raid against the little yellow devils before they left. It was a very bad day and our squadron was the only one that got to the objective—July 27th. They left immediately after that during a very bad spell of weather . . . . Well folks, I'll have to call this a letter, whether it is or not. Have to get going real early in the morning and battle through twenty miles or so (I hope not) of fog." Anna spent Christmas with Arnold and Audrey, after which she took the train to Trail, where she visited with Agnes and family until late January.

■ ■ ■

Arnold and Audrey left Vancouver in late December, when they travelled east and had a vacation together before Arnold reported to Lachine, Quebec, on January 13, 1944. Later, Anna remembered, *"[Audrey] said good-bye to Arnold at the Mount Royal Hotel in Montreal. She said it was the hardest thing she had ever done. She stayed with Arnold until the last and she left Montreal the same morning . . . . Arnold kept up fine until the last half hour, and then he really broke down and said, 'Oh Audrey, I wish I didn't have to go . . .' He left at three o'clock in the morning on the 19th . . . . "* The squadron boarded the SS *Pasteur* at Halifax on January 20, 1944 for their trip to Great Britain.

■ ■ ■

Anna visited at Trail with Agnes (my mother) and our family for about a month after she left Arnold and Audrey at Vancouver. My most vivid memory of Anna was the time spent with her during this visit. She taught me to crochet a sweater for a doll, and taught me several needlework stitches. She was very soft-spoken and gentle, and had a distinctive Norwegian accent. Anna visited with Gudrun's husband, Francis, and his two children.

Anna had an interesting experience on her return train trip to Calgary from Trail. Faye and Lew were greatly worried when they met every train for several days and Anna did not appear. Normally the trip took about twenty-four hours. The train engine had derailed near Kootenay Lake. Passengers were transferred to a boat, and then later transferred back to a second train that came in from the opposite direction. She arrived home in good spirits, to be greeted by a greatly relieved Faye and Lew. Telephone and telegraph systems had failed to relay information about the accident, and the media had scarce technology and scarce resources for covering such occurrences.

Anna wrote to Agnes in February, *"I have been busy with my fancy work. I have finished my lunch-*

eon cloth and it sure is lovely. I couldn't leave it alone before it was finished." She added, "*Faye is pleased with hers. I got her some thread the other day. She said she can do it all right and I think it will do her good.*" She had also encouraged Agnes to do needlework. To fill the lonely hours while living alone, Anna had been working to make crocheted bedspreads, one each for Magnhild, Faye, Agnes and Audrey. Keeping busy helped to relieve the stress of worrying about her loved ones, and she also produced gifts to leave with her children.

Anna wrote to Agnes in late February, " . . . *Audrey is still staying with her folks and she said she is so unsettled that she doesn't know what to do . . . . I sure hope that the Lord will protect him and Ernest so that they can both come home again soon.*" The family could only pray now that the war would go well, and that their loved ones would return safely.

Chapter 18
"We like our Spits very much"

THE TROOP SHIP ARRIVED at Mersey Estuary, south of Liverpool, on January 27, 1944, but because of strong winds in the crowded harbour they lost their docking place, and were delayed four days from deboarding the ship. Number 14 Fighter Squadron finally left by train for the south coast of England, and after ten days at the Reception Centre at Bournemouth, they travelled north again to Digby, Lincolnshire. Here, the squadron would be trained in the Supermarine Spitfire IXB. Theirs became one of six RCAF squadrons, comprising two newly formed wings that would become part of the Second Tactical Air Force for the invasion of Europe in 1944.

Their newly formed wing was numbered 144, and the three squadrons in it were numbered 441-443, following the custom of numbering RCAF squadrons in the European theatre in the four hundreds. No. 14(F) became No. 442(F). The renowned British fighter pilot, J. E. "Johnny" Johnson, arrived at Digby to become wing leader, and to train them in their new aircraft.

Arnold wrote in March, *"We have been travelling in our new aircraft and attending lectures. We like our Spits very much and find them a welcome change indeed."* Their Spitfire was a lighter aircraft than the Kittyhawk, with a powerful engine. This gave the plane a low weight-to-power ratio that made it a delight to fly. It was also lighter than the two German aircraft it would meet in the European skies, the ME109 and the FW190.

■ ■ ■

Finding the necessary personnel and resources for the formation of a wing was a massive undertaking. A wing operated as a self-sufficient unit with a range of skilled staff to care for all needs. Within the wing each squadron functioned separately. The wing included 769 personnel, with 39 officers, of which Arnold was one. The formation of a wing could be likened to setting up a small town and preparing it to go on an extensive camping trip, along with aircraft, parts and supplies of all sorts.

On the 8th of March, the squadron diary noted that there was a "swift increase in tempo of activity throughout the Airfield (Wing). It reminds one of a beehive at blossom time." Three days later, the diary noted that they had " . . . a trying, hectic day. All sections crying for information and 83 Group (administration) is laying it on thick and fast." The whole wing would move five times before D-Day, when the real camping trip began.

■ ■ ■

Audrey wrote to Agnes that she had been a "silly girl and lost ten pounds since Daddy left." She had moved to Toronto in early February, but was so lonely that she packed the children up and returned to Neustadt, Ontario two weeks later, where she had grown up, and where her family lived. *"I have decided that no matter where I am, I will be lonely with-*

out Daddy [Arnold], so I might as well be in a small town." She had already received seven letters from Arnold. He found many items very expensive and very scarce. He wasn't going to have any leave for a while, so he didn't expect to see Ernest or her brother Ray any time soon.

In early March, Arnold wrote that he hadn't seen much of England yet. *"What I have seen so far reminds a person quite a bit of Ontario, only on a smaller scale—even to the trains."* He had written to Ernest as soon as he landed but hadn't had a reply when they moved to their next location. *"I am sure looking forward to seeing him, as I haven't seen him since he joined up . . . . The food is pretty good, but monotonous. We (flying personnel) get an issue of three eggs and three oranges per week, which helps a lot. Our quarters at present are very comfortable, but much colder than we are used to."*

The squadron was living in tents during a spell of cold, damp weather when there was a shortage of fuel. Then snow fell. As luck would have it, Arnold and a number of others in the squadron had colds when they moved to Homesly South on the 18th of March. He was hospitalized with tonsillitis and discharged a week later on "light duties," just in time for the squadron to move to Westhampnett. He had missed the excitement when the squadron went on operations for the first time, escorting Fortresses of the United States 8th Bomber Command on a sweep through northern France attacking German airfields.

■ ■ ■

Since the fall of France, the invasion had been under serious consideration by the Allied High Command. While France suffered under the occupation of the German army, the war raged to the south and the east. In the summer of 1943, the Allied armies had invaded Sicily, taking almost a year to advance as far as Rome. The Russians were eager for the Allied invasion of France to begin, in the knowledge that some of the power of the German army would then be diverted away from Russia.

However, in preparation for the invasion of Europe, the Allied powers had many problems to solve and, in order to gain a strategic advantage, the invasion had to be a surprise to the Germans in both location and timing. In his book *Wing Leader*, Johnson later wrote that although many of the tasks of aerial war prior to D-Day may have seemed unrelated, they were all " . . . part of a well-conceived plan which aimed at denying transport and radar facilities to the Germans."

On the 1st of April, Johnson notified 83 Group that 144 Wing was ready for operations. This occasioned some changes in command in the squadron. Johnson needed men in command who knew well the European environment and geography. Operational flying in Europe was very different from that in Alaska. The No. 442(F) pilots had never met their enemy in the air, or used their guns in aerial combat, an essential skill in Europe where the guiding principle was "kill or be killed." The two flight commanders of No. 14(F), of which

Arnold was one, were relieved of their duties when two pilots who had earned DFCs in the Battle of Britain joined the squadron to assume those duties, F/L H. J. Dowding and F/L L. G. Keltie. Johnson knew that these men had the experience and skill required to lead the pilots of No. 442(F) in operations.

During April, the squadron participated in a variety of missions and on one mission went deep into the Ruhr Valley in Germany. They participated in several ramrods escorting bombers to France. Their duty on such missions was to defend the bombers from any possible aerial attack by enemy aircraft. They also went on numerous sweeps over France looking for targets to shoot up. In the spring of 1944, Allied pilots were rarely involved in aerial combat with the Luftwaffe, as the Germans had sent many of their aircraft to the Russian front. The Germans were short of aircraft and very short of pilots, so they chose carefully where they would meet Allied aircraft in combat. After their trip to the Ruhr, which Arnold participated in, the squadron diary noted " . . . all pilots returned safely in a 'browned off' condition with sore bottoms . . . ." They had flown three hours in the restricted space of the Spitfire cockpit without encountering any German aircraft. For such trips the Spitfire was fitted with an extra fuel tank that the pilots jettisoned when it was near empty. Or, if they met enemy aircraft, the pilots had to rid themselves of the extra fuel tank to make their Spitfire more manoeuvrable in combat.

In mid-April, Arnold flew with No. 442(F) when the wing escorted seventy-two B-26 bombers to Charlevoix in Belgium, when they dropped their bombs on the railroad marshalling yards. Arnold also went on several other bomber escort flights. The Spitfires offered fighter protection for RAF Mitchell bombers and USAAF Marauders, in case enemy fighter aircraft should put the bombers under attack. On all these bomber missions the targets were rail yards and junctions, and airfields in northern France and Belgium. One of the problems of the Spitfire was its short flying range of about 400 miles. The pilots had to nose homeward before their gas tanks got too low, or they would end up ditching in the channel. Many pilots and aircraft were lost in the channel on their return trip to England.

■ ■ ■

The squadron went on a one-week bombing and gunnery course in late April at Hutton Cranswick, in Yorkshire. The course was an occasion to hone the critical skills required, when the Spitfire would act as "a flying machine-gun," and on other occasions would assume the role of a bomber.

The squadron was greatly surprised in early March when their original commanding officer, B. D. Dal Russel, arrived for a surprise visit with the squadron. They had another surprise at Hutton Cranswick, on the 28th of April, when Russel arrived there to become their squadron leader once again. He had been on a rest after his second tour of operations, but he didn't want to miss the excitement of participating in the invasion. Russel had told his old friend Johnson that he would be willing to take a demotion if he could return to his position as squadron leader. Johnson was happy to have him back, so Russel replaced Brad Walker, DFC, as squadron leader for No. 442(F), allowing Walker to go on a well-deserved rest after his tour in Alaska.

■ ■ ■

In the weeks before the invasion, the wing flew hard on a wide variety of operations. On fighter sweeps over France, the Spits roamed around, enticing the Luftwaffe into combat whenever they could. They directed their attacks on armoured cars, trucks, freight yards, etc., shooting up anything that would undermine the mobility and strength of the enemy. They also made bomber attacks on bridges, sealing off future battle areas in Normandy.

The Spitfire was not built to dive-bomb, but was adapted as a bomber by having a rack fitted to the underside of the body, which could carry either a 500-lb. bomb or a fuel tank. One frequent bombing target was the difficult "Noball" site. These were launching sites of a new secret weapon that the Germans were developing to support their diminishing manpower resources. The sites looked like ski jumps and were usually well-hidden and difficult targets. It would be weeks before this secret weapon would be revealed to the Allies.

■ ■ ■

On the 5th of May, Johnson was leading 14 pilots from No. 442 on a sweep to clear the air for bombers heading to Lille, France, when he spotted five FW

190s north-east from Douai at 2,000 feet, and he went down on the chase. After Johnson crippled one of them, Arnold was taking aim to finish him off, when the pilot bailed out. Arnold wrote later, " *. . . Guess he decided to give it up as a bad job. I was quite disappointed, as I really had the goods on him when he jumped.*"

He wrote that their wing was high scorer for the month of April, but their squadron was away on course while the other squadrons were having fun. The fighter wings were engaged in a competition to see which wing could down the most German aircraft. After weeks of training in an aircraft that they loved to fly, the pilots were eager to claim success in shooting down the enemy. And they all understood how essential it was to reduce the power of the Luftwaffe, in preparation for the anticipated invasion of France. However, it would be another six weeks before any 442 pilots would down a German aircraft.

The squadron kept a rigorous schedule throughout May, but in their camping area the pilots relieved the pressures of war in their marquee tent — playing radio or card games, spending time at the pool table, and playing darts and push penny. Their lectures also continued. One lecture focused on army recognition and land-to-air signals, important for their task of aerial protection to the armies on the ground. Also stressed was the importance of aircraft recognition, the ability to quickly and accurately distinguish enemy aircraft from Allied aircraft. Although they met relatively few enemy aircraft on their missions to France and Belgium, they did encounter heavy flak delivered by the enemy from the ground. In early May Arnold returned with a bullet hole in each wing, after escorting Marauder bombers on an evening mission.

■ ■ ■

Arnold received regular letters from home. He wrote to Audrey almost every night, and also had many other letters to respond to. He stated that to keep up he had to write ten to fifteen letters a week—a large assignment for one who detested writing letters.

He was pleased to hear that Ernest was safely back in Canada, and hoped that he was on the mend. *"There is no reason why he shouldn't be, as nervous cases are very common in wartime. They must be, as they have special hospitals for them."* Anna had received a telegram on the 2nd of April, notifying her that Ernest was suffering from a "nervous disability. This does not imply a permanent disability . . . ." Ernest had made a good adjustment to army life and his performance was found to be "very satisfactory." However, in hospital he reported that he had been suffering mood swings, and believed that he had got in with the "wrong bunch." When he felt the blues coming on, he started to drink heavily. In hospital he was depressed, confused and hallucinating. In late April, he was returned to Canada, to Ste. Anne's Hospital at Ste.-Anne-de-Bellevue, Quebec.

Anna wrote in late May that she had a letter from Ernest. *"I was so glad and excited when I got the letter that I just sat down and wrote him a letter right back, and then I went over to Fay's."* Ernest did not like the hospital, where he was in a ward with ten others. *"It is easy to tell from his letter that he is badly mixed up, but I still think that he must be improving some."* She reported that Faye's baby was "nice and fat and good as gold."

■ ■ ■

Arnold had a five-day leave just before D-Day, and he spent it in London. He wasn't impressed with London and found it terribly expensive. He did enjoy visiting historical spots, but even that became boring. *"Besides, two of the days were so terribly hot that a person just couldn't walk around in these heavy uniforms."* He returned to the squadron, at Ford in Sussex, in time for the preparations for D-Day.

. On the 3rd of June, the squadron was shocked to receive the surprise announcement that the ground party would be moving to the concentration area the next morning at 0700. The ground party was up all night preparing for the move, and arrived at their destination on time the following day. The concentration area was at Old Sarum, on the Salisbury Plains near Stonehenge, just three miles from the city of Salisbury. They would remain there until their move to France. The pilots remained temporarily at Ford, while the ground crew would move forward to prepare their new base in France.

On the 5th of June, a false invasion report was broadcast on American radio. The invasion had been planned for that day, but due to rough waters in the channel was postponed one day. That same day the London daily newspapers announced that the city of Rome had fallen to the Allied forces.

On the evening of the 5th of June, W/C Johnson attended a briefing, along with other wing commanders and group captains, on what was expected of them the next day, and Johnson later briefed the pilots at Ford. Later, in his book *Blue Skies*, F/L W. A. Olmstead, DFC, wrote that there was an audible gasp in the room when a large map of the Normandy coast was pinned on the wall. Until then, speculation had been that the invasion would take place at Dieppe.

■ ■ ■

Before the pilots slept they could hear a great armada of Allied aircraft roaring overhead, heading south. They were awakened at 0315 to prepare for their morning missions over the channel.

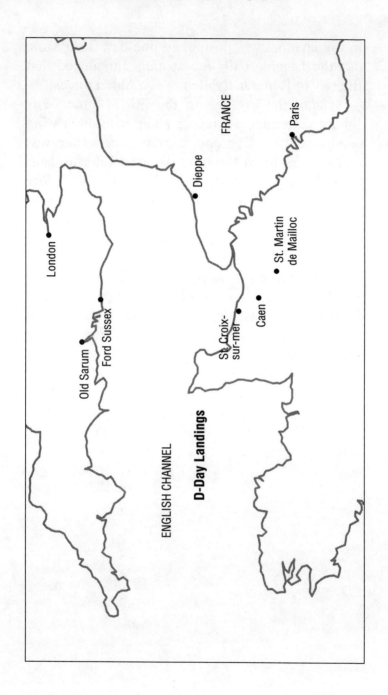

FRANCE

Paris

Dieppe

London

St. Martin
de Mailloc

Ford Sussex

Caen

Old Sarum

St. Croix-
sur-mer

D-Day Landings

ENGLISH CHANNEL

Chapter 19
"I have never been so keen about flying"

"We were over the beachhead 20 minutes before the landing started on June 6th. It was truly a terrific and awesome spectacle." Arnold left at 0630 with the first flight on patrol duty. Rain was falling lightly over a grey, choppy sea, but it brightened up later with a cloud cover at 2,000 feet. Visibility was five to seven miles, reasonable flying weather. As far as one could see the channel was littered with ships of all sizes and descriptions. Above the channel and over the assault area, many Allied aircraft roamed restlessly. Bombers, fighter aircraft and naval aircraft were all swamped in the limited airspace below the clouds. An RAF controller, in a ship below in the channel, helped to monitor the air traffic by radio contact with the leaders of the flights.

The pilots could see flashes of the guns below as naval gunners in the channel shot over and above them towards the German station inland from the beach. Johnson kept his pilots below the 2,000-foot level, out of the line of fire.

The duty of the fighter aircraft was to defend the ships in the channel and the landing forces by preventing any attacks on them from German bombers or fighter aircraft. The Canadian fighters spent the days after D-Day following a fairly rigid schedule. Many tedious hours were devoted to patrolling the ships that were bringing supplies to the beachheads, and monitoring the scrap-strewn beaches. They sighted very few German aircraft. The Allied Command estimated that there were about 300 German aircraft on the Western Front at the time, compared with the 11,000 aircraft that the Allies had allocated to the invasion.

■ ■ ■

On the 7th of June, F/O Goodwin of No. 442(F) ran out of gas and bailed from his Spitfire into the channel. Another 442 pilot spotted him in the water in his dinghy, and then watched as Goodwin climbed up the side of a Polish destroyer. That evening the pilots heard his voice over the radio reporting that he was on the beachhead in Normandy. He returned to the squadron the next day after a four-hour trip in an antisubmarine boat.

On the 8th of June, after his Spitfire was hit by flak, F/L H. J. Dowding made an emergency landing on a new landing strip near the Normandy beaches, at Ste-Croix-sur-Mer. He returned to the squadron at Ford the next day. Both of these men had exciting tales to tell the rest of the squadron. CBC and Canadian Press media came by to interview them. Dowding gave a report of a journey through a minefield, through crowded roads and past snipers, while trying to find a boat returning to England. He had finally made the trip back to the base in a motor torpedo boat.

The new landing strip at Ste-Croix was officially opened on the 10th of June, after being inspected by senior air officers with the RCAF. That day S/L Dal Russel landed there to inspect the runway. A field of clover and knee-high grass had been transformed into an airfield covered with the reliable interlocking steel matting. The entire task was accomplished within two days. Their work had been delayed a little by the necessity of dealing with nearby snipers. For a few more days the field was used exclusively for refuelling, re-arming and emergency landings.

From Ste-Croix-sur-Mer, the city of Caen was about eight miles to the southeast, and the English Channel was about one mile north. The Canadian army had advanced to the northern outskirts of Caen on D-Day, but then lost ground with the fierce resistance of the German army. For their strong defence in Normandy, the Germans were supported by a tremendous number of long-range, high-velocity guns, as well as their effective Panzer and Tiger tanks. The Germans also had a decided advantage for their defensive positions with the flatness of the ground in this area of Normandy, while the same ground was treacherous for the offensive operations of the Allies.

■ ■ ■

On the 9th of June, the ground crew of the wing left Old Sarum for the marshalling area. Two days later the advance party of the ground crew left for Normandy, to prepare for the arrival of the rest of the wing. At that time, the new airfield was right in the middle of the fighting zone and still under shellfire. The remainder of the ground crew landed on the 12th of June at Courselle-sur-Mer, a village in Normandy. They proceeded the short distance to Ste-Croix-sur-Mer, where they spent a sleepless night due to enemy bombing. The next day their airfield was still under mortar fire from a pocket of enemy resistance, about a mile away.

On the 13th of June, the Germans used their new secret weapon for the first time, the V-1 or "buzz bomb." The bombing target was the city of London. The small pilotless plane was capable of flying about 400 mph, and carried an enormous explosive load, creating a great blast upon impact that was very powerful and destructive. Because the buzz bomb was so fast and so small, it was extremely difficult to shoot down. The engine made a distinctive, loud pulsating sound that terror-ized those who heard it. The greatest terror was when the pulsating stopped, as it was about to hit its target.

■ ■ ■

On the morning of the 15th of June, the pilots of 442(F) flew eighteen Spitfires from Ford, Sussex for the last time, and arrived at Ste-Croix-sur-Mer about an hour later. Now that they were stationed in Normandy they no longer faced the risk of ditching in the English Channel on their return trip to Ford. From Ste-Croix-sur-Mer, they would be over enemy territory almost immediately once in the air.

The day was bright and sunny. About noon, ten Douglas Dakotas arrived with the remaining seven pilots, ground officers and ground crew. The pilots were happy to greet their colleagues from the ground crew, who had been working on the base for several days to prepare for their arrival. They had a great respect for the ground crew, who had a vast array of skills that were of utmost importance in the operation of the wing. Of special importance were the skills of those who serviced their Spitfires—the mechanics, the radio men, the armourers, etc. The pilots were the glamour boys of the wing, but they could not have performed without the exceptionally reliable men who carried out important tasks looking after their needs, and servicing their aircraft.

Once landed, the pilots collected their tents and selected their sleeping spot. Some dug slit trenches for extra protection from enemy mortar fire. Most settled in an area of the orchard and gathered grass or stems of wheat to line their in-ground beds. The day was hot and the dust from the runways filled the air. It wasn't long until a number of the men started cutting their hair in "prison haircuts" in an attempt to keep their heads cleaner. As the wing diary noted, " . . . the men breathed the dust, ate the dust and washed in it." The squadron's servicing units were located in tents. The mess tent was on one side of an orchard. The dispersal unit, entertainment marquees, and other facilities were scattered about nearby.

"We find it terribly dusty over here. We sleep in our little dug-out at nights, but on the whole and considering that there is a war on, we are very comfortable. I believe I would rather be here than in England. It is much more interesting, and furthermore, we don't have to fly over a couple of hundred miles of water each trip."

W/C Johnson later described their early days at Ste-Croix in his book *Wing Leader*. On the other side of the orchard was a narrow secondary road that led south from the beach. On this road a continuous procession of vehicles, including tanks and armoured vehicles, moved slowly south, bringing men and equipment from the ships down to the front line. All day long they heard the drone of vehicles on the road, the roar of aircraft landing and taking off, and the constant chatter of artillery and anti-aircraft guns. When darkness came, the enemy reconnaissance and bombers made an appearance and all the guns on the beachhead opened up. Orange tracers from the naval guns in the channel criss-crossed the sky in fantastic patterns, and searchlights constantly swept the night sky. To the southeast, in the region of Caen, large fires brightened the night sky. On their first morning at Ste-Croix, a flight of Spitfires were ready to take off at 0605 when four FW190s strafed their airfield without causing any damage, and then got away.

The new airstrip served a useful function, aiding those in the ground forces who had been wounded in action. On the 18th of June, a special detail of airmen from the wing were assigned to act as stretcher bearers, loading over 100 wounded into Douglas Dakotas. The Dakotas were due to arrive at 1030, but because of a mix-up in orders did not arrive until 1800. The wing diary noted, "It was certainly no joke for those poor devils on the stretchers." Another complement of Dakotas arrived on the 20th of June to take wounded back to

Britain, and on the 21st five more Dakotas arrived to take out injured.

■ ■ ■

The world was eager for news from Normandy, and those at Ste-Croix were eager for news from the rest of the world. At Ste-Croix, they were thankful for their radios and the BBC news broadcasts, and for copies of the London daily newspapers, especially when news from their base was featured. On the 16th of June, they heard that King George VI had travelled by cruiser to a nearby village in Normandy to meet with General Bernard Montgomery, commander of the ground forces for the invasion of Europe. On the 19th, they heard a recorded broadcast by General Charles de Gaulle, who had returned to France from England to speak to the French from a village in Normandy. On the 20th, the wing received copies of *Wings Abroad*, the RCAF newspaper, with the headline, "History Written on RCAF Airfield as Allied Planes Invade Normandy." On that same day, 144 Wing was featured in newsreels in British cinemas with film taken at Ford, Sussex, prior to their departure for their new base. Arnold wrote on the 24th, *"The Russian news certainly sounds very good to-day. It would be wonderful if we could get this end of it over with this year."*

■ ■ ■

While the war went on around them, the base took on a fast-paced life of its own. During the first week the officers enjoyed a movie in their mess, and another evening the British army put on an outdoor musical show, featuring an orchestra and a Negro singer and dancer. On the 19th of June, 121 Wing (Typhoons) from the RAF settled in at Ste-Croix for a few days, because their new location was still under heavy shellfire. That morning the wing saw its first buzz bomb, when one flew low over the base. That same day word was received that W/C Johnson had been awarded another Bar to his DSO and Bar. He had also been awarded a DFC after the Battle of Britain in 1941, one of the first three awarded in the Second World War. Those in 144 Wing had great respect for Johnson, so this became an occasion for congratulations and celebration.

Two days later the wing enjoyed another celebration when a Spitfire arrived from England with a barrel of beer under each wing, fitted into racks that normally would have carried a 500-lb. bomb. A large delivery of mail arrived the next day, to the delight of the airmen. Children from local farms continued to visit regularly.

■ ■ ■

"It was certainly grand to receive some mail once again— after what seemed like a very long wait." Arnold had received two letters from Audrey that day, and other mail. On the 24th of June, he wrote to Anna asking about Ernest, hoping that they would let him go back to Calgary for a while, for a rest. He apologized for not having time to write many letters, and added that *" . . . our weather hasn't exactly been like Alberta weather."*

The wing had arrived in bright sunshine on the 15th of June. The next three days were cool, and either cloudy or hazy—and dusty. On the 19th, rain began to fall and the dust on the ground turned to mud. The dispersal and entertainment marquees each leaked in several places, as did the mess tent. The squadron was grounded for two days because of poor visibility. The sky cleared, and the sun finally came out at noon on the 22nd.

■ ■ ■

For the first few days different flights patrolled the battle areas and channel to keep the sky cleared of enemy aircraft. On two consecutive days, flights went out late in the evening on bombing missions, each flight assigned to bombing particular bridges. Their first target was a bridge near Caen, and on the second night it was bridges near Castroville. As usual, each flight was interrogated upon return, with misses and "near misses" reported. Spitfires were not accurate bombers and a "near miss" was a miss. However, roads were damaged and one bridge was reported partially damaged. Arnold went out on the flight on the second night to Castroville. Only one flight went out in the following three days, on a scramble. On such occasions, after receiving reports of enemy aircraft in the area, pilots got their Spitfires into the air quickly, in an attempt to intercept the enemy before their aircraft could inflict damage on Allied forces.

■ ■ ■

The Luftwaffe began appearing in greater numbers in late June, defending their important rail movements in support of their ground forces. On the afternoon of the 22nd the squadron was in the air again. In the late afternoon, a flight of seven spotted a mixed flight of enemy aircraft, ME109s and FW190s. They brought down three enemy aircraft, with one attributed to the wing commander. Johnson's scoring success was a matter of intense interest to the wing, which at that time was the top-scoring RAF wing. Johnson's personal record was nearing that of Sailor Milan, a South African pilot flying with the RAF, who at that time had thirty-two enemy aircraft to his credit, the highest-scoring pilot in the RAF. Johnson now had thirty to his credit. The members of 144 Wing were all eager to see their commander exceed the record of Sailor Milan. And each pilot was keen to set his own personal record.

"I am really enjoying the work and have never been so keen about flying at any time before—especially in our aircraft, I would pick them ahead of anything," Arnold wrote in late June. On the first of July, he wrote, *"I finally spotted six yesterday and got into them ahead of any of the other boys—right on the deck. Destroyed two FW190s before the rest of the gang really caught up . . . . It really was a thrill—and also a very nice way to start out—with two. It was my first chance, and I was very happy that I was shooting straight— which amazed me!!"*

Johnson also scored again that day for his thirty-third victory. That night Johnson hosted the pilots of 144 Wing at the Officers' Mess to celebrate his scoring success, and later S/L Russel congratulated the pilots of 442 Squadron for being the top-scoring squadron of the wing, with fifteen enemy aircraft destroyed in the last nine days. He then invited them to his tent to carry on the celebration.

■ ■ ■

While the war progressed in Normandy, the family at home waited anxiously for daily news reports. Audrey wrote to Agnes, " . . . *I try not to worry, but since the invasion, I'm afraid a lot of my so-called vim and vigour has completely sapped out of me. I feel like [I am in] a rage. I go around praying half the night and all day. I'm sure our Dear Lord will answer our prayers and keep our loved ones safe and well.*" Arnold had asked her not to worry because the mail might be held up, or he may not have a chance to write. *"All I live for is our reunion, what a heavenly day that will be . . . .*" She added that she was very grateful for the write-ups on Johnson in the newspapers, because she kept tab on Arnold that way. Johnson was a great favourite with the media and was frequently featured in newspaper articles.

Arnold wrote to Anna, *"I'll be so thankful to get back to them and am hoping that I can make it by Christmas . . . . Please don't worry as everything will turn out okay, I'm convinced.*" He added that he had received a letter from the Okotoks Handicraft Club — giving all the latest news of the boys in the services, and also news of the rest of the local population. He thought it was a very clever idea and he got a great kick out of it. *"I had more or less lost touch with them. I'm going to drop them a line of appreciation . . . .*"

He wrote to Agnes that his tour was almost three-quarters complete as he had been over enemy

territory 70 times in all. S/L Russel wanted him to
stay around, because with any luck, he thought
Arnold might be promoted to squadron leader. " .
. *He's put me in for it. They're plenty difficult to get, as
everyone is so darned experienced over here now—not like
it was at the beginning, or even a year or so ago. However,
we'll see. I would like to have my own but I am still perfectly happy just the way I am, as far as that goes. At
present we're top squadron. I'd hate to leave it after two
and a half years. I'm the only original with it, right from
the day it was formed, with the exception of the C.O.
Ugh!*"

On the 19th of June, S/L Dal Russel had
written a report on Arnold. "A first class fighter
pilot, keen and very aggressive in the air . . . . With
a little more experience will make a fine flight commander. His determination will be an inspiration to
the other lads in the squadron."

■ ■ ■

Johnson did not let the pilots get slack after their
successes in June. He lectured the pilots and
warned them all to smarten up their eyesight so that
more opportunities would be afforded the wing. An
unseen enemy aircraft might be the one that would
destroy one of their Spits. Discipline in operations
was critically important in combat. Johnson had
been influential in adopting a formation the
Germans had developed in their war with Spain in
1936. This was the "four-finger formation," as in the
fingertips of the outstretched hand, palm down,
with the middle finger in the more elevated position. This formation allowed for the maximum

visibility for four aircraft. On fighter operations, aircraft were paired. The duty of No. 1 was to seek and destroy, while his No. 2 protected him from the rear. Failure to comply with these safety rules was considered a serious infraction by the pilot.

■ ■ ■

"W/C Johnny Johnson just got his 33rd victory yesterday—one better than Sailor Milan who previously held the record with 32 destroyed," Arnold wrote on the 1st of July. When he wrote his next letter, Arnold gave the details of his own next victory—his third enemy aircraft down in three days. On a patrol south of Caen, a flight from 442 came upon enemy aircraft diving down through the clouds to escape from another Spitfire squadron. He found three Messerschmitt 109Gs and tackled them, but they saw him coming and split up. *"However, I managed to get one of them. I was very amazed to find that I wasn't the least bit excited the second time. I'll admit I was a bit on the first. Since then I've been unlucky and haven't seen a thing."* The July weather continued to be variable with a lot of cloud, and the Luftwaffe were seen less frequently.

■ ■ ■

On the late evening of the 6th of July, the wing witnessed a magnificent spectacle as hundreds of four-engine bombers flew past the base in the direction of Caen. As the wing watched, just a few miles away the bombers saturated the city with incendiaries, while flak was bursting all around the aircraft in the night sky. After dropping their loads, they circled and headed back towards England. The next day the city of Caen fell to the British and Canadian armies. The following day the *Toronto Star* reported, "The Germans have made Caen the keystone of their entire Normandy defence system, packing in at least seven crack Panzer divisions plus other elements to oppose the British and Canadians. This great density of manpower . . . far exceeds that amassed by the Wehrmacht in other areas . . . " The Germans had fought fiercely to hold Caen, to prevent the Allied armies from advancing to Paris. Since D-Day, they had held off the Canadian and British armies on the eastern sector of the Normandy front, and the American army in the western sector. The Allies did not take all of Normandy until the 18th of August, when the German army fell to the Allied forces at Falaise.

On the 6th of July, the *Toronto Star* front-page headline was "ROBOMBS KILL 2,752 IN LONDON." The article further stated, "Mr. Churchill disclosed that the robot bombs were dropping on London at a rate of 100 to 150 per day . . . . More Britons have been killed by flying bombs in southern England than were killed in the first fifteen days of the Battle of Normandy . . ." Another article in the same paper was headlined, "RADIO-CONTROLLED FLYING BOMBS SPIT FIRE LIKE GIGANTIC ROCKETS . . . Spitting fire from their tails . . . the fantastic missiles whooshed across the channel within 30 feet of rooftops singly and in small groups. Others soared to a height of 3,000 feet." Mr. Churchill concluded a speech in the House of Commons with, "London will never be conquered and will never fail in her renown. Triumphing over every ordeal, her light will shine long among men."

■ ■ ■

On the 7th of July, 144 Wing celebrated winning their bet with 127 Wing. They had shot down more enemy aircraft in the first month of operations after D-Day. Number 442(F) was the highest-scoring squadron in 144 Wing. Russel was proud of his pilots, describing them as keen, daring and aggressive. That same day brought about changes in command for the wing. Dal Russel won back his rank of Wing Commander and was appointed wing leader of 126 Wing. Replacing him as squadron leader for 442(F) was F/L Hugh Dowding, DFC. Also joining the squadron that day was F/L William Olmstead, DFC. Arnold finally won a promotion when he was appointed to take the place of Dowding as Flight Commander of 'B' Flight.

On the 11th of July, the weather was again cloudy and cool, but when it improved in the late afternoon, twelve Spitfires from 144 Wing took off towards Caen. A young pilot who had been a member of the squadron for less than twenty-four hours was out on his first flight, and flying No. 2 for Dowding. They were out on their operation for less than twenty minutes when the Spitfire that the young pilot was flying was hit by flak. He was last seen entering a cloud with heavy smoke coming from his aircraft. He was the first pilot lost by No. 442.

It was cloudy again on the 13th of July, when twelve planes left on an armed reconnaissance towards Lisieux at 1630. Squadron Leader Hugh Dowding led the mission, with Arnold commanding the Green section. Pilot Officer Hugh Morse was flying No. 2 to Arnold. They had just climbed above the clouds while crossing enemy territory on return to their airfield, when Arnold and Morse spotted enemy aircraft below. They dove down and took aim at two aircraft that quickly fled into the clouds. Arnold continued the chase but Morse rolled off to the side.

Arnold did not return, and it was some days before word came back through the Red Cross that his plane had crashed near the village of St. Martin de Mailloc, near Lisieux, France.

■ ■ ■

On July 19, 1944, Anna travelled to Okotoks to visit with the Jacobsens for a few days. That evening, Anna and Mrs. Jacobsen went out to pick Saskatoon berries, and while they were gone, Helmer Jacobsen took a phone call from Lew. A telegram had come notifying that Arnold was missing in action. They told Anna nothing that evening, but the Jacobsens slept very little. Helmer received a copy of the telegram the next morning. As they sat around the breakfast table he told Anna that Arnold was missing. Anna was shocked and could not believe it. It had not been a year since Erling's death. It seemed impossible to her that Arnold was gone also. Anna remained quietly at the Jacobsens' home, until Lew came to take her back to Calgary that evening.

■ ■ ■

A few weeks later, at the age of sixty-six, Anna suffered a heart attack. She was hospitalized in the Calgary General Hospital, where Faye visited her regularly. Faye later said that she felt quite helpless, as no one seemed to be doing anything for Anna. Nurses were in short supply during the war, and in the 1940s, modern medicine didn't have many solutions for treating coronary thrombosis, except bed rest. Anna continued to fail, until one evening in the late summer she died quietly, with Faye at her bedside. Later, Faye recalled the tearful and lonely walk home to her family that night, through the shadows of the dimly lit Calgary streets.

Epilogue

IN 1998, while I was visiting with Ralph Cameron in Okotoks, he took me to the cemetery where Grandpa, Hildur, Gudrun and Grandma were buried. The gravesite was marked with small wooden crosses, hand-painted white long ago, with their names painted in black, scarcely legible. I thought they deserved better, so I contacted my cousins and made arrangements to have a new tombstone erected for them. One morning, late in May 1999, I was sitting at the dining-room table preparing to write a cheque for the proposed new headstone. At that moment, the mail arrived with a letter from the National Archives of Canada. The National Archives had my name on file in respect to my research concerning Uncle Arnold, and they had received a letter from the mayor of a village in France in respect to my uncle. They were forwarding this letter to me.

Along with a letter from the Archives was a letter written in French, and a photograph of a monument. Although the monument's inscription was in French, I could see that the dedication included the name of my Uncle Arnold, "F/L A.W. Roseland, R.C.A.F. Fighter Squadron 442," and the date that he died, July 13, 1944. The photo of his monument sat beside the mock-up of the headstone for the other four members in his family who had been buried at Okotoks. That it arrived at the precise

Monument to F/L A. W. Roseland at St. Martin de Mailloc,
France; dedicated July 13, 1999.

moment I was arranging for the headstone for the
others seemed like a voice calling out from the past.
I had the feeling that Arnold wanted to be remembered, too.

Arnold was remembered. The mayor of the
village of St. Martin de Mailloc, in Normandy, had
watched the dogfight in which my uncle's Spitfire
was attacked by several German Messerschmitts.
The mayor, as a young man, had watched my
uncle's plane crash in the village. Members of the
German army came quickly and took Arnold's iden-
tification away, but left behind a cigarette lighter
inscribed with his name. The mayor, Pierre Behier,
never forgot that day or that name. Years later, when
the village wished to erect a monument in honour of
the fiftieth anniversary of D-Day, the mayor recom-

mended that they create a monument to my uncle as their thank-you to all Canadians who fought for the liberation of France. Because of privacy laws, they had been unable to contact a relative for a dedication on the fiftieth anniversary of D-Day, so they hoped to make the dedication on the fifty-fifth anniversary of Arnold's death.

I contacted Arnold's two sons with this information, and they got in touch with the mayor. Subsequently, one son and two of Arnold's grandsons attended the dedication ceremony at St. Martin de Mailloc on July 13, 1999. Although Arnold's two sons had never known their father, his memory was very important to them. Audrey had married again and her two children were adopted by her second husband. She subsequently had three more children and the boys grew up in a secure, loving family.

The war had changed the world and the country forever, but after the war, people got on with their lives. At the same time the economies of the western world began a steady climb, creating a wealth of new opportunities and a stronger social support system. Although most people put memories of the war behind them, or tried to, the impact on individuals and on the country was huge. Reflecting on the days of the Second World War and learning more details of my family history has given me a different perspective on my childhood memories.

■ ■ ■

The experiences of the Roseland family were not unique. Their story takes the reader on a ride through history viewed from the perspective of the working class, where hard work, talent and resourcefulness do not always pay economic dividends. Our immigrant ancestors who built the North America society we know today confronted problems similar to those encountered by this family. Through their words we get a more intimate glimpse of the economic, social and political world in North America during the first half of the twentieth century. *From Sailing Ships to Spitfires* would appear to fulfil the desire of those travellers I met on my bus tour in Norway who said, "I would love to learn more about history, but I don't want to read a history book. I want to read a story."

MEMBER OF SCABRINI GROUP

Québec, Canada
2005